MICHAEL BAIGENT

ANCIENT MYSTERIES

A History through Evolution and Magic

VIKING

VIKING

Published by the Penguin Group
Penguin Books Australia Ltd, Ringwood, Victoria, Australia
Penguin Books Ltd, 27 Wrights Lane, London w8 5tz, England
Penguin Putnam Inc., 375 Hudson Street, New York, New York 10014, USA
Penguin Books Canada Ltd, 10 Alcorn Avenue, Toronto, Ontario, Canada m4v 3b2
Penguin Books (NZ) Ltd, Private Bag 102902, NSMC, Auckland, New Zealand

Penguin Books Ltd, Registered Offices: Harmondsworth, Middlesex, England

Published 1998
Published in Great Britain under the title
Ancient Traces: Mysteries in Ancient and Early History 1998
1 3 5 7 9 10 8 6 4 2
First edition

Set in 12/15.5 pt Monotype Bembo
Typeset by Intype London Ltd

Printed in Great Britain by Clays Ltd, St Ives plc

A CIP catalogue record for this book is available from the British Library

ISBN 0–670–88443–X

Contents

List of Plates

Acknowledgements

I should first like to thank my stepdaughter, Emma Milne-Watson, for beginning the discussion out of which the idea for this book arose.

I should also like to thank my wife, Jane, for her interest and support during what proved a rather intensive period of writing and research.

My thanks too for the criticisms and comments made by Joseph Addison, Isabelle Baigent, Tansy Baigent, David Milne-Watson, Lawrence Harvey and Carl Sandeman.

I owe further debts to many: Brie Burheman; Ann Evans; Andrew Nurnberg; Tony Lacey; and my long-time colleague, Richard Leigh.

Finally, I owe much to the efficiency of the staff of the British Library Reading Room at Bloomsbury (alas, now dragged to the wasteland of St Pancras), the Bodleian Library and the Ashmolean Library.

Picture Credits

I would like to thank the following for their kind permission to reproduce material: Professor Naama Goren-Inbar for 1; the British Library for 2, 16, 17, and 27; Dr Don R. Patton for 3 and 4; the New York Public Library for 5; *Deseret News* for 6; the Natural History Museum, London for 7 and 9; Professor Roy P. Mackal for

ACKNOWLEDGEMENTS

8; the International Society of Cryptozoology for 10; Professor Paul H. Leblond for 11, 12 and 13; the Fortean Picture Library for 14; the Science Library for 15; AKG London for 18; Dr Michel Lorblanchet for 19; WARA, Centro Camuno di Studi Preistorici, 25044, Capo di Ponate, Italy for 20 (copyright © 1988); John Anthony West for 23; Peter A. Clayton for 24; the British Museum for 25 and 26. Pictures 21 and 22 are my own.

The map on page 160 is reproduced from Admiralty chart 4103 by permission of the Controller of Her Majesty's Stationery Office and the hydrographic offices of France and the United Kingdom.

Introduction

In the heat of July 1989, Israeli archaeologist Professor Naama Goren-Inbar, together with her colleagues, began to excavate in the northern Jordan valley. Their site was very ancient, around 500,000 years old, and very waterlogged, for it lay close to the Jordan river.

They would have begun just after sunrise and, with considerable relief, stopped for the day at noon, just as the sun finally stole away all their shadows. Security considerations cannot have been far from their minds as they worked; the Jordan was the front line during the years of hot peace, and occasionally there were problems.

They decided first to expose all the geological levels: a mechanical digger was employed to excavate slowly two deep trenches across part of the site. As each bucketload of earth was brought to the surface it was emptied and its contents examined for bones or artefacts.

One morning, to the archaeologists' amazement, the digger dredged up part of a well-constructed and highly polished wooden plank. Nothing like it had ever been found before.

The plank was of willow wood, almost ten inches long and just over five inches wide. It had a very flat, very smooth, artificially polished surface which had been so expertly prepared that no trace of any tool marks remained. Furthermore, one edge was completely straight and deliberately bevelled. Underneath the plank the wood was roughly convex and unpolished. Both ends were broken off, a probable result of the mechanical extraction. The other pieces were never found.[1]

According to current archaeological thinking, no one living 500,000 years ago had any need for straight, flat and polished wooden planks. Of what possible use would one be to a lifestyle which was devoid of straight edges and flat surfaces? Cavemen, we are told, did not use rulers and set-squares.

Nevertheless, this plank was found. It had been made with considerable care, effort and skill. We must conclude, therefore, that a need for it had existed at the time. But what might this have been? Professor Goren-Inbar was perplexed; she had no explanation for it.[2]

Together with her colleagues, she could only conclude that the technical capabilities of these ancient people had been seriously underestimated. And, she added, there may well be further 'unconventional' finds of this type. Finds which may force a revision of opinion regarding the sophistication of early human society.[3]

We can see that our comfortable picture of ignorant and brutish cavemen, set far distant from our modern world not only in time but in intelligence and capability, is suddenly in serious danger of being exposed as a deception. This find does not just provide solid evidence of an unexpected level of skill and technical prowess but it also constitutes evidence of an unexpected social and mental development – in other words, it shows that at least some inhabitants of this long-lost epoch possessed minds which could visualize and actualize elegantly constructed objects which we normally associate with a more modern world.

This well-worked plank needs a context: it seems to whisper unobtrusively but insistently to all who will listen carefully, 'civilization'. But of *cavemen*?

This raises one possible explanation which the archaeologists did not advance, perhaps because it simply did not occur to them, or perhaps because its implications were just too wild. This plank may have been intrusive. Not in the sense of deriving from a later period, but culturally intrusive. Could the primitive humans at this Jordan valley site have obtained the plank elsewhere, from some other, more advanced, more technically accomplished group who had made and used it?

It seems probable that, in time, the very existence of this plank will force us to rewrite our ancient history. But until then it is likely that this extraordinary discovery will be ignored or, at least, marginalized to the extent that it ceases to pose any threat to the standard story of our past.

The unfortunate truth we need to confront is that history can be rather like statistics: anything can be proved; any fraudulent story of the past can be maintained so long as all unwelcome data is excluded. As we will discover during the course of this book, certain stories about human prehistory have so much money and so many reputations vested in them that they are stubbornly maintained even in the face of steadily accumulating contrary evidence. To the extent, in fact, of supporters taking every opportunity to shout louder and more often than their opponents. Which does not, of course, help towards any search for the truth.

Science demonstrates a rather similar situation. Most people forget that, at its heart, science is simply a methodology, a way of working. Its conclusions are not 'truths' but essentially statistical approximations. If something happens 100 times, then it is supposed that it will happen 101 times, or 1,000 times. And if, on one occasion during these 100 or 1,000 events, something else occurs, then that lone event is quickly excluded as anomalous and therefore irrelevant. It is dismissed and, in time, forgotten.

But just occasionally the anomalies become so frequent and so well known that they force a total revision of the accepted story. This book will look at the situation, for example, of evolutionary theory where more than a century of intensive research into fossil animals and plants has failed to produce the proof needed to support Darwin's concept. Many experts are now looking elsewhere for an explanation.

Similarly challenging conventional theories are new discoveries concerning the sudden appearance of a fully developed city culture in southern Turkey, many thousands of years ago, in an area where no trace of earlier development has been found. There are, too, further enigmas and unexplained curiosities surrounding the Pyramids of Giza and the Sphinx. These, together with the related mysteries of alchemy, have proved unwelcome to the self-appointed guardians of orthodoxy and so have been widely ridiculed or ignored. This book will take an objective look at them.

It is noteworthy that apparently damning criticism has always been found to justify the exclusion of enigmatic and contrary data. Experts have argued, in effect, that, because such discoveries were so strange and ran counter to all that is accepted, they *must* be wrong. This is, of course, an argument based on faith rather than fact.

Nevertheless, such pundits seek to support their faith by casting doubt upon their opponents, accusing them of being incompetent, ill-trained or, even worse, rank amateurs. As if it makes a difference who actually makes the discovery. The Dead Sea Scrolls are no less valid for having been discovered by a shepherd.

Those upholding the orthodox story have always played for time because eventually the reasons for excluding conflicting data might be forgotten and thus never subjected to the critical scrutiny which might expose their hollowness. Meanwhile the data and the disputes would also be forgotten. Deep in the basements of our museums ancient bones have long grown dusty in their cardboard boxes, once-dynamic scholars who vigorously argued contrary ideas were broken in spirit, or grew too weary to continue the fight and left the field. Some even had their characters and careers destroyed, as we shall see in the case of Canadian archaeologist Thomas Lee. He dared find human artefacts far older than the accepted date of humankind in the Americas. And he dared to keep digging them up.

In this book we will be looking at much of that information which directly challenges orthodoxy: information which upsets the comfortable, but confining, boundaries of our modern world. We will look at evidence suggesting design in evolution; at discoveries indicating the existence of very ancient technology; of remnants suggesting that human beings existed millions of years before the present; of human culture emerging in lands no longer available for archaeological study. And, moving into the mystical side of our life and world, we will look at evidence, both ancient and modern, concerning the timeless mystery of death and rebirth. Can we truly have lived before? Increasingly, data is emerging to lead us to answer 'yes'.

All too often we fall into the trap of thinking that we know everything about our world. This book has gathered together information which reminds us that we do not.

1

How Ancient is Humanity?

We are confidently informed that, almost 4 billion years ago, our planet was merely a spinning lump of rock. It took almost a billion of those years for life to begin, forming the bacteria and algae which have left their shadowy traces in ancient rocks. Further great stretches of time slipped sleepily by, and then primitive worms crawled out of the biological torpor.

All in all, life seemed well contented with simplicity.

Abruptly this changed. About 530 million years ago life burst its rural boundaries. It erupted in an intense, unprecedented, unexplained event now called the Cambrian Explosion.[1] This changed the earth's history for ever. In a frenzy of biological invention the earth became covered with creatures which first swam in the sea and, later, crawled, walked, ran and slithered all over the land. The earth changed from a country lane to Piccadilly Circus at rush hour. And it was permanently lunchtime.

During this 'explosion' all known varieties of complex animals and plants suddenly appeared. But, mysteriously, there is no trace of their development to be found in the earlier fossil record. All appear, fully formed, fully evolved, fully functioning, teeth sharpened and scales glistening. No one knows who or what let them out. Or why.

And, given such a push, life never looked back.

In time the dinosaurs ruled over the earth. The earliest appeared

190 million years ago, leading into the huge monsters of *Jurassic Park*: in fact, they ruled for almost 125 million years. But, despite this success and long after the world seemed destined to remain a Jurassic playground for ever, another mysterious event occurred. The dinosaurs abruptly died out, about 65 million years ago. No one knows the reason. Perhaps the cosmos no longer needed dinosaurs.

It was this rather sudden disappearance which gave the early mammals a chance to become widespread, filling up the ecological gaps rendered vacant. Of particular importance to humanity is the apparent evolution, during this period, of one specific branch of mammals, the primates – apes and monkeys. For if humans evolved from the primates, as we are led to believe, then our body shape has its ultimate origin at this time.

Sixty-one million years later – just under 4 million years ago – the first traces of what is believed to be early man appear. Man-like apes or ape-like men descended from the trees – so we are told – to begin a new two-legged life scavenging on the immense African grasslands. But tool-making, one of the defining characteristics of mankind, was yet to come; archaeology has indicated that the earliest use of simple flaked-stone tools began about 2.5 million years before the present.[2]

Our culture is even more recent. It is thought to have begun a mere 10,000 or 11,000 years ago, nurtured in the developing settled farming communities of the Turkish highlands. Even later still is the use of metals; it took perhaps another 5,000 years. And now we can land this metal on Mars.

According to the current scientific theories, humanity and civilization have occupied only a minute fragment of the hundreds of millions of years of earth's history. In the face of the apparently solid geological and archaeological evidence, for anyone to suggest that human artefacts and human culture might long predate the last 2.5 million, or even 4 million years is to invite total ridicule.

Yet how solid is the accepted story of the past?

Does it really accord with all the evidence? Does it provide a satisfactory explanation for all the artefacts which the earth has given up?

The truth is, that it does not.

In California, early in 1848, some forty miles north-east from where the city of Sacramento now stands, a carpenter was building a water-driven sawmill. The mill-stream drew its water to power the wheel from the nearby American river. But the mill-stream proved too shallow and so the carpenter was digging it out, making it deeper to enable the wheel to turn more freely. One morning he discovered, at the bottom of the stream, some small nuggets of gold which had been exposed during the night by the rushing water. He tried to keep his find a secret; inevitably, he was unsuccessful. A stampede for gold rapidly ensued: the Californian 'Gold Rush'.

Within six months, over 4,000 men had abandoned all other occupation in order to mine the immediate area. The land exploited rapidly expanded into hundreds of square miles and the mining population itself grew to 80,000 or more, half of whom had come by sea around Cape Horn to San Francisco, the others overland by the California Trail. Either way, it took considerable effort.

The gold lay in the rivers which ran down from the Sierra Nevada mountains, through the great central valley of California, to enter the sea at San Francisco. Mining soon moved from simple panning and sieving to an increasingly intricate mechanized operation. Sluices were built to create high-pressure streams of water which could be employed to hose away entire hillsides to get at the gold beneath. Channels washed the tumbling water and rubble through a series of ridged tables which separated out the heavier flakes of gold. And, always, close inspection was the norm; every particle of gold meant money which, after all, was the reason behind all the effort and expense.

3

It was soon discovered, however, that this precious metal's primary source was in deeply buried gravels, the former beds of very ancient rivers which lay hundreds of feet beneath the surface. In places they were partly exposed by great ravines cut by modern rivers, ravines which sometimes reached 2,000 feet or more in depth. The miners began to excavate horizontally into the cliff faces or deep beneath steep hills in order to gain access to these gold-bearing gravels. But the work was hard: the gravel was tightly consolidated, like concrete, and heavy pick work, often coupled with explosives, proved the only way to break it up.

The miners found gold by the ton; but, along with it, they also found many curious artefacts and human remains. Rumours began to spread throughout the mining camps of a long-lost civilization which had existed in the area millions of years before and which was the source of these remains. Certain miners began to make collections of these artefacts: skulls, bones, stone spear- and arrow-heads, knives, mortars and pestles, stone dishes, ladles, grooved stone hammer-heads or sinkers, plummet stones and other cultural remnants.

Word of the odd discoveries even reached across the Atlantic. In December 1851 *The Times* of London reported the story of a miner who had dropped a piece of gold-bearing quartz which split open to reveal, firmly embedded in the rock, a corroded but perfectly straight iron nail.[3]

So many anomalous artefacts were found during the subsequent decades that professional organizations began to take an interest – or at least felt that they should take some action to counter what they saw as extravagant claims about mankind's past.

In 1880 Harvard University published a monograph by one of its professors (who was also the State Geologist of California) on some of the finds.[4] On 10 January 1888 a report was read to a meeting of the Anthropological Institute in London.[5] Then, on 30 December 1890, a paper on the subject was delivered to the

American Geological Society[6] and in 1899 the most prestigious American scientific organization of all, the Smithsonian Institution of Washington DC, made a survey and critique of all that had been found by that time.[7]

The Smithsonian noted in its survey that most of the finds appeared to come from gravels dating from around 38 to 55 million years ago. But it noted also that many of the artefacts came either from mines near the surface or from the sluicing away of cliffs.

In consequence the Smithsonian experts quite correctly pointed out that many of the artefacts found could well have come from more recent Indian cultures, either buried in deep graves or having long ago fallen into caves or sink-holes and, over the centuries, been covered over with rubble. It is true, certainly, that some of the human remains found revealed chemical changes which are consistent with this explanation. It is also true that sluicing, being a totally destructive exercise, removed everything wholesale. Artefacts from near the surface would be mixed with those from much lower, and thus much older, rock strata. The miners, who generally lacked discrimination in any scientific sense, regarded all the artefacts which they found, like the gold, as coming from the ancient gravels. Clearly, in many cases, they could be wrong.

In this, the Smithsonian had found a scientifically acceptable and, in general terms, accurate explanation for the appearance of man-made artefacts in the company of rocks of great antiquity. This survey – and others rather similar – achieved the desired result: any challenge which these artefacts might have constituted to scientific orthodoxy was rendered null and void.

But at least the Smithsonian experts were honest: they did concede that there were some artefacts for which their explanation was no answer at all. They were referring to those objects which had been recovered deep within mines often hundreds of feet beneath mountains. They recognized that such artefacts were in a very different category and were not so easily explained away. But they declined to speculate upon the matter further.

Which is a pity. For these artefacts, as we shall see, are as close to definitive proof of an ancient culture as we are likely to get.

Table Mountain

To understand the situation, we need to understand the geology. In the general gold-bearing region the youngest bedrock dates from about 55 million years ago. At various times afterwards, erupting volcanoes laid wide-ranging lava deposits on top, deposits which can be dated reliably. The gold-bearing river gravels themselves, above the bedrock and below the lava deposits, are dated between 33 and 55 million years ago.

Those miners who worked within a specific geological site, rather than simply sluicing away everything indiscriminately, were better able to determine the source of any artefact. They could date with confidence anything which they might find amongst this ancient gravel; anything which long ago had been washed along by a river. Or discarded at its side.

One such site, which was to become well-known for its artefacts, was Table Mountain in Tuolumne County, California, on the western edge of the Yosemite National Park.[8]

The top of this mountain is a huge larva cap, 9 million years old. Beneath this cap and other rock strata lay the gold-bearing gravels, some lying immediately above the ancient bedrock.

Years of searching for gold there created a network of mines. Some were cut horizontally in through the bedrock for hundreds of feet and then shafts were driven vertically upwards into the lower gravel deposits. Other mines ran obliquely down from the mountainside into the upper layers of these same gravels.

The artefacts were all found within the prehistoric compacted gravel. Miners first came upon spear-heads, six to eight inches long, ladles with handles and, uniquely, a curious notched slate object which seemed to be a handle for a bow. They also found a stone-grinding tool and a human jaw-bone.[9] These objects came from gravel dated from 33 to 55 million years ago. It is logical, and correct, to conclude that these artefacts could have a similar date.

This gives a direct challenge to science: man-made objects over 33 million years old cannot be accepted by orthodoxy; science ignores or dismisses them. But we cannot.

There is much more evidence of a similar nature: one mine-owner personally found a large stone mortar – used for grinding food – in a horizontal mine-shaft 180 feet beneath the ground surface, beneath the larva cap. A fragment of fossilized human skull was also found in the same mine.[10]

In 1853 a cartload of gold-bearing gravel was being brought out of one of the mines from a pit-face about 125 feet below the surface. Mixed in with the gravel was a well-preserved mastodon tooth (the mastodon is an extinct type of elephant) and a large bead of white marble, about one and a half inches long and just over an inch in diameter. It had a quarter-inch hole drilled right through it.[11]

In 1858 in a shaft over sixty feet below the surface and some 300 feet into the mountain, a stone axe was found. Its length was about six inches and it had a four-inch-wide cutting edge. A hole had been drilled through it to take a wooden handle. Nearby were found a number of stone mortars.[12]

Yet another stone mortar, just over three inches in diameter, was found in 1862, some 200 feet beneath the surface and around 1,800 feet along the mine tunnel.[13] It had been carved out of andesite, the nearest source of which lay 100 miles away.[14]

Seven years later a top professional became involved. Clarence King, a well-known and highly respected American geologist, was the director of the US Government survey of the 40th Parallel. In 1869 he was looking at the geology of Table Mountain. At one particular area near to the volcanic cap, he noticed that a recent flood had exposed sections of the underlying gravel. He began a search for fossils but during this close inspection he found part of a stone pestle tightly wedged in the compact and hard gravel. After extraction it left a perfect cast of itself in the stone matrix.[15] King had no doubt at all that the pestle had rested there as long as the gravel itself, for many millions of years.

King was an experienced geologist; there is no possibility of doubt over the age of the rock strata in which he found this pestle, over 9 million years old: yet it is man-made. It is now in the Smithsonian Institute where an expert recognized the problem for science that this pestle posed. Nevertheless, he commented, honestly, that this particular artefact, 'may not be challenged with impunity'.[16]

In 1877 more artefacts were found beneath Table Mountain in the lower layers of gravel, within a foot or so of the bedrock. One afternoon during an excavation to put a timber support in place 1,400 or 1,500 feet in from the tunnel entrance, a mine superintendent found several obsidian spear-heads, each about ten inches long.

Intrigued, the superintendent made further investigations and a few feet away found a stone mortar. Shortly after, he found another, this time with its stone pestle. The superintendent later reported to investigators that there was no trace of any disturbance of the gravel or any hole by which these objects could have been placed there more recently, perhaps as a practical joke by one of the other miners. He reported that, 'There was not the slightest trace of any disturbance of the mass or of any natural fissure into it by which access could have been obtained, either there or in the neighborhood.'[17] The site of the find, in the gold-bearing strata close to the bedrock, suggests an age of between 33 and 55 million years ago.[18]

These particular discoveries were the subject of a paper read to the American Geological Society in 1891; the geologist concluded with the comment:

It would have been more satisfactory to me individually if I had myself dug out these implements, but I am unable to discover any reason why [the superintendent's] statement is not exactly as good evidence to the rest of the world as my own would be. He was as competent as I to detect any fissure from the surface or any ancient workings, which the miner recognizes instantly and dreads profoundly.[19]

While the Table Mountain mine workings alone have provided sufficient enigmas for science, objects were found in mines at other sites which similarly indicated very ancient dates for their origin. Near the town of San Andreas, for example, 144 feet below the surface, a number of stone mortars and other unspecified artefacts were discovered.[20] All these were in rock strata dated to over 5 million years ago. From at least twenty-six other mining sites stone mortars, and sometimes pestles, were found, some in rock strata dated to at least 23 million years ago.[21]

It is an uncomfortable fact which needs to be confronted by the scholars that, by the end of the nineteenth century, literally hundreds of ancient artefacts had been excavated in geological strata of great antiquity. Can they all be dismissed as some kind of fraud or misrepresentation by untrained observers? Or as misidentified intrusive objects? In fact, an experienced miner, following the progress of the work, day by day, for his own safety looking out for cracks or old mine workings, is probably a more competent observer than any visiting geologist.

It is worth remembering too that many archaeological discoveries important to science have been found by unqualified amateurs in rock strata which are difficult to date or in circumstances difficult to reconstruct later. Yet they have been accepted into the official record.

One anthropologist, commissioned by the University of California in 1908 to investigate – and demolish – the claims to veracity made by these discoveries, put the official position bluntly. He stated that these remains 'would necessitate placing the origin of the human race in an exceedingly remote geological period. This is contrary to all precedent in the history of organisms, which teaches that mammalian species are short-lived.'[22]

Science has a theory: that man evolved from the primates during the course of some 3 to 5 million years, beginning around 6 or 7 million years ago. Nothing contrary to this is acceptable. But is it so outrageous to suggest that this evolution might rather have taken place around 50 million years ago?

Or could even this date be too recent?

The Morrisonville Chain

On the morning of Tuesday 9 June 1891, the wife of a local newspaper publisher in Morrisonville, Illinois, Mrs S. W. Culp, was filling her coal scuttle. As one of the lumps of coal was too large, she began to break it up. It broke in two, splitting almost down the middle. Inside Mrs Culp saw exposed a delicate gold chain perhaps ten inches long 'of antique and quaint workmanship'.[23]

Mrs Culp's first startled reaction was that the chain had been accidentally dropped into the coal, perhaps by one of the miners. But this thought was quickly proved wrong. When she went to lift the chain out she discovered that, while the middle of the chain had become loosened, the two ends, lying close together, were still firmly embedded. Furthermore she saw that where the chain had come loose, a circular indentation remained in the piece of coal. The chain was evidently as old as the coal itself. She took the chain to an expert. On analysis it proved to be of eight-carat gold and weighed about twelve grammes. Mrs Culp died in 1959 and the chain passed to a relative and has been lost to research.[24]

Due to the strange circumstances of its discovery, it was never taken seriously at the time and neither then or later investigated by any scientist. We do not know, therefore, any manufacturing details which might possibly throw some light upon its origins.

By any standard this find is extraordinary: the coal in this area is between 260 and 320 million years old.[25] The implication is that in some distant epoch a culture existed capable of such fine manufacture as represented by this chain.

Three immediate explanations present themselves: firstly, that our theories of human evolution are wrong, that civilized humans did exist at the time of the early dinosaurs. Alternatively, that our theories regarding the formation of coal may be wrong. Perhaps coal – or a type of coal – was made thousands of years ago rather than the millions we normally accept. Finally, perhaps the most immediately attractive explanation is that this was a simple case of mistake or even fraud. It has, from the first, been a truism that newspaper publishers are always looking for sensational events to sell their papers; this may have been one more.

A look at the newspaper revealed that the report was not sensationalized in any way; if anything, it was handled in rather a low-key manner suggesting a certain discretion on the part of the publisher. It appeared, it is true, on the front page but between the leading report which described a drowning and a droll description of the defeat of the Morrisonville baseball team (due to the lack of a pitcher).

Yet the editor clearly wished to let a wider audience know of an event which obviously mystified all who were aware of it. As the article stated, in its orotund manner, it 'almost hushes one's breath with mystery when it is thought for how many long ages the earth has been forming strata after strata which hid the golden links from view'.[26]

It is hard to see this as a deliberate fraud; it may be some kind of error but exactly what is hard to discern from the context. The account has a naïvely honest tone. Those involved in this discovery and its publication were educated and intelligent; it is fair to conclude that the story they printed is accurate in its details and expressed, however hesitantly, their own belief that an error or fraud had not taken place. It constitutes another anomaly which demands an answer.

Gold and Culture

Cultures produce artefacts. They generate endless quantities of tools, weapons, utensils, religious images and bones; endless quantities of bones.

Any group of people who have progressed beyond a desperate daily struggle for existence also produce art; images for ritual purposes or simply decoration and jewellery, to adorn both women and men. The production of gold or silver jewellery, in particular, is the mark of considerable cultural advance.

The making of a gold chain is a specialist enterprise; it cannot just be thrown together by someone with time on his or her hands between the slaughtering of mammoths or the stealing of wives. In addition, a delicate gold chain cannot possibly be made by stone tools. In other words, a gold chain represents a settled culture which has already undergone many thousands of years of development. A culture rather like that of ancient Egypt, Mesopotamia or China.

Proof of this is that the earliest gold chains which orthodox archaeology accepts come from the ancient civilizations of Egypt and Mesopotamia, their construction beginning around 5,500 years ago. But they are normally of pure gold. They are not of an alloy of eight carats as was the chain found by Mrs Culp.

Gold of eight carats is not really gold at all but an alloy; it is eight parts gold mixed with sixteen parts of another metal, probably copper. This is a curiosity for those who suspect error: in Victorian times gold alloys were common but they were usually of fifteen carats – just over 60 per cent gold. And they were hallmarked. There was no standard of eight carats.

What this discovery by Mrs Culp proves – if we can accept the story – is that such a specialist culture existed before the time of the dinosaurs. Of course, this is an outrageous thought.

Unfortunately for those who prefer the comfort of the orthodox theories, other man-made objects have been found in very early rock formations.

Ancient Artefacts . . .

The Times, Saturday 22 June 1844, contained a curious story. 'A Singular Circumstance', it was headed. Some days earlier, it explained, just below Rutherford on the river Tweed, some workers in a quarry found a gold thread in a piece of rock. They took a small section of it to the local newspaper office at Kelso where it was put on display.[27] The author noted wryly, 'How long this remnant of a former age has remained in the situation from which it was taken will baffle the skill of the antiquary or geologist . . .'

While the exact site of discovery cannot now be determined, the age of the sandstone in the area of Rutherford is 360 million years.

Equally enigmatic is a report which Sir David Brewster delivered to the British Association for the Advancement of Science. He stated that quarrymen in the Kingoodie Quarry, near Dundee, had found an iron nail in the middle of a block of sandstone. After it had been split open, the head of the nail, together with an inch of its shaft, was still firmly embedded in the rock.[28] The sandstone in this area is Lower Devonian, at least 387 million years old.

A similar challenge to orthodoxy emerged in 1885, in an iron foundry in the Austrian town of Vöcklabruck, midway between Salzburg and Linz. A block of coal broke open to reveal a small steel object, almost a perfect cube, measuring 2.6 by 2.6 by 1.8 inches. A deep groove ran around it and two opposing faces were rounded. The foundry owner's son took the cube to the museum at Linz where it was studied. Analysis revealed that it was as hard as steel and contained both carbon and nickel. A cast was made of it, which was fortunate for the original has now been lost – perhaps in the chaos of war – but the cast has survived.[29]

In California, in 1952, an artesian well specialist, Frederick Hehr, accidentally discovered at a depth of thirty-seven feet the apparent remains of an iron chain embedded in solid sandstone. A photograph of it dating from 1955 shows the block of stone with one large ring connected to a number of much smaller ones. Unfortunately, like many of these remnants, its whereabouts is no longer known.[30]

Because of the anomalous character of finds such as these and the fact that they present such a challenge to the accepted scientific perspective – the orthodox 'paradigm' – many of these finds are not reported and those which are fail to receive the attention which would ensure their preservation. With such official disdain, all too often they simply become lost, given away to an interested friend, filed in a box in the bowels of a museum or discarded upon the finder's death.

. . . Or Ancient Ancestors?

The iron nail from Kingoodie could be 387 million years old; the gold thread found in Rutherford was in rock dated to 360 million years; Mrs Culp's gold chain fell out of coal assigned a date of at least 260 million years; the finds at Table Mountain range between 35 and 33 million years: clearly there is no possibility that any of this data can be accommodated into the conventional scientific understanding of the earth's history. It suggests, at least, that those fossils of ape-like creatures which are studied by the palaeontologists have little or nothing to do with the evolution of humans at all. In fact, this evidence – if it can be substantiated even in just one of the cases we have reviewed – indicates that humans, in a modern form, have been walking upon this planet for a very long time indeed.

But while we have listed some of the artefacts found – and it is amazing that any have survived at all – what of the people themselves? Have any bones, skeletons or other remains been found?

In fact, they have.

In 1862 bones judged to be human were discovered by coal miners working ninety feet underground in Macoupin County, Illinois. The miners reported that the bones were first seen with a shiny hard coat the same colour as the coal. This, they discovered, could be scraped off leaving white bones. Recent estimates of the age of the coal there indicate a minimum of 286 million years.[31]

In what is unfortunately a repetitive litany, these bones have long since vanished and no other studies seem to have been made of them. We can have little doubt, however, that the miners reported the events just as they occurred. But were these bones of humans? Or were they of some early primate? Or were they some strange rock formation or mineral accretion? It would have been pleasing if the bones had been measured and described by an experienced geologist or biologist. And even more satisfactory would have been someone who had the foresight to store the remains so that we might study them now.

The thought of bones being found in coal deep beneath the surface of the earth may seem so strange as to cast doubt immediately upon the veracity of the find. However, curious though it might seem, given the great pressures and temperatures involved in the formation of coal, true fossil bones have certainly been found buried deep within coal seams.

During the early morning of 2 August 1958, coal miners working at Baccinello, Italy, 656 feet below the surface, discovered the skeleton of an extinct ape, an Oreopithecus. It was found stretched out and compressed – like a hedgehog on a motorway – in the roof of a gallery. The lignite coal which held it was dated to 10 million years ago. Judging by the bone fragments which had earlier been recovered mixed with coal brought to the surface, an expert from the Natural History Museum of Basle concluded that some thirty skeletons had already been destroyed by mining operations.[32]

Footprints which appear to be human have also been discovered in a number of sites.

In 1938 Professor Wilbur Burroughs, a respected and widely published professional geologist, and head of geology at Berea College, Kentucky, reported finding fossil footprints dating from the Upper Carboniferous age, around 250 million years ago, at a site in Kentucky. He commented cautiously that 'creatures that walked on their two hind legs and had human-like feet left tracks on a sand beach in Rockcastle County, Kentucky'.[33] The Curator of Vertebrate Paleontology at the Smithsonian Institution became interested in these, pointing out that similar tracks had been found elsewhere, in Pennsylvania and Missouri.

Professor Burroughs described the fossil tracks as being on an ancient beach, now an outcrop of hard sandstone on a privately owned farm. The tracks showed both left and right feet, and each print revealed 'five toes and a distinct arch'. The length of each track was about nine and a half inches and the width across the toes six inches. They were quite distinct.[34]

In order to rule out suggestions of fraud, suggestions that these prints had been carved long ago by local people or Indians, Burroughs took a microscope to the site to study the composition of the sandstone itself. He reported that the grains of sand inside the tracks were more closely packed than those outside. This is consistent with the weight of an animal's foot pressing down. In the best-preserved track he discovered that the grains in the arch of the foot, while more compacted than outside, were not as compacted as those at the heel.[35]

In addition to this, the sandstone beside the prints was slightly raised, as it would be from a footprint which, as the foot pushed downwards, would push the surrounding sand up slightly. Two local doctors, well used to human feet, also studied the prints and agreed with Professor Burroughs' conclusion: that the prints were not carvings but true fossils of an unknown creature which walked on two legs.[36]

The trouble with this conclusion is that there were no known bipedal creatures living at that date in history. The largest land animals of the time, according to current knowledge, were primitive amphibians rather similar to modern crocodiles and, like the latter, they moved on four legs and had a heavy tail which too would have left a fossil track.

Professor Burroughs was stumped: the most obvious conclusion for a non-scientist – ignorant of the anomalous dating – would be that these prints were made by humans. But, as a scientist, Burroughs could not accept that, at least publicly (for it seems that he had begun to suspect something quite heretical). Instead he wrote blandly that, 'The creatures that made the tracks have not as yet been identified,' and, together with a biologist, a curator from the Smithsonian and a professor of Latin, chose the species name *Phenanthropus mirabilis*, meaning 'looks human' and 'remarkable'.[37] The Smithsonian has no record of this creature today.

When queried about these prints in 1953, going perhaps as far as he dared, Burroughs replied cautiously, 'They look human. That is what makes them especially interesting, as man according to some textbooks has been here only a million and a half years.'[38]

Humans with Dinosaurs?

One hundred and eleven million years ago much of what is now Texas was a great ocean. On its shores were wide mudflats which were the habitat of a great variety of dinosaurs. They roamed at will, their tracks criss-crossing the mud. Naturally, most of these traces have long since vanished, but with one exception: the region around the town of Glen Rose, Texas. There, fossil dinosaur tracks have long been found. They have always been accepted as genuine by the scientific establishment who have studied them with interest.

For many years, especially in the 1930s, local entrepreneurs cashed in on the interest in dinosaur footprints by chiselling them out for sale to tourists. Before long faked fossil footprints of humans also began to appear on the local market.

Through these ancient fossil mudflats flows the Paluxy river. In 1969, in the bed of this river, a remarkable discovery was made. Mr Stan Taylor found a short trail of human-like footprints, since known as the 'Taylor Trail'.

Unfortunately, this find has become tainted by the local trade in fakes. In addition, since Taylor's discovery the major advocates of the Paluxy site have been of the 'creationist' fundamentalist Christian fraternity. So we need to be cautious; a not-so-hidden agenda is at work here. In fact, the agenda is positively evangelical: the 'Creation Evidence Museum' stands in Glen Rose as a bulwark against the evils of evolutionary theory.

Taylor first saw two human-like fossil footprints under shallow water at the edge of the Paluxy river right in front of a solid limestone bank about eight feet high. He began excavating this bank to see if any more prints were to be found beneath it. Between 1969 and 1972, and with the aid of mechanical earth-moving equipment, he removed tons of rock to reveal that the prints did indeed continue on underneath. It seemed sure proof against any charges that they had been carved or faked in any other way.

Taylor uncovered seven more prints. They were all very convincing. They showed a consistent left–right pattern as would be made by the bare feet of a human walking across mud. Later excavation revealed further prints, bringing the total in the trail to fourteen. In the immediate vicinity, 134 dinosaur tracks of the same age were noted. It seems as though humans and dinosaurs were roaming together on the same prehistoric mudflats.

There is little possibility of fraud with these tracks. No one could have created fake footprints under solid limestone; even the most critical of the sceptics concede this. So, despite the taint from the past, despite the creationist agenda, the evidence speaks for itself. The explanation, it appears, is to accept either that humans were alive along with the dinosaurs tens of millions of years ago, or that some dinosaurs had human-like feet. Or is there some other explanation?

There is, too, one practical difficulty. How would any humans have survived in this flat muddy environment filled with fast-moving predators seeking food?

The critics, and there are many, do not dispute that these are genuine fossil footprints. They argue that they were made by dinosaurs in the same way as many other of the prints in the region. But these particular prints have been either heavily eroded or were never made very clearly in the first place. These critics have shown how a three-toed dinosaur print could be converted into something rather like a worn human footprint: as the centre 'toe' of the dinosaur bears most of the weight and thus goes deeper into the mud, it is this impression alone which would survive after the lighter impression of the two outer toes had been worn away through erosion.[39]

This is a very plausible scenario, but difficulties with it as a definitive explanation still remain. For one thing, the human-like prints of the 'Taylor Trail' actually run amongst and beside some tracks of a three-toed dinosaur. The three toes are clearly visible; there is no suggestion of the outer two having been worn away. Secondly, at least some of the human-like prints show what appears to be the impression of a big toe. Thirdly, each of the prints is eleven and a half inches long, consistent with a large human foot. We should also recall that Professor Burroughs made a point of describing that five toes were visible on the fossil prints he found. This certainly does not accord with any 'erosion' explanation.

Whatever the truth, photographs of the Paluxy river finds are heart-stopping. They defiantly challenge the entirety of modern evolutionary theory. They bring conversation to an end as the enormity of their implications strikes home. And so, despite the creationist taint, and despite the erosion hypothesis, the conclusion must be that here too science has a case to answer. Unfortunately, the experts shy away, scientific journals are hesitant to run research articles about these prints and most specialists who do pass comment do so with a supercilious disdain which only reinforces the impression that they have something to fear.

A similar picture emerges in Russia: Professor Amanniyazov of the Academy of Sciences in Turkmenistan reported in 1983 finding a human-like footprint in rock dated to 150 million years ago. Next to the human-like print was one of a three-toed dinosaur, just as we have seen in the Paluxy river example. The professor concluded, rather reasonably in the circumstances, that while the print looked human to him, there could be no proof that it was.[40]

These cases are not alone: fossil footprints closely resembling those of humans have been found at quite a number of sites in the United States, Central America, Africa and Turkey.[41] Not all, however, are as old as those of Kentucky, Texas or Turkmenistan.

Traces of Fossil Shoe Prints

That fossil footprints have been found in rock so immensely old is extraordinary enough, but the strata have produced even more unusual residues: fossil shoe prints.

In 1922 a mining engineer and geologist, John Reid, was looking for fossils in Nevada. He was astonished to find a fossil of the rear half of a human shoe. The shoe's sole was clearly outlined in the rock. Proof was the visible stitching: around the edge of the sole 'ran a well-defined sewn thread which had . . . attached the welt to the sole'.[42] Inside this, another line of stitches was evident and in the centre of the heel was an indentation just as would be caused by wear.

The fossil was taken to New York by Reid and shown to a geologist from Columbia University and to three professors of the American Museum of Natural History. They all agreed that the fossil was from the Triassic period, 213 to 248 million years ago. They also all agreed that it 'was the most remarkable imitation' of a shoe. Further than that they would not commit themselves.

Microscopic analysis of the fossil was undertaken by an expert from the Rockefeller Institute with the result that, by virtue of the intricate twists and warps of the thread used in the stitching, it appeared conclusive that this was a fossil of a man-made object.[43]

But science rejected this find as a 'freak of nature'. No book on fossils will ever mention it. No professional will ever discuss it. A photograph taken in 1922 is all that remains of it today.

More recently, in June 1968, a second shoe print was found by William Meister in rock dating from the Cambrian Explosion near to Antelope Springs in Utah. This too is rather difficult to dismiss. In his search for fossils, Meister split open a two-inch-thick rock of shale – dating from 505 to 590 million years ago – and, as it fell apart, it did so to reveal what looked like the print of a sandal just over ten inches long and three and a half inches wide.

While scientists who have been made aware of this find are dismissive – as would be expected – there is a curiosity about this particular find which makes it very hard to discard as a freak or a fraud. Crushed into the mud by the front of the sandal, by the weight put on it those many millions of years before, was a small fossil trilobite – a shellfish which has been extinct for 280 million years. The indentation it left is clearly visible.

On the heel was another small trilobite which had evidently crawled or dropped on to the sandal's flat impression after it had been made.[44] This is good evidence against this fossil being simply a geological oddity and, it would seem, conclusive evidence both for its age and for it being the fossil impression of something the shape of a sandal which squashed into the mud so many millions of years ago.

Scientist and author Dr Richard Thompson, who visited Meister to study this fossil, reported that, 'Close inspection of the print revealed no obvious reason why it could not be accepted as genuine.'[45] Apart from the date, that is.

Ancient Humanity

While some readers may disagree, in the face of this evidence it does seem reasonable, even rational, to accept the possibility that intelligent beings were walking the earth many millions of years ago.

Perhaps humanity evolved very early and many times in the past, developed a culture, a civilization, only to see it destroyed by some major incident. The most ancient writings which have been passed down to us record periodic destructions of humanity over long periods of time.

The ancient Indian writings, the Vedas, arguably expressing the oldest traditions known, speak of vast ages of man's existence, the smallest division being the *Kali-Yuga* which amounts to a period of 432,000 years. One yugic period represents 4,320,000 years. A thousand of these *Yugas* form a *Kalpa*, a 'day of God' – which just about equals the modern calculation of the age of the earth.

Every ancient tradition conveys a blend of truth and fable. Could this particular tradition be even partly correct?

Such reports as we have looked at do not, of course, give any succour to either side in the on-going debate between those who believe in the evolution of mankind as opposed to those who believe in a divine creation. But what this anomalous evidence does do, however, is point out a failure on the part of those official custodians of modern scientific theory. For a theory which needs to reject evidence in order to survive is not a theory worth keeping.

2

Problems with Evolution

Few people this century have avoided exposure to Charles Darwin's theory of evolution. His book, *The Origin of Species by Means of Natural Selection*, first appeared in late November 1859 and quickly passed through three editions.

By proposing chance rather than divine purpose as the agent of our origins, Darwin's theory confronted, head-on, the literal understanding of the biblical account of creation. And, by a single reference to an evolutionary connection between man and apes, it became widely ridiculed as the 'Monkey Theory'. In a debate with evolutionary biologist T. H. Huxley, Oxford's Bishop Wilberforce inquired, with silken sarcasm, 'And do you claim descent from an ape on your grandfather's or your grandmother's side?'

It was true, of course, that the implications of Darwin's theory were inimical to religion, for it implied that life was a random process which had no purpose other than survival.

Darwin's theory rests upon two fundamental points:

1) Small random changes in structure or function occur in nature. Those which are advantageous are, by natural selection, retained; those which are not are discarded.
2) This process of evolutionary change is gradual, long-term and continuous: it occurs now just as it occurred in the past. The

23

cumulative effect of these small changes over long periods of time is to create new species.

The theory was certainly attractive: it had logic, simplicity and, reassuringly, appeared self-evident. Within a decade Darwin had gained the widespread and powerful scientific support which continues today. The orthodox scientific consensus was summed up in 1959 by Sir Julian Huxley, Professor of Zoology and Physiology at King's College, London, when he stated that Darwin's theory of evolution was 'no longer a theory but a fact'.[1] Professor of Zoology at Oxford Richard Dawkins expressed himself just as bluntly in 1976, opining that, 'Today the theory of evolution is about as much in doubt as the theory that the earth goes round the sun . . .'[2]

It comes as a shock, then, to read Stephen Jay Gould, Professor of Zoology and Geology at Harvard University, observing in 1977 that, 'The fossil record offered no support for gradual change.'[3] This is a direct challenge to one of the fundamental props holding up Darwin's theory.

In 1982 David Schindel, Professor of Geology at Yale University, writing in the prestigious journal *Nature*, revealed that the expected gradual 'transitions between presumed ancestors and descendants . . . are missing'.[4]

What has happened? Did we all blink at an important moment? Have we all missed something?

We thought the debate over evolution had long been settled, but we were wrong. The origin of species is as much a mystery now as it was in Darwin's day.

The Origin of Species

Darwin argued that the development of any one species from its ancestor would be by a long and gradual progression which passed through a countless number of intermediate forms. He realized that, if his theory was correct, thousands of these intermediate forms must have existed. And he further realized that upon the existence of these forms his theory stood, or fell. He wrote, 'the number of intermediate and transitional links, between all living and extinct species, must have been inconceivably great. But assuredly, if this theory be true, such have lived upon this earth.'[5] But 'Why?' he asked, raising his own doubts, 'do we not find them embedded in countless numbers in the crust of the earth?'[6] He was painfully aware of the lack of such fossils in the geological strata. He stalled: 'the answer mainly lies in the [fossil] record being . . . less perfect than is generally supposed'.[7]

Nevertheless, this fact continued to haunt him and he proceeded to devote an entire chapter of his book to 'the imperfection of the geological record'. Despite his confident arguments, he clearly retained considerable unease about the situation for he felt the necessity to place in print his confidence that in 'future ages . . . many fossil links will be discovered'.[8]

Enthused by his theory and the certainty that a focus upon larger areas of fossil-bearing rocks would satisfactorily resolve this 'imperfection', geologists and palaeontologists (scientists who study fossils) have devoted enormous effort towards filling the gaps in the fossil record. Amazingly, given the vast resources applied to the task over the years, the effort has failed. Professor Gould revealed that, 'The extreme rarity of transitional forms in the fossil record persists as the trade secret of paleontology.'[9]

In 1978 Gould's colleague, Professor Niles Eldredge, confessed in an interview that, 'No one has found any "inbetween" creatures: the fossil evidence has failed to turn up any "missing links", and many scientists now share a growing conviction that these transitional forms never existed.'[10] Professor Steven Stanley writes, 'In fact, the fossil record does not convincingly document a single transition from one species to another. Furthermore, species lasted for astoundingly long periods of time.'[11] No one, for instance, has ever found a fossil giraffe with a medium-sized neck. If the fossil record fails to show the expected links, what then *does* it show? And what *does* it prove?

The Fossil Record

The fossil record, as we know it, starts at a period called by geologists the Cambrian, which they date to about 590 million years ago. Some minute fossilized remains have been found in rocks from the early years of this time: some bacteria and some very curious creatures unlike anything known before or since – the Ediacaran fauna dating from around 565 million years ago. But they were all apparently extinct shortly afterwards. It is as though a few training exercises were scribbled upon the book of life following which a distinct line was ruled across: thereafter real evolution began; or, at least, something began.

And it was dramatic: for the animal kingdom, everything came at once. Such was the sudden and mysterious blossoming of life's variety at this time that, as we have seen, scientists speak of the Cambrian Explosion which they date around 530 million years ago.

The most startling discovery was that every known body shape of animals, either as fossils or alive today, began here. At this time life chose its basic forms and has never seen fit to change.

What is more, even though the full Cambrian period is held to have lasted for some 85 million years, the actual appearance of these new forms probably occurred in about 10 million years or less.[12]

In other words, Life's history on earth reveals about 2 per cent creativity and 98 per cent subsequent development.

It is by body plan that all living creatures were first classified. A complex system has developed which divides all life into two great kingdoms: the animal kingdom and the plant kingdom. These, in turn, are subdivided, firstly into phyla (the plural form of phylum),

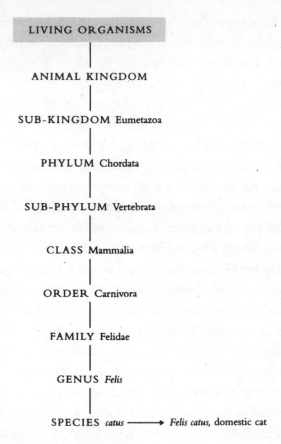

	LIVING ORGANISMS

ANIMAL KINGDOM

SUB-KINGDOM Eumetazoa

PHYLUM Chordata

SUB-PHYLUM Vertebrata

CLASS Mammalia

ORDER Carnivora

FAMILY Felidae

GENUS *Felis*

SPECIES *catus* ———→ *Felis catus*, domestic cat

Simplified diagram of animal classification.

derived from the Greek for 'tribe', then further divided progressively down to species and sub-species.

The animal kingdom is generally divided into thirty-seven phyla. All of these phyla arose during the Cambrian period. Since that time evolution has just tinkered with modification of the basic plan. Furthermore, there is no evidence whatever for any previous development of them. There is no evidence that they 'evolved' as we understand the term in its Darwinian sense. They all just appear in the fossil record as fully formed, highly distinct, creatures.

Scientists are bemused. Drawing attention to the fact that 'all the evolutionary changes since the Cambrian period have been mere variations on those basic themes',[13] Professor Jeffrey Levinton of State University of New York, asks, 'Why are the ancient body plans so stable?'[14] He has no answer.

What is very clear from the geological record is that this stability is the norm. Fossil forms of animals or plants appear, flourish for millions of years and then disappear, but still in much the same shape. Whatever change is seen is gradual and limited mostly to size: the entire animal or plant, or certain of its features, grows larger.[15] It is not seen to change into another form, even one relatively close: a mouse has never evolved into a rat; a sparrow has never become a blackbird.

Furthermore such change as has occurred seems very selective. A great number of creatures still living today have survived for very long periods of time without any evidence of significant change in their form at all. This is contrary to all the expectations of Darwinian evolution.

Oysters and mussels are much the same now as they were when they first appeared some 400 million years ago. The coelacanth and lungfishes have been living for around 300 million years without significant change. Sharks have remained the same for 150 million years. Sturgeons, snapping turtles, alligators and tapirs have all shown stability of form for over 100 million years. Modern opossums differ only in minor details from those which first lived 65 million years ago. The first turtle had a shell like it has today; the first snakes are almost identical to modern snakes; bats too have remained stable, as have frogs and salamanders.

Has evolution then stopped? Or is some other mechanism or agency at work?

An example, often used to demonstrate evolution, is that of the horse. It is supposed to have begun with the diminutive, four-toed, *Hydracotherium*,[16] which lived 55 million years ago and developed into the modern *Equus* which has been living for about 3 million years. Elegant and convincing charts and museum displays showing the progressive evolution of the horse have been widely seen. They cleverly show how the toes gradually reduce to one, how the size of the animal greatly increases and how the teeth change with its change in diet.

However, experts are now generally agreed that this line of slow but sure alteration from an animal the size of a dog into the large horse of today, is 'largely apocryphal'.[17] The truth is, as usual with the fossil record, that there are many gaps between the various species of fossil horse which are placed into this series. Beginning with the first, *Hydracotherium*, its own ancestry a mystery, there is no known link to the assumed 'second' horse, and so on.

What we have is not a line of development, nor even a family tree leading to modern *Equus*, but a great bush of which only the tips of the many branches are apparent – leaving open any question regarding the existence of its trunk. At any one time several differing species of horses were alive, some with four toes, some with fewer, some with large teeth, some with small. Horses too grew large, then small, and then large again. And, as a constant irritation throughout, there is a lack of interconnecting species.

Finally, we must also admit that the supposed ancestral horse is not so different from a modern horse. Apart from a few minor changes with feet and teeth and the increase in size, little of significance is different. This very minor alteration, championed as proof of evolution, even if true, is hardly impressive given the 52 million years involved. Bluntly, to regard this pseudo-sequence as in some way a proof of evolution is less an act of science than one of faith.[18]

The Abrupt Origin of Species

The fossil record is characterized by two aspects: the first, as we have seen, is the stability of the plant or animal forms once they have appeared. The second is the abrupt manner in which these forms emerge and, for that matter, subsequently vanish.

New forms arise in the record without obvious ancestors; they leave just as suddenly without any obvious descendants. One could almost call the fossil evidence a record of a vast series of creations, related only by choice of shape, not by evolutionary connections. Professor Gould summarizes the situation: 'In any local area, a species does not arise gradually by the steady transformation of its ancestors; it appears all at once and "fully formed".'[19]

We can see this process occurring almost everywhere. When, for example, about 450 million years ago, the first fossils of terrestrial plants appear, they do so without any previously recorded development. Yet, even this early, all the major varieties are evident. According to the theory of evolution, this is impossible – unless we can accept that *none* of the expected linking forms has been fossilized. Which seems rather unlikely.

Similarly, although the period preceding the appearance of flowering plants is one of great fossil diversity, no ancestral forms have ever been found for them; their origins too remain obscure.

The same anomaly is found in the animal kingdom. Fish with backbones and brains first appear about 450 million years ago. Their direct ancestors are unknown. And in a further blow to evolutionary theory, these first jawless but armoured fish had a partly bony skeleton. The commonly produced story of a cartilaginous skeleton (as seen in sharks and rays) evolving into a bony skeleton is, bluntly, wrong. In fact, these non-bony fish appear in the fossil record some 75 million years later.

Furthermore a significant stage in the apparent evolution of fishes was the development of a jaw. But the first fish with a jaw appears abruptly in the record without any earlier jawless fish able to be designated as the source. An additional curiosity is that lampreys – jawless fish – still happily exist today. If a jaw provided such an evolutionary advantage, why should such a fish still live? Similarly

Total number of living orders of land vertebrates:	43
Total number of these found in the fossil record:	42
Therefore, percentage discovered as fossils:	97.7%
Total number of living families of land vertebrates:	329
Total number of these found in the fossil record:	261
Therefore, percentage discovered as fossils:	79.3%

We can conclude that the fossil record is a competent record giving an accurate sample of the life forms which have existed on earth. Therefore, appealing to an imperfection of the fossil record as a way of explaining the gaps is not very convincing.

The accuracy of the fossil record.

enigmatic is the development of amphibians, aquatic creatures yet able to breathe air and live on land. As Dr Robert Wesson explains in his book *Beyond Natural Selection*,

> The stages by which a fish gave rise to an amphibian are unknown . . . the earliest land animals appear with four good limbs, shoulder and pelvic girdles, ribs and distinct heads . . . In a few million years, over 320 million years ago, a dozen orders of amphibians suddenly appear in the record, none apparently ancestral to any other.[20]

Mammals too show this abrupt pattern of development. The earliest was a small animal skulking furtively around during the era of the dinosaurs, 100 million or more years ago.[21] Then, after the mysterious and still-unexplained demise of the latter (about 65 million years ago), a dozen or more groups of mammals all appear in the fossil record at the same time – around 55 million years ago. Fossils of modern-looking bears, lions and bats are found at this period. And, to complicate the picture, they appear not in one area but simultaneously in Asia, South America and South Africa. On top of all this uncertainty, it is not sure that the small mammal of the dinosaur period was actually the ancestor of the later mammals.[22] Gaps and enigmas abound wherever one looks in the fossil record. There are no known fossil links, for example, between the first vertebrates and the primitive earlier creatures – the chordates – which are the presumed ancestors.[23] The amphibians alive today are markedly different from the earliest known: there is a 100-million-year gap in the fossil record between these older and later forms.[24]

Darwin's theory of evolution would seem to be crumbling away before us. His idea of 'natural selection' may conceivably be saved, but only in a significantly modified form. It is clear that there is no evidence for the development of any new plant or animal forms. It is only once a living form has appeared that perhaps natural selection has a role. *But it can only work on what is already existing.*

Students at school and university, as well as scientists, carry out breeding experiments with the fruitfly, *Drosophila*. They are taught that they are demonstrating the proof of evolution. They create mutations of the fly, give it different coloured eyes, a leg growing from its head, or perhaps a double thorax. They might even manage to grow a fly with four wings instead of the usual two. But these changes are only modifying already existing features of the fly – four wings, for example, are but duplicates of the original two. A new internal organ has never been created, neither has a fruitfly ever been turned into something resembling a bee or a butterfly.[25] It has not even been turned into another type of fly. It remains, always, a variant of the genus *Drosophila*. 'Natural selection may explain the origin of adaptations, but it cannot explain the origin of species.'[26] And even this limited application runs into problems.

How, for example, can natural selection explain the fact that humans – a single species – have dozens of different types of blood group? How can it explain that one of the earliest fossil types known, the Cambrian-period trilobite, has an eye of such complexity and efficiency that it has never been bettered by any later member of its phylum? And how could feathers evolve? Dr Barbara Stahl, author

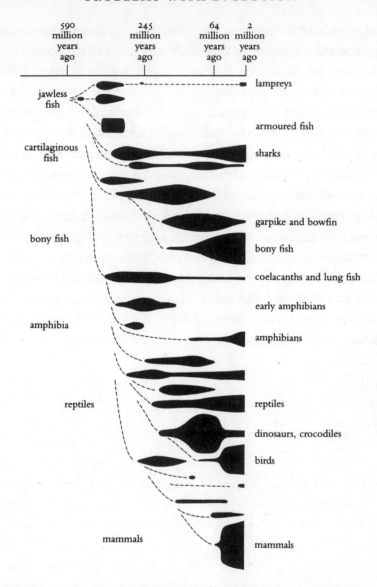

Apparent evolution of vertebrates. This diagram represents the abundance of vertebrate groups over time. The dotted lines are the missing links required by evolutionary theory to link these groups. *These links have not been found in the fossil record.*

of a standard text on evolution, admits, 'How they arose, presumably from reptiles' scales, defies analysis.'[27]

Even at the beginning Darwin knew that he faced profound problems. The development of complex organs, for example, strained his theory to its limit. For until such an organ was functioning, how could it be sufficiently advantageous for natural selection to encourage it to endure? As Professor Gould asks, 'Of what possible use are the imperfect incipient stages of useful structures? What good is half a jaw or half a wing?'[28]

Or perhaps half an eye? In the back of Darwin's mind the same question had arisen. In 1860 he confessed to a colleague that, 'The eye to this day gives me a cold shudder.'[29] As well it might.

The final example – proof if you will – that natural selection, if indeed a valid mechanism for change, has more to be understood, is the case of the waste-disposal habits of the sloth given by Dr Wesson:

> Instead of defecating on demand, like other tree dwellers, a sloth saves its faeces for a week or more, not easy for an eater of coarse vegetable material. Then it descends to the ground it otherwise never touches, relieves itself, and buries the mass. The evolutionary advantage of going to this trouble, involving no little danger, is supposedly to fertilize the home tree. That is, a series of random mutations led an ancestral sloth to engage in unslothlike behavior for toilet purposes and that this so improved the quality of foliage of its favorite tree as to cause it to have more numerous descendants than sloths that simply let their dung fall . . .[30]

Either evolution has other modes of 'natural selection' that we have not yet even guessed at, or something else entirely must be used to explain the abrupt scatter of the fossil record – a cosmic sense of humour perhaps?

Irregular Evolution

The problems with the fossil record have been known from the very first. For a century or so scientists simply hoped that they would go away, removed by some discoveries which bridged the gaps. Or, perhaps, by the discovery of certain proof that the gaps were caused by an intermittent geological process rather than any problems with evolution. Eventually, however, the strain became too much. The consensus broke in 1972 when Stephen Jay Gould and Niles Eldredge jointly submitted a radical paper to a conference on evolution.[31] Their paper directly contradicted Darwin's theory.

They put forward the argument that even though the fossil record was certainly far from satisfactory, the observed abrupt appearances of new species was not evidence of an imperfect fossil record; rather, it reflected reality. The origin of species might not be a gradual evolutionary process but a process in which long periods of stability were occasionally punctuated by sudden massive changes in living forms. By this argument, Gould and Eldredge could account for the absence of 'missing links': they held that they did not exist.

However well this idea might account for the fossil record, it is still based upon a perspective which holds life's development to be random, by chance. Yet it can be demonstrated that evolution, however it may have occurred, is unlikely to have been a random process.

The instructions for the plant and animal forms are contained within the genetic code. This code is complex and the amount of variation which could be involved is immense. Could this code have evolved randomly? A simple look at the figures suggests that it could not have done. If, for example, a monkey sat at a typewriter striking a key every second, how long would it take, by chance, for this monkey to create randomly an English word twelve letters long? The answer is that, by chance, it would take him almost 17 million years.[32]

How long would it take for this same monkey to produce, randomly, a meaningful sentence in English of 100 letters – a chain much less complex than the genetic code? The answer is that the probability is so low, the odds against it exceed in number the sum total of all the atoms in the observable universe.[33] Effectively, it is impossible for a meaningful sequence of 100 symbols to be produced by chance. We must conclude that it is similarly impossible for life's complex genetic code to have been produced by chance as the theory of evolution would require.

The astronomer Fred Hoyle, never one to suppress a pungent phrase, wrote that the chance creation of the higher forms of life is similar to the chance that 'a tornado sweeping through a junkyard might assemble a Boeing 747'.[34]

If, then, the genetic code is not arrived at by a random process, then it must be arrived at by a non-random process. Where could this thought lead us?

Directed Evolution

In 1991 Wesson's *Beyond Natural Selection* threw a new and powerful challenge into the arena. He dismissed the attachment to Darwinian evolution as 'indulging the old daydream of a universe like a great clockwork'.[35] Wesson points out that we cannot look at any animal in isolation. He proposes that we should consider a wider perspective: 'organisms evolve as part of a community, that is, an ecosystem . . . which necessarily evolves together. One might better speak not of the origins of species but of the development of ecosystems . . .'[36]

In a truly radical move Wesson suggests that we apply the findings of Chaos Theory to evolution in order to make sense of all the staggering oddities which we see both in the fossil record and in living creatures today.

Creatures of Chaos

Chaos Theory is a means by which very complicated systems – such as evolution – might be understood. But understood as a whole, not broken up into pieces as is usually the case.

Normal physics is baffled when trying to understand and predict behaviour in such complex systems as weather patterns, the turbulence of water as it rushes down a pipe, or population growth – to give but a few examples. Chaos Theory has created a technique which is able to capture the underlying structure of such apparently random events which make up these systems; a structure which appears as a pattern.

The Chaos explanation was discovered in 1961 by Dr Edward Lorenz, a scientist working on weather prediction. He had decided to repeat a computer sequence in order to examine one particular section further. To save time, he began midway through the sequence and instead of entering the exact data, which was accurate to six decimal places, he dropped off the three last decimal places of each figure. He assumed that any change would be minimal. He ran the program fully expecting that it would replicate the first. He then wandered off to drink a coffee.

When he returned he found something quite unexpected had occurred: the result of the repeated sequence, a graph, initially looked identical to the first he had already printed, but then rapidly began to diverge; first a little, and then wildly. This rapidly escalating rate of divergence is now termed a 'cascade to Chaos'. The very tiny, apparently insignificant, error which Dr Lorenz had introduced by dropping the final decimal places from his figures had rapidly caused a completely different result.[37]

Lorenz established two principles of Chaos: the first, sensitivity to initial conditions; small events can ultimately create large effects. The second, the importance of feedback from the environment. There is a constant interaction between the developing system and its surroundings, each affecting the other, backwards and forwards in an endless cycle: the system changes in a totally unpredictable way.

Chaos theorists have an eye for pattern and the patterns of chaotic systems share similarities: the same patterns seen in snowflakes are also seen in turbulent water, in heartbeat patterns, in patterns of waves breaking upon a beach. In some way nature is playing the chaos game.

In short, events which appear random turn out to have an underlying order.

The entire ecosystem within which we and all other creatures live is part of a global entity which is constantly and progressively cascading into Chaos and has done so ever since the very beginning of life. It will be seen that this idea solves the problem of the existence of millions of weird and unlikely forms of animals and plants which seem impossible to account for by Darwinian natural selection. These oddities *no longer have to be seen as advantageous to be selected*. The development of genetic variation chaotically cascading through the millennia can account for this incredible diversity. In comparison Darwinian natural selection seems linear, mechanistic and simple-minded.

There is a further surprising point revealed by Chaos Theory: evolutionary intent.

Because of the importance of feedback, from the environment and back again, on the creation of chaotic patterns, we can see that life is not so much helplessly modified by a one-way traffic of chance effects but actively involved in creating its own future direction.

The increase in the complexity of living creatures over the aeons is in complete accord with the theory of Chaos; a system cascading away from its starting point into unpredictable complexity. But there is more: this move towards complexity, evident in evolution, indicates that it is not random. Rather, it appears to be the expression of some deeper design: 'Evolution can be conceived as a goal-directed process insofar as it is part of a goal-directed universe, an unfolding of potentialities somehow inherent in this cosmos.'[38] And, as proof of a goal-directed universe, Wesson points to the sun and planets: they have moved naturally from a 'fireball to solar system'. This is evidence of a progression, a cycle perhaps, where inherent potential is unfolded.

Is something seeking to express itself?

An Act of Faith

Darwin's theory was a child of its times. Victorian man had an innate feeling of superiority over the rest of the world and Darwin appeared to have given scientific sanction to this belief.

Once the later scientists had added the discoveries of genetics to the theory, they felt that it had then become unassailable. Despite this, it remains far closer to religious faith than scientific fact. It may satisfy some scientists personally, it may give meaning to their lives, but it cannot account for the data.

A war rages over the area: some experts make an almost ideological commitment to it – like Oxford's Professor Dawkins who is the modern equivalent of a seventeenth-century fundamentalist preacher in his fervent demand for adherence to an orthodoxy.

Under pressure, not only from the creationists, science is trying to present a united front. It is as though scientists fear that to abandon Darwin is to fall into the hands of the creationists. This is nonsense and a measure of how weak many feel their scientific explanations really are.

In the end, Darwin's theory of evolution is a myth; like all myths it seeks to satisfy the need for understanding the origin of humanity. To that extent it may work, but that does not prove it is true.

3

Could 'Extinct' Creatures
Still Exist?

In 1972 the USS *Stein*, an antisubmarine frigate recently commissioned into the United States Navy, left its base in San Diego on a routine patrol which took it down the coast of South America. Shortly after it crossed the equator, its underwater tracking gear mysteriously malfunctioned and all efforts at repair failed. Forced to abandon its mission, USS *Stein* returned for repairs to a dry-dock at Long Beach naval base. There, the reason for the malfunction was quickly discovered. The large sonar dome protruding from beneath the ship had been savagely attacked by some massive marine creature; a creature which had left embedded in the dome hundreds of hollow, sharp teeth, up to an inch long. Specialist scientists studied the evidence and, eventually, it seemed reluctantly, conceded the obvious: that the destruction had been wrought by some 'extremely large' creature 'of a species still unknown to science'.[1]

In the 1960s and 70s the small American submersible *Alvin* was used in a research programme to study the strange life existing in the extreme ocean depths, in particular that existing around the deep ocean vents. The 'pilots' of this versatile craft had become well used to strange creatures and sudden emergencies for each trip was operated at the edge of both knowledge and technology. But even they could be shocked.

On one dive thousands of feet below the surface, a regular pilot, 'Mac' McCamis, was gazing out of his observation port when, without any warning, a huge deep-sea creature slid suddenly and rapidly past and quickly vanished into the deep black gloom. Despite his experience of the seas, McCamis was left shaken. He reported seeing a 'monster or something . . . at least forty or fifty foot of it'.[2] Its identity continues to be a mystery.

Scientists aboard another research submersible, *Deepstar 4000*, saw a similar monster in the late 1960s. They were 4,000 feet from he surface planting instruments on the sea floor of the San Diego trough when a huge fish, about forty feet long, of an unknown species swam right up to them. 'The eyes were as big as dinner plates,' the pilot reported.[3]

It is true that there are monsters in the sea. It is not always necessary to invoke unknown species to account for them. Sceptics will point out that monsters are well known: the whale or the whale-shark, for example; even the Great White shark moving at speed might seem bigger and more fearsome than it already is. It is a common and confident belief that no unknown animal of any size could have escaped the increasingly sophisticated search of the sea by fishermen and naval vessels as well as by the specialist ships engaged in scientific research. But this belief is really just an excessive attack of patronizing over-confidence. Large, unknown sea-creatures have been found.

In 1976 a United States research vessel operating off the coast of Hawaii hauled up its sea anchor to find, entangled in it, a large and totally unknown shark about fifteen feet long. This shark proved to be not only a new species but – astonishing biologists – also a new family and genus. Due to its huge mouth – four feet or more wide – it was quickly dubbed the 'Megamouth' shark.[4]

Megamouth was unlike all other sharks. Its head was large and chunky in relation to its body and its mouth contained a luminescent lining and 256 rows of tiny teeth. It lived on plankton which it strained out of the water. It was a slow and shy fish, unlikely to ever pose a threat to man. Nevertheless, it is extraordinary that it should first have been seen only twenty years ago.

In 1990 a slightly larger Megamouth shark was caught alive and, to gain a better knowledge of its habits, it was released back into the ocean with two small transmitters inserted beneath its skin. These revealed that the shark daily migrated up and down in the sea following the plankton it fed on: at night it would rise to a depth of about forty feet; by day, it would descend to 500 feet or more. This is one of the reasons why it had managed to stay out of human contact for so long. By 1995 seven examples of this shark had been caught, the longest measuring seventeen feet; it is thought that larger examples might exist.

Survivors from the Fossil Record

It is probable that creatures long thought extinct, known only by examples found fossilized in the rocks, are still living deep beneath the surface.

During the unexplained disasters which killed off much of terrestrial life, more often than not life in the sea survived. This is because it is an environment which remains remarkably stable, especially in the deeper regions. It would certainly be possible for large ancient creatures to survive there and remain unknown to science – if not to those who, for millennia, have made their living from the sea. Is it surprising that these fishermen speak of creatures not yet accepted by science? That such creatures exist is hardly in doubt.

A huge and terrifying shark, the ancestor of all nightmares, is known to have prowled the oceans long ago. It grew to at least twice the size of the largest known Great White, reaching a length of fifty feet or more. Its teeth were formidable weapons, triangular daggers up to six inches long.

This monster is the *Carcharodon megalodon* and is thought to have become extinct a million years ago. Perhaps early man, making primitive attempts to cross the sea, was familiar with its power and his desperate fear has since reverberated down through the millennia.

Perhaps, though, the cessation of fossils has more to do with geological processes than biological reality; perhaps *megalodon* did not die out. After all, there is no obvious reason why such a tough and resilient creature should survive for millions of years simply to succumb suddenly. Especially when its fellow sharks continued to flourish. The sea has not changed; why should a single species of shark?

Twice this century, in the region of the Polynesian Tuamotu Archipelago, north of Tahiti, a huge and unknown species of shark has been seen by experienced shark fishermen. It was described as being forty to fifty feet long, yellowish in colour with obvious white speckles. Its head alone measured ten feet or more across.[5]

A monstrous shark, 'ghostly whitish', was observed off the coast of New South Wales, Australia, in 1918. Frightened and subdued fishermen described how their heavily weighted crayfish pots, each three and a half feet in diameter, together with all tackle and mooring lines, were quickly and easily scooped up by an immense shark over 100 feet in length. The Australian shark expert who, together with a Fisheries Inspector, recorded this story from the fishermen themselves, accepted a measure of exaggeration in the telling but conceded that something strange and unknown had unnerved these experienced fishermen who, as he pointed out, were readily familiar with the normal species of sharks in that area. And, he noted, for several days after this attack they all refused to put to sea.[6]

The Polynesians, whose lives are closely intertwined with the sea, have ancient tales of a fearsome huge shark which they claim grows to 100 feet or more in length. Such is their respect for its power that they call it 'Lord of the Deep'.[7]

Could this shark be *megalodon*? If it lived one million years ago, could it be alive in the sea's depths today?

It is at least possible; it can be proved that *megalodon* was living much closer to our era than the fossil record would allow. While it is true the fossil remains suggest an extinction, there are other, *non-fossilized* remnants which suggest quite the reverse.

In 1875 the British survey ship HMS *Challenger* dredged two *megalodon* teeth, five inches long, up from the seabed 14,000 feet below. They were actual teeth, not fossilized. In 1959 these teeth were dated. The most recent proved to be a mere 11,000 years old.[8] They were found in Polynesia, just a few days' sail from Tahiti, in the region where the sightings have occurred.

In geological terms this tooth was modern. *Megalodon*, in all its powerful and terrifying fury, was alive at the time the first settlements were being built in Anatolia, at the time when communities were forming in Egypt – and, if some arguments are correct, about the time the Sphinx was being carved.

The Living Fossil

Certainly there are cases of creatures, known only in the fossil record, which have subsequently been found still thriving in the modern world. While this is not a common occurrence, the existence of even one example is sufficient to prove the possibility of others existing. One such is the coelacanth.

This fish first appears in the geological record around 450 million years ago; its heyday was about 50 million years later. Most varieties are considered to have been extinct for 200 million years, although a single fossil has been found dating from 70 million years ago.

In December 1938 a living coelacanth was found quite by chance in South Africa. The young curator of the Museum of East London, on the Indian Ocean coastline, had an interest in fishes. She was in the habit of looking at the day's catch as the fishermen returned. A few days before Christmas she was on the quayside when she noticed an odd-looking fish beneath a pile of freshly landed sharks. It was large, about five feet long, with, she noticed, very curious lobe-like fins and tail. She had never seen such a fish before. Its scales too were astonishing: large, thick and rough. She took it back to the museum where it was eventually identified, to considerable world-wide excitement, as a living descendant of the fossil coelacanth.

Since that initial discovery a hundred or more examples of the fish have been found. It lives at depths of up to 900 feet, mostly around the Comoro Islands, which seem to be some kind of breeding ground or home-base for it. Indeed, long before science recognized its existence, the natives of the islands were well aware of it. They valued its rough scales as alternatives to sandpaper in their repair of punctured bicycle tyres. For them this fish was simply another useful creature of the sea.

None of these living fossils has yet been caught elsewhere in the world. Yet, tantalizing evidence suggests that a similar, or related, fish lives in the depths around the Mexican Gulf.

In 1949 a scientist at the US National Museum received in the post a single strange fish scale with a request that he identify it. The letter came from a woman in Florida who made souvenirs out of fish scales and had received a bucketload of these strange scales in one of her regular consignments from fishermen. The scientist saw that the scale was very similar to that of a coelacanth. He tried to contact the woman but failed. Worse, he managed to lose the single scale.[9]

In 1964 a finely detailed antique silver model of a strange fish which had been made in Mexico in the seventeenth or eighteenth century was discovered in a village church in Bilbao, northern Spain. It was a very exact representation of a fish which the silversmith had obviously seen. A year later a second such silver fish was found in an antiques shop in Toledo, central Spain. They were exact representations of a coelacanth.[10]

In the 1970s a US naturalist attending a craft fair happened to see one stall-holder wearing a necklace made of large scales, just like those of the coelacanth. The owner said that he had found them on a shrimp boat which plied the Mexican Gulf. The naturalist tried to buy the necklace but the owner would not consider it.[11] This evidence too has vanished from the reach of the scientific world.

Whether, as seems likely, the coelacanth also thrives in the Mexican Gulf as well as the Indian Ocean, its importance is that it defies evolutionary theory by remaining essentially unchanged for upwards of 450 million years, and it defies the fossil record simply by still existing.

The importance of this single example of survival is that it must be considered possible for any other such creature of the past, especially one which can live deep in the sea, to have survived over tens of millions of years.

The way is opened not only for *megalodon* but also for other huge sea-creatures of the fossil record such as plesiosaurs, and other creatures of the dinosaur era, to still live deep in the sea, unnoticed by science. Of course, they may not be unnoticed by fishermen or other seafarers.

Sea-serpents

No scientist had made any methodical attempt to come to grips with the many reports of unknown animals and fishes until the 1950s, when the French zoologist Dr Bernard Heuvelmans embarked upon a project to gather and to analyse many reports from around the world. His first book was published in France, in 1955. In 1958 an augmented version of it appeared for the English-speaking audience as *On the Track of Unknown Animals*. This book caused a sensation and began a movement amongst scientists which led to the formation, in 1982, of the International Society of Crytozoology with Dr Heuvelmans as its president.[12] The Society publishes an annual journal, *Cryptozoology* – the term which it defines as 'scientific research into hidden animals', that is, those which are known only by hearsay, not yet by sound evidence. It is the sound evidence which the Society seeks to find.

In 1968 Heuvelmans published a work which dealt solely with unknown sea-monsters: *In the Wake of the Sea-serpents*. This too caused a sensation. In it Heuvelmans gathered 587 reports of sea-serpents witnessed throughout the world; 238 he dismissed as either hoaxes, mistakes or as too vague to be useful. The remainder he considered sufficiently solid to analyse. He divided the sightings into categories which allowed him to propose the potential existence of nine species of unknown large sea-creatures.[13] One of these monsters had been seen on a number of occasions off the coast of Canada: a monster called locally 'Caddy', from 'Cadborosaurus', a name given it by a local newspaper since it was seen in Cadboro Bay, off Vancouver.

Heuvelmans's book intrigued two young scientists working at the Institute of Oceanography in Vancouver. They were already aware of the reports of this strange aquatic creature and had begun to collect data about it. As a result of Heuvelmans's systematic survey, these young scientists, Dr Paul LeBlond (now Professor of Oceanography at the Institute) and Dr John Sibert decided to pursue this local creature in a scientific manner. Late in 1969 they began a serious survey to gain further evidence and hopefully, by this, to gain a greater idea about the form and the life of these unknown animals or fishes. Their hope was that sufficient data might be forthcoming as to lead to a scientific search for these creatures.[14]

They began by searching for eyewitnesses and interviewing them directly. They were quickly contacted by all those witnesses still living and willing to talk. Of these witness reports, twenty-three described a creature so unusual as to be unlike anything known to science, a creature sighted down 1,000 miles of sea-coast from Oregon to Alaska.

Many of the descriptions revealed features in common which led LeBlond and Sibert to conclude that up to three types of unknown creature were involved. Two were distinguished by a horse-like head on a long neck – perhaps five or ten feet long – with a body which, when swimming, revealed three humps. One of the creatures had large eyes and was covered with short fur; the other had smaller eyes, short horns on its head and often a large mane like that of a horse. Both were very rapid swimmers. They may perhaps be male and female of the same species. The third creature was like a large snake, with a sheep-like head and a jagged fin running down its back. As it swam, loops of its body would break the surface of the water.[15]

In November 1950 a lieutenant commander in the Canadian Navy reported seeing the 'Cadborosaurus'. He was fishing in a small open boat out from the naval base at Esquimalt Harbour, on the southern tip of Vancouver Island. 'Caddy' crossed behind him, less than seventy feet away. The officer reported that the creature was 'thirty feet long, head to tail, and created a heavy wash'.[16] And then

> He surfaced about every thirty-five feet. Each time he lifted his head from the water he opened his mouth wide and showed two rows of large teeth which had a saw-tooth appearance. Before he dove he snapped his teeth together with a terrifying sound.

The naval officer described the creature's head being about two feet long and eighteen inches wide; its eyes were black and two or three inches across. The head and body were covered with brown hair. Its neck was long, about six feet to where it joined the creature's body at what seemed to be shoulders. It swam by means of large flippers and a big flat tail.[17]

During March 1961 a trained biologist saw the creature. She was walking with a relative and her two small sons on a beach near to the entrance of Puget Sound, the shipping route into Seattle. While they were watching a freighter far away, moving down the channel, they suddenly became aware of something strange in the sea closer to them:

> We could see that it was some kind of creature and distinctly saw that the large flattish head was turned away from us and towards the ship. I think all of us gasped and pointed. We could distinctly see three humps behind the long neck.[18]

As they watched, the creature sank beneath the water. It then reappeared shortly after, closer to them: 'we could distinctly make out colour and pattern, a long floppy mane and the shape of the head'. Her small son cried out and began to clutch at her in fear. At this the creature appeared to notice them for the first time and sank. It again reappeared close enough for them to see its details clearly. She confessed later that, as a biologist, she found it very difficult to accept what she was witnessing.

One curiosity reported with 'Caddy' is a readiness to add sea-birds to its diet. In December 1933 two friends were duck-shooting on the coast. One duck, wounded, landed on the sea and headed for the safety of a large mass of seaweed. The friends rowed out to retrieve the bird. As they neared it, ten feet from their boat, two large coils of some sea-creature rose six feet out of the sea. Then a head appeared – they described it as like a horse's. To their horror, 'it gulped the bird down its throat'. The creature then turned and looked at the youths in their small boat. One recalled, 'It then looked at me, its mouth wide open, and I could plainly see its teeth and tongue . . . I would swear to the head being three feet long and two feet wide.'[19] The creature then snapped at some swooping seagulls before disappearing beneath the sea. A short time later the creature appeared again, this time only twenty yards from the shore where eleven other people saw it, including a local Justice of the Peace, who immediately recorded legal affidavits from all the witnesses.

This was not a unique occurrence. At other times it has been witnessed catching and eating ducks.[20] And it has several times been seen snapping at seagulls. Once, watched by three observers, it caught and devoured one.[21]

By 1995, LeBlond and a colleague, Edward Bousfield, former Chief Zoologist at the Canadian Museum of Nature, had compiled a total of 178 sightings, sometimes by several witnesses, dating from 1881 until 1994.[22] In addition, they found eleven occasions when strange carcasses had been drawn from the sea or found on the shore, some or all of which might have been the remains of unknown sea-creatures.[23]

One of these carcasses was photographed and it is this evidence which has led LeBlond and Bousfield to name officially this particular creature *Cadborosaurus willsi*.[24]

The photographs were taken in summer 1937 at a whaling station in the Queen Charlotte Islands, near the Alaskan border. A recently caught sperm whale was being cut up when a very strange creature was discovered inside the whale's stomach,[25] a creature which had remained largely intact. It had been killed and swallowed shortly before the whale itself was killed and very little digestion had taken place. The station manager realized that this creature was very unusual and decided to make a photographic record of it. These photographs survive as the best evidence for the existence of at least one mysterious sea-creature in the British Columbian coastal waters.

The photographs reveal a thin serpentine creature, ten and a half feet long, with a head rather like a dog's but with no noticeable hair. Its tail appears to have flippers at its end and there are small fore-flippers at the base of its neck. This seems damaged, probably by the sperm whale which caught and killed it. A witness present when it was removed from the whale's stomach reported that its long body was covered with fur except for its back, which had overlapping spiked plates of horn or something similar.

The file of photographs found by LeBlond has a note stating that it was sent to the Pacific Biological Station at Nanaimo on Victoria

Island. But there is no record at the laboratory of it ever having arrived.

In 1987 a sea-captain, Captain Hagelund, reported having once captured a baby 'Cadborosaurus'. During a family sailing trip, he had anchored for the night when he and other members of his family saw something odd moving on the surface of the water. Upon investigation it was found to be a small 'eel-like sea-creature swimming along with its head completely out of the water, the undulation of its long slender body causing portions of its spine to break the surface'.[26]

This small creature was caught in a net and brought back to the yacht. It was about sixteen inches long, an inch thick with a lower jaw holding small sharp teeth. On its back were scales like plates while underneath its body was a covering of soft fur. It had two small flippers at its shoulders and two flipper-like fins at its tail. It seems to have been a young example of that found inside the sperm whale in 1937.

Captain Hagelund, realizing that this was something very unusual, resolved to bring it to the scientific laboratory at Nanaimo and so put it in a plastic bucket of sea water. Into the night this little creature fought and scratched in attempts to escape. Listening to this increasingly desperate splashing and scratching Hagelund became filled with compassion and so returned to the deck and lowered the bucket back into the sea. He saw the little creature swim quickly away.

No other has yet been caught.

Mysterious Aquatic Animals

In the face of this considerable weight of evidence, eyewitness accounts by credible witnesses, together with photographs, it is not difficult to accept that one or more very strange species of animal live in the north-west Pacific Ocean. This evidence also adds credibility to the many eyewitness statements regarding other unknown aquatic animals living either in the oceans or in lakes.

The most famous of these is undoubtedly the Loch Ness 'Monster' but it is not alone. Large creatures have been reported elsewhere for many years, not only in other Scottish lochs. Lake Nahuel Huapi in the Argentinian Andes has a plesiosaur-like 'Nahuelito';[27] a large, long-necked creature with a long fin running down its back was seen in 1964 by a Russian scientist in Lake Khaiyr, Siberia;[28] another long-necked creature is reported from Siberia, in the lake of Labynkyr and, like 'Caddy', it has been seen to catch low-flying birds in its mouth.[29]

A possibly related creature has been reported in Sweden's Lake Starsjön, since at least 1635. This lake lies midway up the country, at the edge of the mountains, and is Sweden's deepest. The creature is described as ten feet long with two pairs of large flippers, a long thin neck and small head. Large fins reported on its head or back are probably a dorsal crest rather like that seen on the creature from Lake Khaiyr. The creature has become something of a tourist attraction for the adjacent town of Östersund.[30]

Japan too has its monster, 'Issie', a resident of Lake Ikeda. This has never been seen clearly but it is large, perhaps up to sixty feet or more long judging by its humps, which have been seen moving rapidly across the lake.[31] New Guinea has its *migaua* on the island of New Britain. In January 1994, a Japanese television team managed to get it on video from a range of almost three-quarters of a mile: it showed a creature about thirty-three feet long swimming with an undulating movement.[32]

North America also has some strange creatures apart from 'Caddy'. Lake Okanagan in Canada has its very old tradition of a creature called 'Ogopogo' which is serpent-like and reportedly grows up to fifty feet in length. To date over 200 sightings have been recorded.[33] Lake Champlain, near the Canadian border, has provided many sightings of a monster, up to twenty-five feet long, with the head of a horse, a long neck and humps, the *chaousarou* or 'Champ'. Sightings stretch back far into Indian times. The first European to visit the area – and after whom the lake is named – Samuel de Champlain, saw the monster himself during summer 1609.[34]

Champlain also reported seeing a further strange creature, a fish five feet long, with a small head, a long snout and two rows of sharp teeth. This was probably a garpike, the *Lepisosteus osseus*: it belongs to a type of armour-plated fish with heavy ganoid scales which mostly became extinct many millions of years ago. Examples have survived only in North America.[35] If one such prehistoric survivor still flourishes there, should we really be surprised to find another?

The Ancient Survivors

Given the great similarities in the various aquatic monsters reported from around the world, both sea- and lake-dwelling, it has been suggested that, of all the known extinct creatures, two in particular would be possible ancestors of some modern surviving species. Naturally, over the tens of millions of years certain changes and adaptations would be expected: changes in size, in habitat, even in the emphasis of various body features.

The first such candidate is the plesiosaur. This was a fish-eating, toothed, long-necked creature which lived in the seas at the time of the dinosaurs and supposedly died out along with them 64 million years ago. However, as we have seen with the coelacanth, the absence of later fossils need not preclude a survival. There is some evidence to suspect that the plesiosaur survived at least another 9 to 10 million years after the disappearance of the dinosaurs.[36]

The plesiosaur best fits many of the eyewitness reports. Its neck was up to twenty-six feet long, its body perhaps twenty feet. Like a turtle, it came on to the land to lay its eggs. However, it did not have the fur, whiskers or mane which have been reported. But over the last 64 million years some changes may have occurred in its structure.

The zoologist Dr Karl Shuker, in his important study of unknown animals, *In Search of Prehistoric Survivors*, is of the opinion that remnant plesiosaurs provide the best explanation for many of the aquatic monsters seen.[37] Referring, for example, to the famous 'flipper' photographs taken in Loch Ness in 1972 by Dr Robert Rine, he thinks that they provide good evidence for 'Nessie', at least, being a developed plesiosaur type.[38]

As a curious addendum to this, it is worth noting that in many isolated environments various large animals, devoid of predators, over the millennia developed into pygmy versions of their species. In Mediterranean islands, for example, the elephants of Malta and the hippopotami of Cyprus grew ever smaller until finally the last of the species, which died out in historical times, was only two or three feet in length. In the island of Mallorca, a dwarf antelope developed in the same manner. Dwarf deer remnants have been found on Jersey in the English Channel. And in the Russian Arctic, on Wrangel Island, recent work has shown that dwarf mammoths lived there until as late as 3,700 years ago – later than the building of the Egyptian pyramids.[39]

In Venezuela, in 1955, on the isolated plateau of Auyan Tepuí, a naturalist reported witnessing three strange creatures lying in the sun on a ledge above a river. His drawings and description fit that of a plesiosaur. Except that the creatures he described were only three feet long.[40]

The second possible candidate for prehistoric survival is perhaps the ancestor of those many reports which describe a sinuous, serpentine creature which swims in a vertically undulating manner. Certainly, no known modern creature such as a watersnake or eel swims in this way. But the fossil record reveals one such creature: the zeuglodont which, according to the palaeontologists, has been extinct for 25 million years.

This is a very long, serpentine mammal growing up to sixty feet long. Fossils show that it was widely distributed around the world, both in shallow and deep water. It has a very long, very flexible backbone and it is thought that it swam in an undulating manner. Cryptozoologists regard remnant zeuglodonts as the main candidates for the unknown serpentine creatures reported the world over.[41]

It is easy to see that some unknown monstrosity, a remnant dinosaur, or some other adaptation, could hide from the scrutiny of mankind in the remote depths of the oceans or lakes. As we have seen, this process has occurred with the coelacanth and the Megamouth shark. However, it is less easy to think of this process occurring on the land, since most of the earth seems to be either covered with humans or well explored by them.

In fact, neither of these statements is true. Vast parts of the earth are rarely, if ever, visited by humans. And, as with the oceans and lakes, animals unknown to mankind, some of them thought extinct, have been found.

In 1992 an international zoological team mounted an expedition along the jungle border of Vietnam and Laos. They found four animals previously unknown: a fish, a bird, a turtle and, most dramatically, the Vu Quang ox. This grows to around three feet high and has two parallel pointed horns sweeping back from the top of its skull. The team came back with three skulls. It was not until June 1994 that scientists successfully captured a live example.[42]

In 1995 a team of French and British explorers were making their way across a remote region of Tibet when they found their route blocked by an unseasonally early snowfall. They detoured through a valley which had never been mapped and were surprised to find it filled with large trees which protected several herds of small horses. These diminutive animals were about four feet high with wedge-shaped heads. The leader of the expedition stated later that they looked just like the horses depicted in the prehistoric cave paintings in France and Spain.[43]

These are just recent examples of a long line of discoveries which have continued ever since scientists began classifying animals; and the discoveries are not likely to cease suddenly. This century alone, seven sizeable creatures, previously unknown, have been found.[44]

The two examples above show us the kind of environment in which discoveries are being made: remote areas of mountain or jungle. It is not surprising, then, that there is a jungle region out of which come tales of a creature resembling nothing less than a great dinosaur. A creature which holds the local population in a state of fear.

4

Living Dinosaurs

On 19 February 1980 Professor Roy Mackal of Chicago University, a biologist with an enduring passion for cryptozoology, was wading through the virtually unexplored Likouala swamps in the northern jungles of the African Republic of Congo. As he pushed through the stinking mud, biting insects and a humidity which touched 100 per cent, he must have wondered why he had left the comfortable life of a university for such hazardous terrain. Accompanying him was a zoologist, James Powell, whose previous experience of the African jungles still had not fully prepared him for the hardships they were facing. Both were driven by a certainty that somewhere in this dangerous region lived large unknown beasts which, just possibly, might be remnant dinosaurs.[1]

The Likouala swamps, however awe-inspiring their beauty often is, are one of the most forbidding and inhospitable places on earth. They are a constantly sodden marshy jungle area which extends over some 55,000 square miles, an area slightly larger than England, about the size of the US state of Illinois or Iowa, stretching across the Republic of Congo to Zaïre, Chad and the Central African Republic. They represent terrestrial life in overload, the thick jungle hiding leopards, panthers, gorillas, hippopotami, antelope and the dangerous wild buffalo, together with a number of unknown species which dwell in the shallow waters.

The region is very hot and very humid. It is infested with

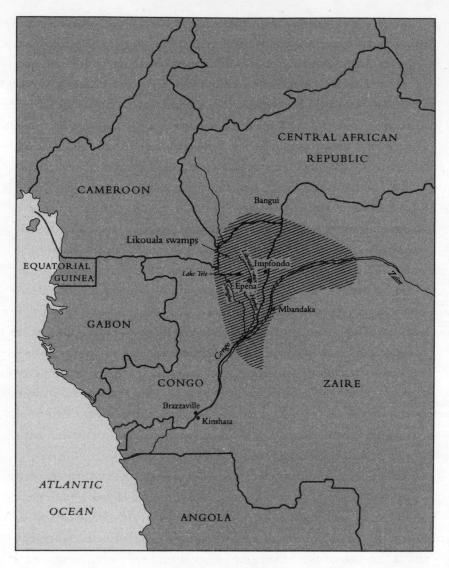

The Likouala swamps: possible home to relict dinosaurs.

poisonous snakes – vipers, mambas, cobras – voracious ants, belligerent crocodiles, scorpions, tarantulas and malaria-carrying mosquitoes. The region has endless tracts of stinking mud which must be laboriously waded through, each step bringing up discharges of stinking gas. It is filled with diseases of every type. Even the local inhabitants, as acclimatized to the region as any humans could be, are rife with intestinal parasites, skin diseases and malaria.

Few hunters venture into the heart of the swamps. Even fewer live there in villages. The largest are only a handful of isolated huts, many miles' and many hours' travel from any neighbours. Those who do live in the area do so on the main rivers, the Likouala-aux-Herbes, the Bai and the Sangha. In this vast swamp a large beast, adapted to the conditions, could survive, rarely seen, indefinitely.

A notable curiosity of this region is that despite its fearsome appearance it is, in ecological terms, an 'island' of stability.[2] It has remained much the same for 60 million years – almost since the time the dinosaurs are thought to have died out. During this long period it has not experienced any of the changes which have distorted the rest of the world. It has never seen earthquakes, Ice Age glaciation, flooding or the mountain-building effects of continental drift. Over these millions of years it has remained environmentally constant. A creature adapted to the conditions, and living here successfully in the past, would have every expectation of continuing to live there today. Indeed, some known creatures have done just that: crocodiles, for example, have thrived there virtually without change for some 65 million years.

It cannot, therefore, be regarded as a complete surprise that here, in this vast jungle swampland, local hunters have occasionally reported seeing a huge hostile monster described as a large reptile. Science may not have recognized it, but the local people certainly do. They know it as the *mokele-mbembe* and take care to stay well clear of its path.

It was the reports of this monster which drew Professor Mackal and James Powell into the swamps. Their decision to mount an expedition, in the face of considerable scholastic disdain, took considerable academic courage. The expedition itself necessitated physical courage.

The African Dinosaurs

It is undoubtedly true that the native peoples who have lived in the Likouala swamps over the centuries have always known of this monster and have seen no reason to feel anything about it but great fear. It is a common belief amongst certain groups in the area that to even talk about witnessing such a creature would, in some occult manner, bring about one's death.

The first Europeans to realize that something strange and monstrous was alive in Central Africa were the French missionaries who, during the eighteenth century, were tramping through the jungles seeking to make converts to Christianity. While engaged in this task they also reported on the daily life of the people and on the animals and plants which they saw, most unknown to Western science at the time. In 1776 the French Abbé Proyart drew from these reports for his *Histoire de Loango*: missionaries had come across the tracks of some huge and unknown animal which left claw-marks about three feet in circumference, with seven to eight feet between each print.[3]

Nothing further was recorded until the early twentieth century. Then rumours of the existence of some very strange beasts began reaching the scientific community in Europe.

One of the earliest official records of these stories was made by the German captain Baron von Stein zu Lausnitz, just prior to the First World War. At that time these swamps fell within the German colonial empire, the Cameroons, which extended through the north of modern-day Congo, in which territory the region lies today. The captain had been ordered to make a general survey of the area which he completed in 1913–14. In his report back to Berlin – which unfortunately was never published because of the outbreak of war – he mentioned an unknown beast, the *mokele-mbembe*, which lived in certain rivers in the swamplands.

This beast, he wrote, was 'feared very much' and lived in an area bounded by two rivers, the Likouala-aux-Herbes and a tributary, the Sangha. Both feed water into the Congo river which flows down the border between Congo and Zaïre before emptying into the Atlantic.

The captain described an animal about the size of an elephant but with a long and flexible neck. Some reports describe a single horn on its head. Its skin was reportedly smooth and grey-brown in colour. It was said to live in caves washed out by the current beneath the river bank and to eat certain plants along the banks. The local natives were terrified of its long powerful tail which was rather like that of an alligator. It was reputed to attack any canoes which came near it, killing the occupants but not eating their bodies for, although vicious, this animal was not carnivorous.[4]

During the succeeding decades, anecdotes and rumours about this beast, and perhaps others equally unknown, kept surfacing, not only in the Likouala area, but in other parts of Central Africa. In the Cameroons, a monster, the *n'yamala* was spoken of in almost identical terms. A water-dwelling monster, the *mbilintu* was noted in the jungle area where the borders of Zaïre, Zambia and Tanzania all come close to one another. This was described as resembling a huge lizard with a long neck, a small head and heavy legs similar to an elephant's.[5]

Another German official, the magistrate Dr Leo von Boxberger, who served in the Cameroons for many years while it remained a colony, reported that in the Congo basin there were many reports of a 'mysterious water beast' described as a huge reptile with a long thin neck.[6]

The earliest European hunters and animal collectors who heard these stories concluded that some relict dinosaur was the likely explanation. Such suggestions briefly made lurid headlines which did the thesis no favours in the scientific community and, even worse, led to a number of sensationalized frauds.[7] These drove the subject well beyond the boundaries of orthodox science.

Nevertheless, apparently genuine sightings continued: in the

1920s a local ruler in what is now Zambia was informed, with great excitement, that a monster 'taller than a man, with a huge body, a long neck with a snake-like head, and sturdy legs'[8] had been resting on the edge of a nearby swamp; upon the approach of the men it had quickly vanished beneath the waters. The ruler immediately visited the site where he could easily make out traces of a large animal. In an area about four and a half feet wide, the reeds were pressed into the mud as though from the weight of a bulky creature and, from this point, a wide muddy track led to the river. This was consistent with what the excited natives had seen. The ruler deemed the incident of sufficient importance to send a report on it to the local British administrator.

In May 1954 an Englishman, working in what is now Zambia, was taking a short fishing holiday at Lake Bangweulu. While fishing, he was astonished by the sudden appearance, about twenty-five yards away, of a small head atop a long thick neck, rising up out of the water. His first impression was that it was some sort of snake but he quickly realized that he was witnessing a much more mysterious creature. He remained tight-lipped about this sighting until the 1990s, when he told his story to cryptozoologist Dr Karl Shuker, who concluded that it represented a *mokele-mbembe* type of creature.[9]

Dr Shuker's informant described the animal's neck as about twelve inches thick and of a grey colour. Its head had a blunt nose with an obvious jaw-line and brow. After a few seconds the creature sank back below the water of the lake.

Other observers have recorded such creatures and have noted that they regularly leave the water because footprints and other marks have been found on the shore; these revealed that it had a foot with three toes or claws and a thick tail.[10]

Local Traditions

In the late 1970s James Powell approached Professor Roy Mackal, who had been delivering a lecture on cryptozoology at a Texan university, with an interesting story.

In 1976 Powell had been based in Gabon conducting a study of crocodiles. During this time he had befriended local people who, knowing of his interest in such animals, told him of a mysterious creature which they called the *n'yamala*.[11] It was said to be a very dangerous long-necked monster, to be avoided at all costs.

Mackal and Powell pooled their information and began to plan an expedition to Central Africa in order to seek out this unknown monster. Both thought plausible the suggestion that it might be a relict dinosaur. Firstly, though, Powell decided to return to Gabon for a fortnight's preliminary investigation. He arrived there at the end of January 1979. His findings were to prove important.

Through his contacts Powell was introduced to a local shaman, a man of high intelligence and great knowledge of the area. Powell reported:

> First I showed him pictures of African animals found in the Gabonese jungles – leopard, gorilla, elephant, hippo, crocodile, etc. – and asked him to identify each one, which he did unerringly. I then showed him a picture of a bear, which does not occur in Gabon. This he could not identify.
>
> 'This animal not live around here,' he said. I then showed him a picture of a *Diplodocus* (a brontosaurus-like dinosaur) . . . and asked him if he could recognize it.

'*N'yamala*,' he answered, quite matter-of-factly.[12] Powell then showed him a picture of a plesiosaur. The shaman also identified this as a *n'yamala*. When shown illustrations of other dinosaurs the shaman replied honestly and bluntly that these did not live in the region.[13]

Powell was cautious but concluded that the shaman was a plausible witness and so accepted that there was, or had been in the recent past, a dinosaur-like creature concealed deep in the swamps of Gabon.

The next day Powell travelled eighty miles downriver to another small settlement where he put the same questions and illustrations to the local people. He reported identical results: 'Pictures of a leopard, gorilla, hippo, elephant and crocodile were all correctly identified. The bear was unknown. Pictures of a *Diplodocus* and a plesiosaur were both identified as *n'yamala*.' The latter was said to be, 'a rare animal that was found only in remote lakes deep in the jungle. Only the very greatest hunters have seen the *n'yamala*.'[14]

The natives told Powell that these animals lived on 'jungle choc-olate', the name given to a plant with large fruit – like nuts – which grows near the banks of rivers and lakes. They added that these animals did not coexist with hippos; consequently, in any areas where the *n'yamala* lived, hippos were conspicuously absent. Mackal and Powell were later to find certain areas abounding with hippos and other parts of the same river complex curiously devoid of them. Could they assume that this indicated the presence of the unknown beast?

The shaman eventually confessed to Powell that he had personally seen one of these beasts about 1946, when he was camping near a small lake. Early one morning, he recalled, a *n'yamala* left the water and climbed on to the land to eat 'jungle chocolate', allowing him a good view of it. The beast was about thirty-three feet long with a long neck and tail and appeared to be as heavy as an elephant.[15] The shaman added that its usual feeding times were between mid-night and dawn; the remainder of the day it would spend under water.

It seemed evident that this *n'yamala* of Gabon was the same creature as the *mokele-mbembe* of the Congo. Enthused by this information, Mackal and Powell decided upon an expedition to the latter region to try and find one of these beasts. They organized rapidly; on 30 January 1980 they flew out of O'Hare Airport, Chicago, *en route* for the northern Congo.

The Expeditions

From the very beginning Mackal and Powell had three aims: firstly, and most ambitiously, to photograph or capture a living *mokele-mbembe*; secondly, to gather all the information they could about the creature, its habits, its environment and particularly when and where it had been most recently spotted; thirdly, to meet and interview as many eyewitnesses of the beast as possible.

They had chosen their area of search well for they soon found cooperative witnesses who testified to the continued presence of the creatures. Mackal and Powell were in the upper basin of the Likouala-aux-Herbes river, based for a time at the riverside settlement of Epéna, near which a number of sightings had occurred in recent times. They interviewed about a dozen men and women, most of whom had personally witnessed the creature.

One, a high-ranking army officer who had been born in the area and maintained a home there, had seen the creature twice. Once, in 1948, when he had been paddling in a canoe with his mother, upriver from Epéna, they saw a *mokele-mbembe* crossing the river about thirty feet ahead of them. The same year, also in a canoe, he had actually run into one lying just under the surface in the middle of the river. He vividly described his amazement when the obstruction suddenly moved away and proved to be a monstrous animal.[16]

Another witness described when, aged seventeen, he had been out in his canoe about 7 a.m. and decided to hunt some monkeys he had spotted. He landed and had just pulled his canoe out of the river when, with a sudden rush of water, a huge animal rose out of the river shallows. It was almost completely visible for several minutes. It had a long reddish-brown neck which, at its base, was as thick as a man's thigh. It was about thirty feet long and around six feet or so high with a tail longer than its neck.[17]

Yet another local resident described that as recently as July 1979, just seven months earlier, at a settlement fifty miles downriver from Epéna, a *mokele-mbembe* had been progressively stranded in a swampy jungle pool by the lowering of the water level with the onset of the dry season. The local people observed it over the course of several months until one day when it emerged from the jungle, walked over a small sandy island and disappeared into the river. It left footprints similar in size to those of elephants, together with claw-marks and a trail of flattened grass six feet wide.[18]

During these interviews a very intriguing story emerged from several informants. At some time in the past, a *mokele-mbembe* had actually been captured, killed and subsequently eaten. This was said to have occurred at Lake Tele, about forty-four miles inland from Epéna, deep in the jungle almost midway between the Likouala-aux-Herbes river and a tributary, the Bai.

About forty years earlier, two or three *mokele-mbembes* had been disrupting the fishing of the local inhabitants who decided to prevent them entering the lake. Around Lake Tele were a number of large lagoon-like pools, each connected by a channel to the main lake. The creatures were living in one of these pools and entering the lake via the channel. The natives chopped down a number of trees, each around six inches across, and sharpened one end. When they knew that the beasts were in the lagoon they drove these heavy stakes across the connecting channel with the points angled upper-most, like a row of medieval pikes. This barrier, they hoped, would keep the monsters out of the main lake. One of the creatures attempted to break through this barrier of stakes and while it was doing so the natives fell upon it with spears, killing it. To celebrate their success, they cut the beast up and ate it. But shortly thereafter, according to the story, all who had eaten the flesh died.[19]

Mackal and Powell ran out of time and did not make it to Lake Tele. But the next year Mackal returned with a slightly larger team, including, this time, a native Congolese zoologist. While they gathered many more reports of sightings they again failed to see or record any of the beasts at first hand. They did, however, find some evidence which might just derive from the *mokele-mbembe*.

While they were at Dzeke on the Likouala-aux-Herbes river, they were told of a site a short ride upriver where, about a year before, one of the beasts had been surprised; it had rushed to the river leaving a clear trail behind.

Mackal and his team, together with a local hunter as guide, visited the site. There, they found that the river bank was fairly firm and covered with grass about three feet high. The thick jungle started some fifty yards in from the bank. 'Jungle chocolate' plants grew in profusion with their fruit the size of a small orange. The guide took them to an area where there were a number of small pools and there showed them the trail which had been left. Near the edge of one pool they could see the traces very clearly: 'Branches, broken and weathered, attested to the passage of some creature 1.5 to 2 metres in height and half as wide. This was certainly the right size for a *mokele-mbembe*, but, of course, also for a smallish forest elephant.'[20] The trail led through the jungle and contained large footprints, a foot or so in diameter, pressed into the soft earth. This trail was readily visible until it entered the grass growing at the river bank where the recent year's growth had since obscured it.

Their guide pointed this out and explained that originally the grass too had been flattened in a six-foot-wide track leading into the river. He added that no elephant makes such a trail and, in any case, elephants always come out of the river again. The other possibility, that the trail was made by a large crocodile, would seem impossible since crocodiles do not leave foot-wide footprints or break the jungle to a height of six feet.

Mackal realized wryly that this creature they were hunting had been living here when, the year before, he and Powell had been upstream at Epéna.

In all, over the two expeditions Mackal took over thirty detailed descriptions of the beast, of which a little more than half came from eyewitnesses, some of them having seen it several times.

Fascinated by the media reports, other investigators began to also arrange expeditions to this part of Central Africa. Since Mackal's and Powell's first there have been over eleven expeditions, occurring almost annually. They include two from Japan and one official Congolese scientific group. None have returned with either photographs or film of the beast. It remains elusive to this day.

The regular arrival of researchers and curious amateurs to the area has had its effect on the local economy. The writer Redmond O'Hanlon, who mounted his own mini-expedition to look for a *mokele-mbembe*, reported that at Boha, the nearest village to Lake Tele – a mere two days' walk away – a prominent shack bore a large sign reading: BOHA PILOTE DINOSAURE.[21]

But the *mokele-mbembe* may not be the only strange creature in the Likouala swamps. Mackal and Powell collected stories of others, two of which might also represent relict dinosaurs.

The Animal with 'Planks on its Back' and Others

Among the interviews which Mackal and Powell conducted, one was decidedly odd. One woman, who had hitherto only repeated local stories about the *mokele-mbembe*, was leafing through a book of dinosaur illustrations carried by the two scientists when she opened a page which had an illustration of a stegosaurus. She suddenly smiled. 'Yes, that animal was spoken of by my ancestors. My parents told me about this animal with the planks growing out of its back. I was told to hide behind a tree if I saw it coming through the forest.'[22] She explained that this animal, the *mbielu-mbielu-mbielu*, also spent much of its time in the water and that the 'planks' along its back dripped with growths of green algae. She added that she had seen the creature herself on only one occasion – or, at least, had seen its back sticking out of the water.

Mackal, on his second expedition in 1981, was to obtain further information on this animal. He met with an elderly local man, a former civil servant who had previously worked for the French administration. He had maintained very detailed records of all sightings of *mokele-mbembes* known to him, noting some fifteen sightings and the places where they had occurred. Near the end of the interview he also mentioned the creature with 'planks on its back'.

He described one which had been a little upriver from Epéna, and which, although he had not personally observed it, had often been seen around dusk in the dry season, when the water was at its lowest. It had 'much green vegetable growth on its back' which was very obvious whenever the creature emerged from the water.[23]

Mackal also found many of his informants talking of another monster which they called the *emela-ntouka*, or 'killer of elephants'. It was said to resemble the *mokele-mbembe* in being semi-aquatic, having the bulk of an elephant and similar thick strong legs, but it lacked the *mokele-mbembe*'s long neck and its head had a sharp horn growing out of it.[24] It had been known to attack and kill water buffalo or elephants but never to eat them. It too was herbivorous.

Other creatures were also mentioned: there were sightings of a giant snake-like or lizard-like creature with a forked tongue which walked on four short thick legs, the *nguma-monene*. It was distinguished by a serrated bony ridge running along its back.

This creature was clearly seen by an American missionary interviewed by Professor Mackal. In late 1971 this pastor was travelling upriver in the Likouala region. The river at that point was about 200 feet wide. Suddenly, ahead of him he saw a creature unlike anything he had ever seen before. It was about thirty feet long and had 'a back like a saw'. He stopped his outboard and drifted in the current watching as this creature swam across the river, climbed out at the other side and disappeared into the jungle.[25]

Finally, there were reported in the same area three giant examples of known creatures: a huge crocodile up to fifty feet long which was said to dig out long underground tunnels, which it then inhabited – this was first mentioned in the nineteenth century by a Belgian explorer; a giant turtle with a shell twelve to fifteen feet in diameter; and a large bird, perhaps some kind of eagle, which had a wingspan of almost thirteen feet and which attacked and ate monkeys.

There is clearly much scope for cryptozoologists in Central Africa.

Ancient Man and Extinct Creatures

Many thousands of years ago ancient peoples created visual records of their world. They recorded, in pictures and carvings, their society, the animals they hunted or tamed and, later, events of importance. Amongst these records are some which are very curious indeed: they defy any easy explanation.

At the very beginning of the Egyptian royal dynasty, around 3100 BC, when writing was in its infancy, there was production of highly decorated slate palettes, a ceremonial development of those used for mixing pigments for make-up. A number of these have been found, particularly in Hierakonpolis, the ancient capital of southern Egypt. All are covered with exceptionally skilful carvings of hunting or political scenes. Many animals and humans are shown with great attention to detail. The animals, in particular, are instantly recognizable; there is nothing about them which seems to derive from the realm of fantasy.

It is all the more surprising, then, that two of the palettes found – one now in the Ashmolean Museum at Oxford and another in Cairo's Archaeological Museum – show long-necked creatures identical to the reported characteristics of the *mokele-mbembe*. The palette of King Narmer in Cairo is particularly forthright. At its centre – framing the circular depression in which pigments could be mixed – are the long curving necks of two strange beasts with strong limbs and long tails. Both these creatures are shown as captive: each has a rope around its neck held tight by Egyptian keepers. This, perhaps, is the nearest the illustrations come to fantasy: no one man could alone restrain such a beast.[26]

Naturally, as no creatures as these are today accepted by science they have quickly been labelled 'mythological'. Yet a moment's study reveals that this conclusion cannot be justified.

Leaving aside modern scientific prejudices, the logic of the palette itself – which is the only logic relevant in this situation – demands that we consider these two long-necked creatures as real, as known, as any of the other animals and humans also depicted. Therefore we cannot avoid concluding that the ancient Egyptians had captured examples of some great beast which either no longer exists or does so only in some distant habitat unknown to science. A beast extraordinarily similar to that reportedly seen in the Congolese swamps.

But the ancient Egyptians were not the earliest humans to record strange creatures which must have inhabited their world and which may still inhabit ours. Millennia earlier, during the last Ice Age, similar monsters were depicted.

It is well known that many caves have been found in Spain and France which hold illustrations made by early man. Some of these are incised by sharp stones; some are drawn in charcoal; others are painted in colour. The most dramatic fact of these illustrations is the very high degree of artistic skill demonstrated by people we otherwise tend to disdain as 'cavemen'. And further, the very life-like aspect of the animals represented allows the vast majority of them to be easily identified. Which fact makes it all the more astounding when, on only two known occasions amongst these thousands of illustrations drawn, carved or painted, there are depictions of long-necked animals unlike anything known today.

The first comes from the cave of Pergouset in southern France and is dated to 12,000 or more years ago. It is a well-executed engraving of an animal with a very long neck bearing a head rather similar to a horse. Is it a giraffe? Unlikely because of the almost arctic Ice Age conditions which existed outside. Is it, then, something like a *mokele-mbembe*? Or perhaps a marine creature rather like Vancouver's Caddy? No one knows. The archaeologists who drew attention to it in 1997 noted, 'The very long neck is no accident; the lines have been reinforced or re-cut several times . . .'[27] They speculated that this and other engravings may be fantasies created under the influence of psychedelic drugs. This is possible; but it is much more likely that, as with other drawings, this creature was something seen by the artist living in the world beyond the cave.

The second example is even more enigmatic. In the Spanish cave of Casares, also dating from the Ice Age, is an incised illustration of a group of three monstrous, dinosaur-like, creatures. Two are large, perhaps adults, and the third is small, seemingly a young animal. They all have long necks, substantial but ill-defined bodies and strange reptilian heads. They look dangerous.[28]

As in the other cases, the logic of the caves themselves suggests that these are creatures which have been actually witnessed by the artists while outside the enclosed safety of the deep caverns.

Were our ancestors, until comparatively recently, confronted by true monsters as they hunted in the forests or fished in the rivers? These drawings would seem to prove that this was so. In any case, whatever the truth, to dismiss these creatures as 'mythological' or 'fantasy' is to cast premature judgement upon them and risk ignoring potentially important historical data.

Perhaps somewhere we will dig up their bones. Unless, of course, they were maritime or partly aquatic river-dwellers – in which case their bones have probably long been washed far out to sea.

Flying Monsters

Between 1911 and 1922 Englishman Frank Melland served the British colonial authorities as a district magistrate in what is now Zambia. He had a keen interest in natural history and had been made a Fellow of the Royal Anthropological Institute, the Royal Geographical Society and the Zoological Society. In 1923, when he returned to England, he published *In Witch-bound Africa*, a study of the tribal shamanism which he had observed during his colonial service. In it he described how his zoological interests were piqued one day when he was told of a special magic charm used on certain river crossings to avoid the attack of some greatly feared creature the natives called the *kongamato*.

When he asked, 'What is the *kongamato*?' he received a surprising answer. It was a type of bird, his informants said, or rather, a flying creature like a lizard with bat-like wings, wings which were four to seven feet across. Not only this, its beak contained many sharp teeth. Melland wrote: 'I sent for two books which I had at my house, containing pictures of pterodactyls, and every native present immediately and unhesitatingly picked it out and identified it as a *kongamato*.'[29] It was said to live in the jungle swamplands, in particular those up the Mwombezhi river which arises near the border with Zaïre.

Further south, in Zimbabwe, tales of a similar creature have emerged. The English journalist G. Ward Price related a story told to him by a colonial officer whose administrative region contained a huge swamp which was so feared by the local people that they generally refused to enter it.

One man, however, proved sufficiently foolhardy as to venture in. He emerged some time later with a deep wound in his chest reporting that he had been attacked by a large bird with a long beak. The colonial officer obtained a book containing illustrations of prehistoric creatures and showed these to the wounded man. He looked through it without comment until he came upon an illustration of a pterodactyl. He cried out and immediately fled.

The officer said to Price, 'It seems to me quite possible that in that vast, unpenetrated area pterodactyls still survive.'[30]

But it is not only the peoples native to the area who have seen these strange creatures. In 1941 a British army officer and his men witnessed one flying above them.

That year, Lieutenant Colonel A. C. Simonds was in the Sudan under the command of Orde Wingate who was preparing his invasion of Ethiopia to restore the exiled emperor Haile Selassie. As part of the preliminary strategy, Simonds, commanding a very small group of officers and men, was ordered south. He and his men left the southern Sudan town of Roseires and crossed into Ethiopia, heading east through the jungle towards the Belaya highlands which they reached fifteen days later. It was during this march that they all saw a strange flying creature fitting the description of a pterodactyl.

In a private memoir written for his daughter, Lieutenant Colonel Simonds described what happened:

On our march we were continually seeing and hearing wild animals, and although I told this story when I came back to civilization I do not think anyone believes me, even now. All of us saw an enormous bird gliding above us which seemed to have a second sort of wing on the end of its wing tip – almost like a hand. There was a great wing-span, and then another little wing-span. When I arrived in Cairo, I reported this to naturalists, who, having checked the information, said that what I had seen was a Pterodactylos which had been extinct for over a million years![31]

Creatures of the New World

Pterodactyl reports are not restricted to the isolated jungle swamp 'islands' of Africa. They occur elsewhere, in an area which would seem one of the most explored areas of the world, North America.

On 26 April 1890 the *Tombstone Epitaph* (one of the most delightfully named newspapers in the world) ran a story, replete with the usual exaggerations, that, several days earlier, two riders travelling through the Huachuca desert south of Tombstone, about fifteen miles north of the Mexican border, came across a huge flying monster. It was reported to have been over ninety feet long with wings 160 feet across: wings which were bat-like, leathery and devoid of feathers. Its head was eight feet long with a jaw bearing a row of sharp strong teeth. The two riders were said to have shot and killed it.[32]

In 1969 a magazine repeated this story with all the exaggeration of the original and it was seen by a then elderly man who had, as a child, personally known the two original witnesses and the original story. He decided to set the record straight and related a sober and credible account of the incident. He explained that the two riders were well known and respected local ranchers. They had indeed come across a very strange creature that day, something totally unknown to them with large leathery wings. These were not the vast size reported by the newspaper; rather, the wingspan was estimated as between twenty and thirty feet; still huge, of course. They had shot at it with their rifles but failed to kill it; twice it managed to take to the air before plunging down again. They left it, wounded, still struggling in its attempts to fly off.[33]

Much more recently in Texas, on 24 February 1976, three schoolteachers were motoring down a country road near the Mexican border when a great shadow fell across them. They saw, flying close above them, a huge creature with very large wings of tight-stretched skin over long fine bones; wings rather like those of a bat. Except that these wings were fifteen to twenty feet across. They had never seen or heard of anything remotely like this creature before. Subsequently they spent some time rummaging through reference books looking for anything, alive or dead, which might explain this bird – if that was what it was.

They finally found a creature which appeared identical: a pteranodon – a very large-beaked pterosaur with wings reaching thirty feet across. Unfortunately, this had been extinct since the time of the dinosaurs, almost 65 million years ago.[34]

Strangely, several days earlier, a similar flying creature – perhaps the same one – had been seen by two other witnesses also near to the Mexican border.

Such creatures may even have flown further north. On the morning of 8 August 1981, a couple were driving across Tuscarora Mountain in Pennsylvania. Ahead two large bat-like creatures, evidently surprised by the sudden appearance of the car, were running towards them, skin-covered wings outstretched, in an attempt to take off. Their wings spanned the width of the road: at least fifteen feet. They took to the air and for the next fifteen minutes the couple watched them gradually soar into the distance. They later identified them as 'prehistoric birds' like pterosaurs.[35]

The world of orthodox science cannot explain these sightings. It is forced to either ignore them or dismiss them as mistaken, fantasy or fraud. But science can provide proof that identical creatures once existed and in the same area. Between 1971 and 1975 the fossil remnants of three pterosaurs were excavated at a site in western Texas. These were dated from the last years of the dinosaur period. While the skeletons were not entirely complete, sufficient bones were found to be able to estimate their wingspan at around fifty feet.[36]

Not only are these the biggest such flying creatures ever found, but they are also the most recent pterosaurs ever found dating from the very end of the dinosaur period. According to the fossil record, this species was the very last in existence. Some day, perhaps, we may unearth some more recent fossils of this type – or perhaps some remains.

We have seen how isolated yet stable areas can harbour large unknown animals, animals long thought extinct. The sea, already demonstrating some of its mysteries with the coelacanth and Megamouth shark, may yet reveal the existence of more un-known creatures, a *megalodon* perhaps or a 'Caddy'. The jungles of central Africa apparently hold one or more semi-aquatic mon-sters which may represent relict dinosaurs. Could Texas be such an area?

It has long been a deeply held claim that everything is biggest in Texas. Could these stories represent a Texan exaggeration of some close encounter of the large bat kind? Could it really be possible that such unknown creatures could find a refuge in North America where the skies seem forever filled with aeroplanes and helicopters? Are there any isolated and remote areas like those of Central Africa near Texas, where some large, as yet unrecognized creature might live? In fact there is one.

Northern Mexico is dominated by the largely unexplored Sierra Madre mountain range which runs like a bony spine up the country from Oaxaca to the United States border. This region is a perfect place for unknown creatures still to survive, hidden away from human contact. Cryptozoologist Dr Karl Shuker suggests that it is here that they might be sought.

Dr Shuker notes a further intriguing possibility: in 1968, an archaeologist found a curious carved relief at the ruined Mayan city of El Tajin which sits in the south-eastern foothills of the Sierras. This carving depicted a 'serpent-bird' which the archaeologist argued was not some fabulous legendary beast but an accurate depiction of some flying creature well known to the ancient Mayans. This 'serpent-bird' is a very good likeness of a pterosaur.[37] Could this archaeologist be correct? If so, it indicates that such a creature was alive in historical times, perhaps as late as the final collapse of the Mayan civilization 1,000 years ago.

Dr Shuker comments:

> Cryptozoology is full of curious coincidences, but few are more curious . . . than the undeniable fact that modern-day reports of giant pterosaurian look-alikes just so happen to emanate from the very same region that was once home to a bona fide creature of this type.[38]

From before the Dinosaurs

What are the chances of a creature found in fossil strata 64 million years old being alive today? Rather slim, one would think. What of a creature twice that age? Would the chances be twice as slim? The survival of the coelacanth shows how foolish such appeals to reason are in this subject. It would seem possible that any earlier animal, under the right conditions, might have a chance of surviving. It could be objected that the sea is a far more stable environment than anything to be found on land. And this seems a reasonable argument. But the truth is far stranger than this.

As an example, there is one animal whose survival gives all zoologists, however sceptical they might be, pause for thought: the tuatara.

The tuatara is a very primitive reptile, superficially resembling a lizard, with three eyes – the third only partly functional. It grows about two feet in length and lives a mostly isolated nocturnal life. Fossil remains of its type have been dated to as far back as over 200 million years ago and since that time the animals have changed very little. In every part of the world except the South Pacific, the fossil record ceases with that of the dinosaurs. If it were not for the South Pacific remnants, it would have been believed that all the tuataras vanished in the same cataclysm which took away the dinosaurs. But the tuatara saw the dinosaurs come and go; it may well do the same with humans.

It still lives today on a few, very small, very remote islands near to the coast of New Zealand. A second species lives on a ten-acre islet in the Cook Islands about 2,000 miles away. Of all the world, how did these small islands, far apart from each other and thousands of miles away from the major continents, end up with the only living tuataras?

What would be the chances of science predicting this situation? It is fair to say that, however much reason was stretched to its limits, such a survival in these so isolated environments could never have been considered even remotely possible.

We can only conclude that, with nature, anything is possible. And to forget that simple truth is to live in a fantasy world. The approach of the cryptozoologists must be correct: it is more, rather than less, likely that large unknown species still exist, still continue to elude our gaze, in the sea, on the land or in the air.

This scientific adventure is set to continue.

5

The Mysteries of Human Evolution

It was the evening of 30 November 1974. In Ethiopia's Afar Desert, at Hadar, American anthropologist Donald Johanson was celebrating. He had, late that morning, found a fossilized fragment of a potentially human skull which, together with other bones, represented about 40 per cent of an ancient female skeleton. These were, he considered, the earliest such remains of humans or human-like creatures ever found.

Johanson was excited: he had been searching in this area for two seasons, impelled by the certain hunch that he would find something of importance. And that day, as he wrote later, he had awakened feeling lucky.

As the night rapidly fell, Johanson sat with a beer in his hand and a tape recorder at his side belting at full volume into the night. He was playing a much loved recording: the Beatles' 'Lucy In The Sky With Diamonds'. The song played time after time as Johanson and his colleagues drank their beer and talked excitedly of the implications of their find. Johanson wrote later of that exuberant and high-spirited night, 'At some point during that unforgettable evening – I no longer remember exactly when – the new fossil picked up the name of Lucy . . .'[1]

And it is as Lucy that she has been known ever since; Lucy, who died over 3.5 million years ago, in or beside what was once a large lake.

The Ascent of Mankind: Rounding Up the Usual Suspects

Lucy wasn't human, but neither, argued Johanson forcefully, was she an ape. Nevertheless, she was no more than three and a half feet high, she walked upright but her hands reached to her knees, and her shoulders, ribs and waist bones, together with evidence of strong muscles, seemed better adapted for tree climbing. Lucy was aged about thirty years but already her vertebrae held traces of the onset of arthritis or a similar disease. She had died rapidly, perhaps by drowning.

Unfortunately, the front of her skull was never found and so the exact size of her brain could not be determined. But from the fragments it was estimated to be only a little larger than a chimpanzee's: around 230 to 400 cubic centimetres (14.0 to 24.4 cubic inches).

Lucy was placed in a group of creatures seeming to share elements of both apes and humans. They had been first discovered in South Africa in 1925 and were named 'southern apes', or in Latin, *Australopithecus* – (*austral* means 'southern', *pithecus* 'ape'). It is now thought that at least six species of this half-way human or half-way ape creature existed, of which Lucy, at the time, was the oldest known.

There is no evidence that any of this group learned to make tools. Yet they seem to have survived until around 1 million years ago when they were certainly in contact with early man who, at the time, was skilfully constructing a variety of stone implements.

This raises the unwelcome question of whether this primitive creature can truly be seen as an ancestor of humankind, as many (but not all) modern scientists propose; and as most journalists writing on the subject seem to accept with uncritical obsequiousness. The most vocal supporter of this idea – that Lucy and her clan are ancestral to humans – is Johanson himself who has proved adept at gaining scientific and media acceptance for his ideas.

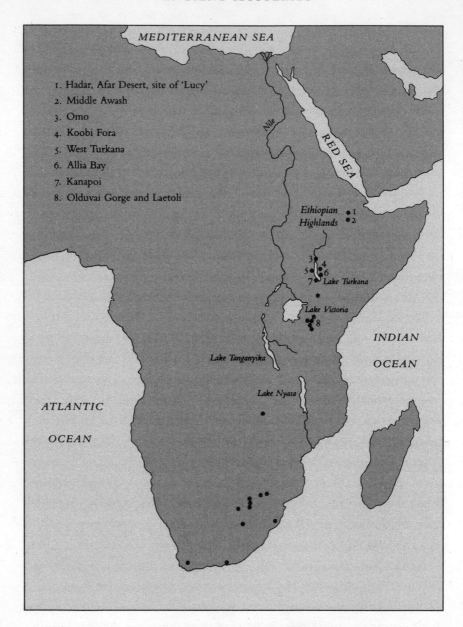

1. Hadar, Afar Desert, site of 'Lucy'
2. Middle Awash
3. Omo
4. Koobi Fora
5. West Turkana
6. Allia Bay
7. Kanapoi
8. Olduvai Gorge and Laetoli

African discoveries of fossil hominids considered ancestral to humans.

The Arguments: Lucy as Ancestral or Parallel

The human species has been allocated the genus *Homo*. Modern man – anatomically speaking – is called *Homo sapiens* (which includes such 'cavemen' as Neanderthal and Cro-Magnon). Our immediate ancestral species is considered to be a more primitive type of human called *Homo erectus* whose remains are found spread over wide parts of the world, from Africa and Europe to China.[2]

But here fierce arguments amongst experts begin: quite a number of apparently older, apparently more primitive types of early man-ape exist but they do so in something of an archaeological limbo. So few fossils have been found that all the theories are based upon extremely tenuous evidence.

Donald Johanson argues that Lucy's people were ancestral to true humans. He believes, in other words, that the genus *Homo*, modern man, over time developed from ape-like creatures like Lucy.

His assertion is fiercely contested by a member of the most famous dynasty of experts on early humanity, Richard Leakey, whose base has always been the National Museum of Kenya, Nairobi. His father Louis and his mother Mary were both pioneers in the field, and his wife Maeve also has great expertise and experience. She continues to excavate and publish on the subject.

Richard and Maeve Leakey are cautious; they do not accept that Lucy and her type are the direct ancestors of modern mankind as Johanson argues. The Leakeys, while accepting a family tree of the various *Australopithecus* species so far discovered, will not commit themselves to connecting the line of *Homo* development to any of them.[3] Although they do accept that a connection should probably be made somewhere, they prefer to await further information. They have considerable support for this position amongst other scientists.

Richard Leakey avoids direct confrontation on this issue, contenting himself with pointing out what seems conclusive evidence that Lucy and the other *Australopithecus* remains found are far more like apes than humans.[4] He considers that humans derived from some much earlier creature, originating perhaps 7.5 million years ago, whose fossil remains have not yet been found.[5] He concludes that humanity has a far older history than supposed by those such as Johanson. Leakey's father, Louis, originally considered that the origins of mankind might reach back to over 40 million years ago;[6] though in the modern scientific world this is no longer considered a tenable hypothesis.

Clearly the fossil record, as it presently stands, is not going to clarify matters regarding human evolution. To do so we would need to find a great many more fossils including some substantially complete finds. Yet already over sixty years have passed since the Leakeys first began work at Olduvai Gorge in East Africa, during which time an extensive and detailed search has been made in likely geological strata. If such evidence existed, surely some trace of it would have been found?

Perhaps the experts have been looking in the wrong place? Or failing to identify correctly the fossils which have been found? Or both?

To investigate these possibilities we need to approach matters from another angle: firstly, we need to ask what kind of environment could have given rise to the oddities of the modern human body and where in Africa, or elsewhere, that environment might be found.

The Orthodox Position: The Savanna Theory

Around 25 or 30 million years ago huge forests covered the greater part of the earth's land masses. Within these forests primates – apes and monkeys – evolved from a small ground-dwelling, four-legged creature about the size of a squirrel.

Twenty million years ago we find evidence of the widespread existence of many types of apes living in the trees. But about 15 million years ago the forests began gradually to vanish. Ten million years ago apes still ruled the remaining forests but then, shortly after that time, for some mysterious reason, virtually all the ape fossils disappear. Why this should be is an unsolved mystery.

From around 8 million years ago until the era of Lucy, some 4.5 million years later, is a 'Dark Age' for primate fossils. Until recently, excavations, while revealing tens of thousands of other fossilized animals within this period, had revealed only an arm bone, a tooth and a fragment of jaw containing another tooth. Encouragingly, from the mid 1990s following research at new sites, the situation has improved marginally.

In 1995 Maeve Leakey and her colleagues established a new species of very early *Australopithecus* with a number of fossils including almost complete jaws, part of a tibia and pieces of skull and teeth, which they had excavated near Allia Bay, eastern Lake Turkana. These have been dated to just over 3.9 million years ago.[7] An even earlier find in Ethiopia of fossil teeth, part of a lower jaw, skull and arm fragments by Dr Tim White and his team was placed into another supposedly ancestral genus and species in 1995. It was dated to around 4.4 million years ago.[8]

Despite the excitement which attended these finds, it is not much to show for a period of almost 4 million years. Furthermore there is no explanation of any worth which might account for this lack of evidence.

According to the orthodox 'Savanna' thesis, it was during this 'Dark Age', following changing climatic conditions, that the forests gradually became so reduced in size that the increasing population of primates within them found themselves under pressure from limits on the available resources of food. In time this pressure grew so great that one primate group decided to seek beyond the forests for their food. They moved out into the great grassy plains of Africa – the savanna.

It was upon this vast grassland, continues the theory, that the characteristics we now know as human were advantageous. So, by natural selection, those creatures showing them gained ground over those which did not. The human traits evolved: man stood up, walked on two feet in order to see over the tall grass, grew his brain and lost his covering of thick fur.

This theory, of course, leaves much unexplained. None of the most prominent physical characteristics of humans would be an obvious advantage in this new environment: a huge grassed plain filled with fierce and fast predators.

Of all the primates which lived in the declining forests only one, our ancestor, stood up from its four limbs and moved upright on to the savanna. Why?

Under the same pressure of population, no other apes or monkeys also reacted in this way. Why?

The environment of the savanna, with its lions, hyenas and other voracious carnivores, was truly hostile. Yet we are asked to believe that some type of proto-intelligent ape entered it, having given up its normal, and rather fast, running on four limbs for an upright gait which would slow it down. One would expect all of these foolhardy apes to have been rapidly wiped out.

From an animal's point of view, running on two limbs is entirely foolish; much of the energy expended in activity is used in simply holding the body upright rather than in propelling it forward at speed. It is a very inefficient means of locomotion.[9] Something of a problem when being chased by predators seeking food.

Why did any of our ancestors change? How could the force of natural selection on the open savanna cause such an alteration in structure?

The answer is, it cannot.

Why Are There Human Beings?

How are we different from other primates, from apes and orang-utans, for instance? Obviously we have a larger brain and the power of speech. We also have bodily differences: we are not covered with fur and we walk upright on two legs. But those are just the immediately apparent distinctions. In fact, there are hundreds of differences.

Almost unbelievably, science does not have any viable explanation for the evolutionary development of any of these crucial characteristics. Certainly scientists have tried: theories have been advanced to account for them and, at times, these theories have been deemed sufficiently competent to become fixed in the evolutionary 'mythology'. But not for long. All the explanations have soon been found wanting. Too many human traits seem impossible to explain, and so scientists, unable to clarify the issue, have generally shied away from the difficulties such ignorance presents.

Biologists, in particular, have called attention to those aspects of the human body which seem to have defied evolutionary process. The growth of the brain, for example – not seen in any of the apes or other primates – the loss of bodily hair, a unique mode of breathing which also allows speech, and a distinctive mode of sexual behaviour.

The size of the brain appears to have steadily increased: from the chimp-sized brain of Lucy; the 440 cubic centimetres (26.8 cubic inches) or so brain of *Australopithecus*; around 650 cubic centimetres (39.6 cubic inches) for what is considered to be early true man; 950 (52.9) to 1,200 (73.2) for *Homo erectus*; 1,350 (83.3) as an average for modern man, *Homo sapiens*. This increase in brain size has led to an increase in head size.

This growth in head size has meant the need for considerable bodily adaptation from ape-like creature to human-like creature simply in order that a female can give birth to an infant with such a large head. For this reason, a human mother has a pelvis of a very different shape from that of an ape. And so important is this increase in brain size that, in modern man, for the first year after birth, the brain continues to grow so much that it effectively doubles in size. A woman could not give birth if the brain were to be fully developed from the beginning.

The loss of hair, of the thick body fur which is so evident in apes, is also something of a curiosity with modern humanity. This hair would protect the body from the sun's heat and from the cold temperatures at night. How would living in the savanna – hot by day and often very cold at night – cause this trait of hairlessness to be developed by natural selection?

Another enigma is our ability to speak. This is a function of our peculiar mode of breathing which is quite different from that of apes, or, in fact, from any other animal alive upon this earth. *It is unique to humans.*

A New Look at Evolution

It is salutary to consider that while these changes occurred in some of the apes – those which apparently developed into humans – they did not occur in any other. The other apes have continued without much evolutionary development for several millions of years, perhaps much longer. Why should the evolutionary forces choose only one species on which to exercise their art? This remains unexplained.

By standard thinking, for any evolutionary or adaptive change to take place two factors must be present: firstly, the change must give an immediate advantage to the creature within its environment. It is not a viable argument to suggest that the creature struggled on, hoping perhaps that in several hundred thousand years all would become easier.

Secondly, the animal and its breeding population need to be

isolated from others of its species so that there is no further opportunity for any exchange of genetic coding. This isolation is usually
by means of some physical boundary such as a desert, a mountain
or a sea. These boundaries prise apart, and keep apart, two groups
which originally were one. The savanna does not fulfil these
conditions.

Humans are mammals: highly specialized, certainly, but sharing
many bodily features in common with others. Yet we humans are
unique among land-dwelling mammals in that we can breathe with
equal ease through our nose or our mouth. Similarly unique is our
inability to breathe and drink at the same time. This is because of a
special feature we have called a 'descended larynx'.[10]

Mammals – apart from ourselves – all have one channel linking
the nose with the lungs, the windpipe. They also have another, the
gullet, which connects the mouth with the stomach. These two
channels are kept separate. Such animals can therefore drink and
breathe at the same time.

This occurs because the mouth and nose are separated by the
palate, the forepart of which is the bony roof of the mouth. The
rear part is comprised of soft tissue. In all terrestrial mammals, apart
from man, the windpipe passes up through the palate by way of a
circular sphincter muscle. Thus, normally, the windpipe is above
the mouth cavity and is connected only to the nose.

However, under certain conditions, the sphincter muscle can
relax and allow the top of the windpipe – the larynx – to descend
into the mouth cavity. This lets air from the lungs be either expelled
through the mouth, or drawn in. It is this feature which allows, for
example, a dog to bark.

Following the barking, the windpipe rises upwards again and the
sphincter muscle tightens, thus once again establishing the separation
between the air and food channels.

However, in humans the windpipe has no connection with the
top of the mouth and is in the throat, beneath the root of the tongue.

It is this condition which is termed the 'descended larynx'. We have no sphincter in the palate to keep the windpipe and gullet separate. Rather, the rear of our palate is open, allowing both air and food to enter either our lungs or our gullet.

This is, of course, a potentially hazardous arrangement. A design fault in natural selection. It makes swallowing a complex action since we have to ensure that food or drink does not enter the windpipe rather than the gullet.

If, for some reason, our control breaks down – through illness, accident or intoxication – we might, for example, suffocate in our own vomit. In fact, the accidental choking on food is a rather common cause of death in humans.

How this anomalous biological construction evolved by natural selection – or any other means, for that matter – between the forest and the savanna is a complete mystery to biologists.[11] While all the experts are agreed on its singular character, none has come up with any viable explanation for its origins. But we possess such a feature; it developed, therefore at some point in our evolutionary history we must have needed it. It must have given us an advantage in our environment.

What environment could that possibly be?

The case of the proboscis monkey provides a clue. This monkey lives in the coastal mangrove swamps of Borneo. While it normally resides in the trees, when it descends it more often than not steps into water rather than on to dry land. Accordingly, these monkeys have learned to swim well and for long distances.

In shallow water they will pick themselves up from four limbs and wade in on two legs only. They are also known to exit the water on to dry land while remaining upright. The ability of these modern monkeys to walk even a short distance upright on two feet confers an immediate advantage in their partly aquatic environment.[12]

This example points to a possible solution to the problem of the enigmatic features of the human body.

An Aquatic Life

While no other terrestrial mammals have the descended larynx, there are other mammals which do possess it. But they are only those which live in the sea or lakes; mammals such as seals, whales, dugongs and sea-lions. They are all animals which need to dive for long periods beneath the surface of the water.

While the descended larynx confers no advantage to terrestrial creatures, it does give a distinct advantage to those which are aquatic. With the means of breathing through the mouth, the animal can inhale or exhale a considerable volume of air in a short time. This is important when surfacing for a moment before a dive. It also allows the animal to exhale very slowly under fully conscious control.

This latter is another, related characteristic which we share with aquatic animals: conscious control over the lungs giving control over breathing. An example of this is seen with the Aboriginal musicians of Australia who employ a disciplined circular breathing pattern to play upon the didgeridoo. A similar example is seen with monks who use complicated breath control for their Gregorian chants. For other terrestrial mammals, breathing is as uncontrollable as the beating of their heart.[13]

In us this has produced something even more unique: the ability to speak. This conscious control of the breath is the means by which we can produce the wide and subtle range of sounds which speech depends upon. Why this should be a gift granted only to humans is a mystery which so far has no solution.

Our face-to-face mode of sexual copulation too is more akin to the aquatic life. Land mammals do not practise this mode of sexual relations but it is the norm with whales, dolphins, sea-otters and others.

Our mode of perspiration is also as unique to humans as is walking on two legs or the ability to speak. It is a surprisingly inefficient mechanism: it wastes water and salt, is slow to begin – leading to the danger of sunstroke – and slow to respond when the water and salt levels of the body become dangerously depleted.

To allow a salt deficiency to continue is to court trouble. A human body, sweating heavily, can expel all its salt in a mere three hours. This leads to the onset of violent cramps and, if not quickly treated, to death.

It is difficult to see how this wasteful system could have evolved in the African savanna where water and salt loss would have posed a frequent and serious problem.[14]

Humans have a prominent layer of fat just under their skin. Indeed, it comprises over 30 per cent of all our bodily fat. This is absent in other terrestrial primates. But this fat layer is the norm amongst aquatic mammals: whales, seals and dolphins all have it.

Biologists who have studied this layer note that it provides an excellent insulation against loss of body heat – but only in the water. In the air it is much less effective than the normal terrestrial design of a layer of body fur.[15] For all those scientists who study the evolution of human features, the existence of this fat layer continues to be enigmatic.

In the face of this evidence it is very unlikely that the savanna was the defining environment for evolving mankind.

For natural selection to favour such a naked ape as a human being, the best environment would be a life in water. With water, the ability to stand and walk upright on two legs would confer an immediate advantage: the ape would avoid its land-based enemies and it would be able to survive by breathing above the surface. As the biologist and writer Elaine Morgan notes, walking upright on land gave few immediate advantages and required thousands of years for it to become efficient. On the other hand, 'Walking erect in flooded terrain was less an option than a necessity.'[16]

Where Could an Aquatic Ape Have Developed?

Where could this aquatic environment have been? There are many theories of African origin. And it is in Africa, according to the orthodox theory, that the oldest traces of mankind have been found. But it seems that we could not have developed in Africa, or, at least, on the mainland of it. This is indicated by the genetic 'baboon marker'.[17]

In 1976 three American cancer researchers investigating a virus carried by baboons made a startling discovery. In the distant past this lethal virus had caused a veritable plague amongst the primate population of Africa. It was an extremely infectious virus which caused a fatal disease. To survive it, primates evolved a genetic sequence which served to oppose its ravages. These researchers found that while the virulence of the virus had long disappeared, the protective genetic sequence remained. It was present in every primate of African origin. It was not present in any primates from elsewhere, from Asia or South America, for instance.[18]

The existence of this genetic sequence – the 'baboon marker' – could then comprise an indication of African origin. Checking, then, the genetic structure of man, the scientists found an absence of this sequence. They thus concluded that this was a sound indication that man's origins were not to be found in Africa: they suggested Asia.

Elaine Morgan thought that this suggestion was unnecessary. She began looking for a region in Africa where apes might have left the jungles and moved into the water. And where, millions of years later, they might have moved back to the land.

Now it is unlikely that these moves were made deliberately: that an ape left its comfortable tree and stood in the water thinking that in a few million years some descendants would love it. Or that a comfortably adapted aquatic ape climbed out of the water – confronting the dangers of sunburn and new predators – and consoled itself with the thought that it all might become easier a million or more years down the line.

The most probable cause of these changes is that the environment altered. No land is totally stable and the great African Rift Valley, stretching from Tanzania to Ethiopia, is less stable than most. Paradoxically, this instability is important. It would foster a need for any resident species to adapt or die. And there is one particular part of Africa where these changes were just as the scenario requires.

Geologists have found that around 7 million years ago an inland sea became established in the northern Afar region in Ethiopia.[19]

The sea swept into this forested area and, in time, this water became trapped. Its entrance to the Red Sea and the Gulf of Aden was blocked by geological movements which isolated the Afar sea from the outside. After millions of years it gradually dried up to leave the salt plain, thousands of feet thick, which we see today.[20] To the east of this vast dry salt plain is a mountainous region known as the Danakil Highlands. When the sea was in place this was a forest-covered island.[21]

Elaine Morgan concluded that the conditions of isolation were thus fulfilled: certain apes, isolated in this sea and on this island could begin their unique development into *Homo*. And, as they were isolated in this way, the baboon virus would not have reached them, thus explaining why humans lack the genetic 'baboon marker'.[22] In this region, the apes would have been driven into the water as the seas rose, and, millions of years later, driven back to land as the seas receded.

Consequently, it is in this area that fossils could usefully be sought, fossils which might provide archaeological support for the biological arguments. In fact, it has received recent attention and looks set to receive much more. In December 1995 a group of scientists from Italy and Eritrea were exploring what is now the salty Danakil Desert. They discovered part of a skull, part of a pelvis and a fingerbone which they dated at around 2 million years ago. These

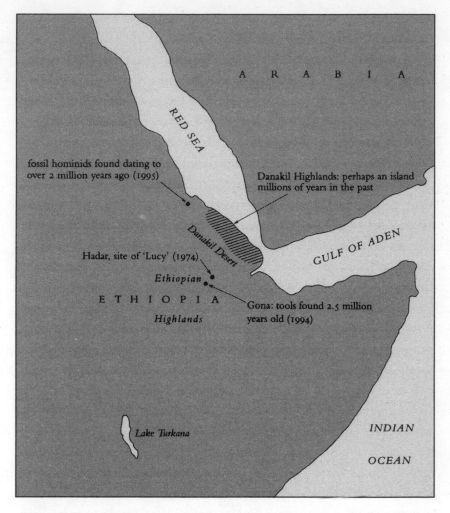

The Danakil Desert and Highlands: showing the possible Danakil 'island'.

are the first human bones ever found in the region. 'We are,' said geologist Ernesto Abbate of the University of Florence, 'just at the beginning.'[23]

It was in the desert further south of this region that Johanson found both Lucy and, later, a large group of human-like fossils comprising at least thirteen individuals who seemed to have drowned together.

Whatever Lucy's true place in human or primate ancestry, could she be associated with an aquatic environment?

It was found that Lucy's knees had not fully developed and could not lock in the modern manner: walking or standing would have been uncomfortable. As we have mentioned, the structure of her bones makes it likely that she may well have spent most of her time climbing trees. Many experts in the field support this position despite the well-publicized image of Lucy as queen of the savanna.[24]

All members of her species, according to Richard Leakey, could comfortably walk upright only for short periods.[25] But that is on dry land. Such movement would not be a problem in water where much of her body weight would be supported. Lucy's feet were never found, but those of other *Australopithecus* individuals proved proportionally much larger than ours, wider, with longer toes. Good for swimming and hanging in trees; bad for walking.

The site where Lucy was found suggests an affinity with water. It seems to have been the swampy edge of a lake, perhaps wooded. Her bones lay amongst remnants of crabs' claws, together with crocodile and turtle eggs. Her bones were not attacked and scattered by any predators, which might indicate that she died by drowning. Of course, the savanna supporters argue that she was simply visiting the swamp to obtain water. But was she? Why could she not have lived in and about the water itself?

Studies of primitive contemporary cultures have shown that, in Africa, no land-dwelling humans choose to live at the edge of a lake or water-hole. The reason is that this locality is frequented by predators such as lions and hyenas which wait there to capture prey rendered vulnerable while drinking. This would not be a safe environment for proto-humans to live and raise children. But if, like the proboscis monkeys, these primitive creatures lived in the trees and swamps themselves, they would be protected from these predators.

There is just one small problem, however. While an aquatic phase of human development does appear to be the most likely means by which our physical attributes developed, when might this have occurred? At first sight it would seem logical to suggest that this development might have occurred during the 'Dark Ages' of primate fossils, from around 4 million to 8 million years ago. But what if mankind were to prove far older?

What if the development in isolated seas or lakes occurred many millions of years earlier? Would this mean that humans anatomically identical to modern *Homo* were living long before Lucy and her fellow creatures? If this could be demonstrated, then the latter would be excluded from any relevance to human evolution at all; every textbook on the subject would need to be rewritten.

Is this unreasonable? Is it perhaps a wild theory going far beyond the evidence?

Not at all.

The Laetoli Footprints

In 1978 an expedition led by Mary Leakey based at Laetoli, in northern Tanzania, about thirty miles south of the Olduvai Gorge, discovered the fossilized footprints of three walking humans. These early people had walked across some recently fallen volcanic ash, perhaps in an attempt to escape an eruption. Some fifty footprints extending for seventy-seven feet were excavated. They were dated to between 3.6 and 3.8 million years ago.[26]

These footprints are earlier than Lucy, thus they are the very earliest evidence so far discovered for erect walking. Yet there is a mystery about them which is unwelcome to Donald Johanson and his supporters. For these footprints were not made by a creature such as Lucy – no matter how often Johanson argues that they were.

In fact, although they were up to 200,000 years *earlier* than Lucy, they were made by feet *anatomically the same as those of modern humans*.[27] There is no possibility that they were made by creatures such as Lucy.

The foot of an *Australopithecus* – the genus of Lucy – has long toes with, as in apes, a divergent big toe. The best example of such a fossil foot which has been found cannot be fitted to the prints. The Laetoli prints, like those of modern humans, have a non-divergent big toe and the space between it and the second toe is the same as it would be today. Professor Russell Tuttle of Chicago University writes bluntly that, 'It is difficult to imagine a foot . . . [like that of Lucy] fitting neatly into the footprints at Laetoli.'[28]

Many experts who have studied these prints have concurred that the feet which made these prints are, in the words of Professor Tuttle again, 'indistinguishable from those of striding, habitually barefoot humans'.[29]

Professor Tuttle continued his criticism. In February 1997 he was reported by *National Geographic* as maintaining that, 'The tracks were made by a mystery hominid whose fossils have yet to be found.'[30] These facts have not been well publicized: popular accounts of Lucy and her compatriots ignore it.

But the Laetoli footprints are just one of many facts which call into question the importance of Lucy in the evolution of humans. Unfortunately the self-appointed guardians of orthodoxy have ensured that their interpretation has found its way into all the standard scientific presentations.

But not without action on the part of dissenters. The prominent zoologist, the late Professor Lord Zuckerman, speaking to the Zoological Society of London in 1973, criticized the claim that *Australopithecus* was a human ancestor. He complained that, 'The voice of higher authority had spoken, and its message in due course became incorporated in textbooks all over the world.'[31]

Almost a quarter of a century later the claim is still being called into question, but this time in the light of much more extensive knowledge. In 1997 Liverpool University's former Dean of the Faculty of Medicine and expert on human anatomy Professor Bernard Wood maintained in *National Geographic* that humanity has 'no clear path of descent from the australopithecines'.[32]

But the arguments over the place of Lucy and her people in human evolution are just the beginning of the complexities.

The truth about humanity's development is far stranger than we can imagine. Science does its best with the few fragments of early primates and hominids which have been found. But behind every interpretation of these finds lies the assumption that these bones represent progressive stages of mankind's evolution over the last 4 or 5 million years. Without this assumption some of the finds would receive quite a different explanation. This assumption has quietly attained the status of an ideology which clouds the modern perspective on the past.

In fact, it seems likely that humans had already evolved, were already living, when Lucy was born 3.6 million years ago. The Laetoli footprints, at least, are evidence for this.

Perhaps the required aquatic stage of human development occurred during the 'Dark Age' period from around 8 million years ago. Or perhaps it occurred many millions of years earlier.

Louis Leakey may have originally been closer to the truth when he considered human development as being 40 million or more years in the past rather than the 4 or 5 million accepted today.

There is, as we shall see, some support for this.

6

Suppressed Facts Concerning
Ancient Mankind

Victors tend to rewrite history in their own image; those yet to achieve victory have often already started scribbling. They know that the control over information and its interpretation is the control over belief.

Such attempts to dominate belief are manifest in many different academic disciplines, notoriously, in recent years, with the Dead Sea Scrolls. But human prehistory has not escaped such ambitions either. Professor Charles Oxnard, of the University of Southern California, pointed out that when *Australopithecus* was first discovered there was a sharp public dispute amongst experts as to whether such creatures were nearly human or nearly ape. With the result, he commented acidly, that the '*opinion* that they were human won the day'. Then he added a warning: this did not just defeat the alternative opinion but, much more seriously, it risked burying all the evidence which supported it.[1]

This is remarkably tough talking. We can be sure that it arises from a real concern that certain material, despite being perfectly sound, has been deliberately excluded in the hope that future generations of scientists will forget it even exists.

The continuing fight to maintain Lucy and her australopithecine cousins' position as human ancestors is carried on without much evidence of compromise or goodwill. While scholastic profession- alism tends to contain the bitterness, jealousy and mutual derision which are endemic, the battle lines remain drawn and explosions still occasionally occur. Dr Donald Johanson and Richard Leakey once had a very public airing of their bitter disagreement, live on a coast-to-coast American television show.[2] Subsequently, a species of guerrilla warfare seems to have continued.

The title of Johanson's book (in collaboration with writer Maitland Edey), *Lucy: The Beginnings of Humankind*, published in 1981, left little room for misunderstanding his claim. Richard Leakey, writing in 1992 in *Origins Reconsidered*, does not challenge the position of Lucy directly. Rather, the book gives considerable space to the work of other experts who prove very critical of the claimed 'humanness' of the *Australopithecus* species, of which Lucy was an early member. This has the overall effect of allowing but one conclusion: that they were tree-dwelling apes; they were not ancestral to humans.

Yet in 1994 a colleague of Johanson, anthropologist Dr Tim White, opened a paper for *Nature* with the confident statement that, 'Work in southern Africa established *Australopithecus* as a human ancestor . . .'[3] There is no sense here that the situation might be rather more contentious.

However, doubts seem to be slipping through the cracks of the great ship 'Lucy'. Even *National Geographic*, a bastion of orthodoxy if ever there was one, in a major series on human origins published in the late 1990s made it clear – in a mealy-mouthed sort of a way – that the issue over the place of Lucy in the ancestry of humanity was far from being resolved: 'Some scientists,' it reported grudgingly, 'are now even questioning Lucy's position as the mother of us all.'[4]

Forbidden Archaeology

The same year that Professor Oxnard pronounced his warnings, Dr Richard Thompson, an American scientist with many papers to his credit in mathematics, geology and physics, began to collect together all the contrary evidence relating to the prehistory of mankind. Dr Thompson was a member of the spiritual Bhaktivedanta Institute, and his perspective on history was that expressed in the ancient Vedic writings of India: that mankind has been in existence for a very very long period of time.

In collaboration with writer Michael Cremo he produced a volume explaining and analysing this evidence, most of which had been suppressed or dismissed by modern science. After nine years' work it was published in 1993 as *Forbidden Archaeology*. It was one of the most remarkable books of the decade. And, it must be acknowledged, notable for its dignified restraint. There is, the authors found, amongst the finds of geologists, archaeologists and palaeoanthropologists, evidence to suggest that modern-type humans lived many millions, or tens of millions, of years ago in Europe, Asia, Africa and the Americas. They used tools, hunted and coexisted with other near-human or near-ape species such as the diminutive Lucy.

The authors point out that there is every reason for thinking that the situation in the distant past was rather similar to that today: humans and apes of different species living at the same time. We have already noted the enigmatic fossil footprints found at Laetoli – proof that humans and certain *Australopithecus* species were alive in the same area at the same epoch.

The very thought that the present reconstruction of our evolutionary past might be so seriously askew is heresy of the highest order against the dominant orthodoxy.

Cremo and Thompson voice their suspicions that the views of those who do not accept either the 'Lucy' or 'out of Africa' hypotheses are not being passed on to the wider community beyond the specialist academic enclaves. They suspect that these opposing views are being deliberately suppressed in order to maximize the impact of the orthodox theories on schools, universities and the interested public.[5]

A further, probably unintentional, effect is that the well-publicized clashes between the Leakeys and Johanson have served to divert attention from an even greater argument: whether Africa is truly the cradle of humanity or not. This, both the Leakeys and Johanson agree on. But many others do not; and with good reason, as we shall see.

To maintain the exclusion of contrary evidence and to shore up the wobbling superstructure of the orthodox viewpoint, a double standard has long operated. Fossil bones or ancient tools which fit the modern theories are quickly accepted and published in the scientific literature; those fossils or artefacts which are contrary to current thinking are dismissed as wrongly identified, intrusive to the early rock formations in which they have been found or, in the last resort, they are carefully placed into 'missing files' amongst the clutter of museum basements.

A classic example of this – sadly not the only one – is the case of Canadian archaeologist Thomas Lee, whose excavation produced evidence unacceptable to the reigning orthodoxy. This scandal centres upon traces of human activity from a much later date than we have been discussing but it demonstrates well the power of an entrenched establishment in manipulating the view of history towards its own perspective. It demonstrates too the utter ruthlessness and self-interest with which these academic battles are fought and won.

The Manipulation of Evidence

During the last Ice Age, so much water was locked up in the vast polar ice-caps that the sea-level worldwide dropped by hundreds of feet. Eastern Siberia was joined to Alaska by a great ice-free tundra plain. According to accepted wisdom, it was across this that the first humans walked from Asia into North America. Since the 1920s the date of this migration has been put at around 10,000 BC.

Even now, despite several contrary finds which directly and fatally challenge this theory, the orthodox position remains the same.[6] Uncompromising criticism is aimed at any archaeologist who should prove sufficiently maverick – that is, sufficiently honest with the data – to suggest otherwise: for the champions of orthodoxy take no prisoners.

Thomas Lee had for many years worked as assistant curator of Indian antiquities for the National Museum of Canada in Toronto. In summer 1951 he was engaged in an archaeological survey of Ontario. While examining Manitoulin Island in Lake Huron he discovered, at its eastern end, near the present village of Sheguiandah, evidence of early human settlement; he began to excavate.[7]

During the course of his archaeological digging Lee turned up dozens of stone tools which seemed to have been constructed by people with an advanced level of skill. Excited by these finds, he continued his 'inch-by-inch' excavations until 1955. The problem was, though, that these tools he found seemed far older than 10,000 BC.

In order to be certain that his dating of these implements was correct, he sought the advice of a number of geologists who, by a study of the strata in which they were found, together with the known history of the North American Ice Ages, determined that all the implements were at least 65,000 years old and could have been much older, perhaps as old as 125,000 years.[8] In 1954 some forty or fifty geologists visited the site on a field trip and agreed with this geological analysis of the strata.[9] In fact, over the years, more than 100 geologists visited the site while the excavations were under way and so had ample opportunity to observe the strata and the objects found in them. Yet, despite the accord of geologists over the dating, the finds presented an insoluble problem to the current view of man's antiquity in North America: they were, quite simply, unacceptable.

In 1970 a geologist from Wayne State University in Detroit, Dr

John Sanford, reviewed all the evidence gathered by Lee and others at the Sheguiandah site. He reported that

> the stratigraphic sequence of the sediments and the artefacts contained in each layer is definite and unequivocal. Careful digging and observation of the sediments and artefacts in place leave no room for doubt regarding the stratigraphy.[10]

Discussing the interpretation of the finds, he concluded that the artefacts 'certainly date from early rather than late Wisconsin time'.[11] This is the way geologists refer to the last of four great Ice Ages which have covered North America. The Wisconsin period dates from around 80,000 years ago. But Dr Sanford added that the very deepest artefacts from the site probably date from the later stages of the previous Ice Age period, the 'Sangamon', which ended around 100,000 years ago.[12]

Lee's discoveries were therefore unwelcome to those whose careers were closely tied to the orthodox theory that humans first came to America across the ice-free Bering bridge.

Lee related the following story:

> while visiting the site, one prominent anthropologist, after exclaiming in disbelief, 'You aren't finding anything down *there*?' and being told by the foreman, 'The hell we aren't! Get down in here and look for yourself!' urged me to forget all about what was in the glacial deposits and to concentrate upon the more recent materials overlying them.[13]

As a result of Lee's refusal to collaborate with such a charade, his opponents played a merciless game. Lee's publication possibilities were eliminated. Simultaneously, and taking advantage of his inability to justify himself in print, the evidence he had uncovered was seriously misrepresented by a number of well-known specialists in the field, thereby discrediting both Lee's reputation as a professional and his finds. Finally, large numbers of the artefacts he had found disappeared into the bowels of the National Museum of Canada, to be forgotten.[14]

However, Lee initially had the support of the Director of the National Museum of Canada, Dr Jacques Rousseau, who refused to dismiss him; in fact, he wished a paper to be published on the subject. This heresy added to the pressure on the Director who was himself soon replaced. Lee too lost his job with the Museum; Sheguiandah was contemptuously dismissed by other archaeologists as a 'non-site'.

And, as a terminal injustice both to Lee and to the finds, the discovery site was turned into a tourist resort.

By such derision important evidence is easily marginalized or removed entirely. In this case everything was done to suppress and discredit the data which emerged from the site. This was crucial for Lee's opponents, for if they had not successfully achieved this then, all the texts describing early man in North America would have needed rewriting. It was that important. Academic careers built upon elaborate but mistaken theories would have been in jeopardy. As Lee bitterly wrote, 'It had to be killed. It was killed.'[15]

The Origins of Man

The theories of human origins are based upon fossils found in a geographically limited area, Africa, and represent only a few species spread over many millions of years. It is necessary to stress how small, and how geographically specific, these samples are. All the evidence really serves to tell us is about the situation in East Africa between 1 and 4 million years ago. Any wider claims remain conjectural.

It remains true, however, that to date, the earliest proto-human creatures accepted by science have been found in Africa. They are represented by seventeen fragments of fossil bones found in Ethiopia between 1992 and 1993 and dated to 4.4 million years ago.[16] The earliest *Homo* ancestors accepted are also from Africa, represented by parts of two skulls, one from Uraha in Malawi and another from Lake Baringo in Kenya: both are considered to be 2.4 million years old.[17] But we should recall that the Laetoli prints, made by a human foot, are dated to 3.6 million years ago. The earliest tools are also from Africa; just over 3,000 of them were found at Gona, in Ethiopia, between 1992 and 1994. They are assigned a date of around 2.5 million years.[18] There is no indication of what sort of creature made and used these tools as no bones were associated with them, but they are presumed to derive from some early human species. They are very primitive artefacts of flaked stone which nevertheless reveal that whoever made them already had considerable understanding of stone-fracturing techniques. There is also evidence of blunted tools being sharpened by having additional flakes chipped off. This is conscious and deliberate tool-making and planning for the future. Africa, then, is the focus for most modern efforts to find evidence of ancient mankind and ancient tool use.

It is not well known that Europe too has revealed similar evidence but this evidence is so astonishing, so controversial, so politically incorrect, that the scientists have long pushed it to one side hoping that it will gradually be lost under the dust of passing years. For if this evidence were to be accepted, it would destroy utterly every modern theory of human prehistory.

The Mysterious Prehistoric Tools of Europe

Compelling evidence for the very early use of tools in Europe was presented to a meeting of the Anthropological Institute in London, Monday 8 April 1872. Fellows present were shown a collection of fossil sharks' teeth which had been excavated from the so-called Red Crag formation of Suffolk, the residue of an ancient sea which had existed 2 to 2.5 million years ago. While the existence of sharks' teeth in this maritime geological formation is not anomalous, they none the less confronted all present with a challenge: each sharks' tooth had a small hole carefully drilled through its centre.

A close examination of these holes revealed that each was tightly filled with the Red Crag rock matrix from which they had been excavated, proving that the holes had been drilled *before* the teeth had been dropped into the ancient sea. This point alone indicated an age greater than 2 million years.[19]

These drilled teeth reveal that an unknown early European man was using tools at much the same date as those recently found in Ethiopia. But the tools used to drill such a small hole are immensely more sophisticated than the simple flaked stone choppers and cutters of Gona. But, like these, the Red Crag finds had no human bones associated with them. We cannot therefore even speculate as to what kind of early European man might have created them. Or whether they were the same species as those unknown inhabitants of ancient Ethiopia.

During October 1875 Professor Capellini, a geologist at Bologna University, had visited the Siena region to pursue his interest in the small fossil whales found there. He had been fortunate enough to find the major part of a fossil whale which he chipped out of the rock himself and brought back to his university. As he cleaned one of the bones, he discovered a slice had been cut into it before it had been fossilized. It seemed deliberately cut by a sharp edge. Yet this bone had come from a geological formation allocated to the Pliocene, an epoch dated from 2 to 5 million years ago.

Closer inspection of the bone revealed three additional but superficial cuts. Professor Capellini concluded that he was viewing the traces of some very ancient butchering because these particular marks were very different from those which would have been made by the teeth of carnivores such as sharks. It appeared most probable that the flesh had been removed from the bones of this ancient whale by humans using a sharp tool which, during the process, cut and scraped the whale's bones. To check, he inspected bones of modern animals which had been butchered and then placed in museum collections: they showed a similar pattern of cuts. As a further test, using some ancient flint tools he had found in the area, he experimented on modern bones proving that he could reproduce the same type of cut. It was, too, easy to demonstrate that the fossil bones had not been cut recently; he later explained to his professional colleagues that the fossil bone was so hard, a steel point could not scratch it.[20]

Recent work has supported the distinction between butchering marks and those of predators. A study of ancient butchering marks found on bones from Olduvai Gorge concluded that

No process has yet been discovered which produces marks that mimic slicing, chopping or scraping marks on a micro-scopic level. Tooth scratches and gnawing of carnivores produce grooves with rounded or flat bases respectively; both lack the fine parallel striations of slicing or scraping marks.[21]

Professor Capellini discovered these marks on quite a number of the fossil bones but was intrigued to find that they occurred only on the top of the spine and the outer face of the right-hand set of ribs. From this curious distribution of the evident butchering marks he surmised that the whale had been beached in some shallows of the ancient sea and was lying on its left side when humans cut the flesh from its right, using flint knives.

He concluded that these marks proved that humans were living in Tuscany over 2 million years ago, at the same time as these whales.[22] He presented these findings to his scientific colleagues at international gatherings in 1876 and 1878. A debate ensued with the result that a number of prominent scientists came out in his support despite the very early date for mankind that was implicit.

Other bones revealing a similar pattern of cuts were subsequently found. A large collection of fossil whale bones, recovered from the Tuscan valley of the Fine, had been donated to the Museum of

Florence. Professor Capellini searched through these and discovered several that showed identical cut marks, presumably also from butchering. These findings were supported by several other scientists including a professor of palaeontology and a professor of zoology and comparative anatomy.'[23]

A small number of other bones showing traces apparently from human action were also found in Italy. One fossilized animal bone had a round hole through it, perhaps drilled; another appeared to have been sawn part-way through and then snapped. Both dated from 2 million or more years ago.[24]

In France similar evidence appeared. A rhinoceros thigh bone was found in limestone at Gannat, in central France. There were parallel cuts across the top of it which would seem to duplicate the marks butchering would leave. This was much older than the Italian fossils, being dated to the Miocene period – from 5 to 25 million years ago – but other fossils found with it are now placed even earlier by modern authorities. The bone could, then, be much older.[25]

Ancient fossil bones of a prehistoric aquatic mammal, rather like a sea-cow, were discovered near Pouancé, north-west France. On an upper forelimb several deep and sharp cuts were evident. It was clear that the bones had never been disturbed in the rock from which they were extracted and so these cuts must have been made prior to fossilization. What is particularly mysterious about this find is that the marine deposits in which it was found are dated today to the *early* Miocene period: around 20 to 25 million years ago.[26] The thought that humans might have lived at that period is serious heresy. But that is the implication of this fossil.

But what of the tools themselves which might have been used for such early butchering? Records reveal that stone tools, some quite sophisticated, have been discovered in many very ancient rock formations in Europe.

Archaeologists working over the last decade have dramatically increased the acknowledged age of human artefacts found in Europe. Well-made hand axes are turning up at Boxgrove in southern England, at a site dated to at least 500,000 years ago, perhaps more. At both Gran Dolina in north-east Spain and Ceprano in Italy, south-east from Rome, simple choppers have been found dating from at least 800,000 years ago. These recent finds amount to literally hundreds of tools.

Even older is a cutting tool from the million-year level at Gran Dolina. This is the earliest find in Europe of a tool together with fossilized human and animal bones. Some of these bones, including those of humans, reveal the cut marks from butchering; dead humans were also a valuable source of protein.[27]

The fact that humans using tools at least 1 million years ago in southern Europe is now scientifically acceptable begins to remove the taint of heresy from the finds we have already mentioned such as the drilled sharks' teeth or the butchered whale found by Professor Capellini, even though they date in excess of 2 million years ago. But even this date may become scientifically acceptable soon, when the argument over another find of flint tools in France is resolved.

In 1989 a French archaeologist, Eugène Bonifay, discovered some simple stone artefacts at the site of Saint-Eble in central France. He dated them to between 2.2 and 2.5 million years ago. Nearby is an extinct volcano which erupted 2 million years ago covering the area; these tools are beneath the volcanic debris.[28]

Stone tools, crude, but remarkably similar to those found by the Leakeys in East Africa and termed 'Oldowan', better than those found by Bonifay in France, were discovered on the Kent plateau near Ightham last century. By the late nineteenth century several hundred had been recovered from various sites there. In the early twentieth century the strata they were found in were dated to between 2 and 4 million years ago.[29]

The Red Crag area dating from 2 million years ago to back as far as 55 million years, where the drilled sharks' teeth were discovered, has also produced flint tools – but of a rather higher level of skill. Large numbers of flints which had all the appearance of being modified were found there at several sites: scrapers and hand axes with elaborate flaking to create a sharp surface similar to tools found in many other excavations.[30]

Considerable controversy was engendered by these finds and an international commission of experts in prehistory was convened to look into the matter. In 1923 the commission decided in favour of the finds and of the dating to 2 to 5 million years ago. But who knows of these now? Today they are either unknown or dismissed sarcastically as erroneous. For they do not fit the theories which have emerged from the African excavations.

But what if the specialists were wrong? What if the humans in Europe at the time did not come from Africa but had already been in Europe and Asia for many millions of years?

The most astounding finds, however, have been in France. A little north of Paris, at Clermont, several well-worked flint tools were found in very ancient strata indeed. In 1910 the famous French prehistorian and university professor Abbé Henri Breuil wrote of one which he had personally extracted and thus was 'absolutely certain' of its age; yet, because of its manufactured appearance, 'Its discovery in place, at the base of the Eocene sands of Bracheux . . . caused me a profound stupefaction.'[31] A stupefaction indeed. The Eocene dates from 38 to 55 million years ago.

Drawings of this and a second tool also found by Breuil and published in 1910 reveal unambiguous evidence of deliberate manufacture. But Breuil, unable to avoid the early date – since he had removed the tools himself – and unwilling to even hint at the possibility of humans living so early, declared each stone tool to be created naturally.[32] Of course, that such a sophisticated tool could occur through geological action alone is effectively impossible. And Breuil must have known this.

1. (*above*): Section of a shaped and polished wooden plank around 500,000 years old, excavated in the northern Jordan valley, Israel, 1989.

2. (*right*): Stone mortar and pestle found under Table Mountain by a mine superintendent in 1877, over 1,400 feet from the tunnel mouth in an ancient river bed at least 33 million years old.

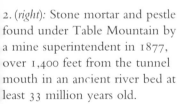

3. The Paluxy river, Texas. 'Taylor Trail' of fossil human-like footprints crossed from the left by the prints of a three-toed dinosaur. This ancient rock is dated to over 100 million years old.

4. (*inset*): Close-up of one of the human-like fossil footprints in the Paluxy river showing what appears to be an impression of toes.

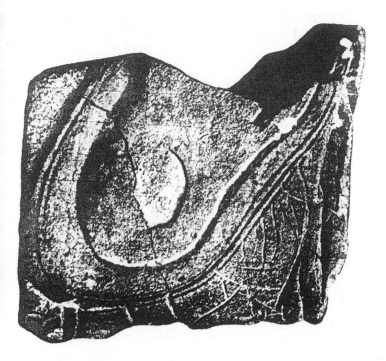

5. Part of a fossilized shoe sole found in a rock over 213 million years old. With magnification, details of the stitching could be seen. The only known photograph was published in a New York newspaper in 1922.

6. Fossil print, apparently made by a shoe, which was found in Utah in 1968, in rock strata over 500 million years old. The small fossil trilobite in the heel has dropped on to the print *after* it was made; another, in the toe, has been crushed by the weight of whatever made the impression.

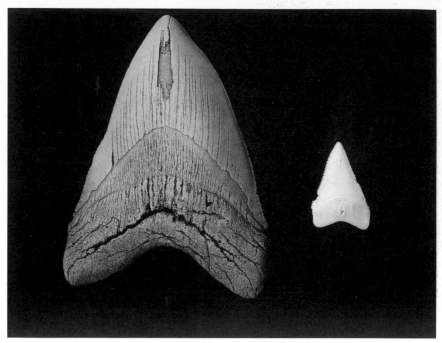

7. Comparison between the teeth of the huge, supposedly extinct shark *megalodon* (*left*), and that of a present-day Great White shark. Reports suggest that *megalodon* still exists in the South Pacific.

8. Artist's impression of the Central African *mokele-mbembe* as a small dinosaur.

9. The coelacanth, thought to be extinct for 70 million years until re-discovered in 1938. At the moment it is only known in the Indian Ocean.

10. Silver model of a coelacanth found in a church in Bilbao, Spain, in 1964. A second was found in Toledo in 1965. Both date from the seventeenth or eighteenth century and originate from Mexico, where the fish must have been known at that time.

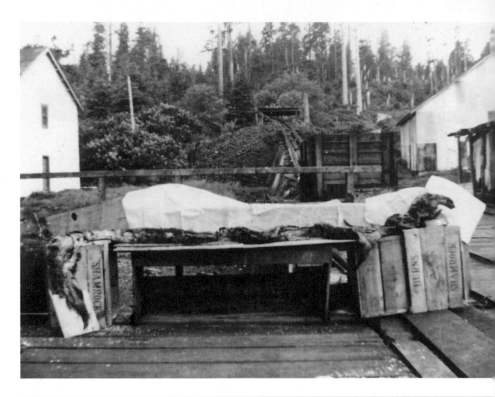

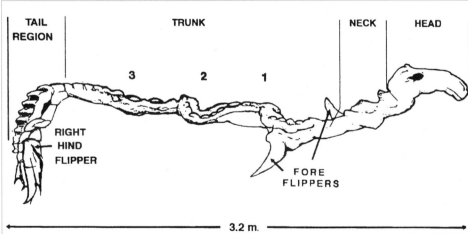

11. (*top*): Photograph of the enigmatic carcass found inside a sperm whale at Naden Harbour, British Columbia, Canada.

12. (*below*): The drawing gives an interpretation of its features.

13. Drawing of mysterious Canadian sea-creature 'Caddy' snatching at birds off Vancouver Island in 1945, by eyewitness Wilfred Gibson.

14. Reconstruction of the fossil bones and artist's impression of the zeuglodont, a species of which might still survive in the sea.

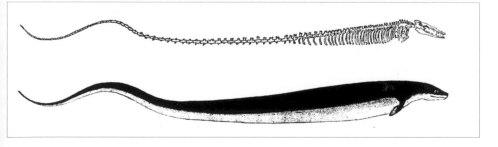

15. The Laetoli footprints, made over 3.6 million years ago by feet anatomically similar to those of modern humans. They were discovered in 1978 by a team led by Mary Leakey.

The uncomfortable fact that he must have quietly agonized over is that, despite their great age, these tools are identical in sophistication to human artefacts of the *Homo erectus* era, known to archaeologists as Acheulian. And, in passing, we might note that they are similar in age to the artefacts found last century by the coal miners of California.

The Earliest Examples of Man

Three to 4 million years ago, a warm sea lapped at the base of the Italian Alps; it has left many rock layers containing marine fossils. In the summer of 1860 an Italian geologist and academic, Professor Giuseppe Ragazzoni, was searching for fossil shells at Castenedolo, near Brescia. In this ancient maritime formation he found some fossilized human bones; an upper cranium fused with fossilized coral, together with other limbs and ribs. He showed them to other geologists who considered it impossible that human bones could be in such an ancient stratum and concluded that they must have come from an intrusive burial – that is, a deep burial of a far later date, which reached down into lower rock layers. And so Professor Ragazzoni discarded them.

Then, in January 1880, more bones came to light. They were found lying between an ancient coral reef and fossilized clay containing shells. Professor Ragazzoni was notified and he and his assistant went to the site to remove the bones themselves. Quite a number were found: parts of the skull, jaw, teeth, vertebrae and limb bones. Later that month jaw fragments and teeth, differing from those previously found, were discovered seven feet away. Remembering his earlier experience, Ragazzoni made a careful study of the site to exclude the possibility of these bones having derived from an intrusive burial. There was no such evidence and, as he wrote, all the bones were 'completely covered with and penetrated by the clay and small fragments of coral and shells', thus allaying any lingering suspicion. This, furthermore, proved that they had once been within the ancient sea.[33]

About three weeks later, during February 1880, an almost complete skeleton was found. Again Ragazzoni supervised the extraction of the fossil remains. The bones revealed the skeleton to be that of a woman. In all, the remains indicated four people, a male, a female and two children. The bones had been rather dispersed, which would be in line with the suggestion of wave action on the bodies following a drowning at sea. They may have been in a boat.

The fact that the bones could be so securely placed within the ancient maritime fossil layers made a date of 3 to 4 million years ago very safe.

Ragazzoni showed the bones to a professor of anatomy at the University of Rome who studied both the excavation and the bones. This expert noted that there was no indication at all that the female skeleton in particular might have come from a burial. He also noted that the skull was so entangled in the clay that it took considerable careful effort for him to extract it.[34]

This professor concluded that the bones, 'are an irrefutable document for the existence of man . . . man of a character fully human'.[35]

As late as 1969 worried experts were still trying to discredit these finds. Scientific tests conducted that year by the British Museum of Natural History purported to show a recent age for the bones but the tests were easily shown to be flawed: insufficient attention had been given to the risks of contamination not only from acids, saprophytes and roots while the bones lay beneath the ground but also afterwards, when for eighty-nine years they had rested in a museum with no protection from the atmosphere or small organisms.[36] However, the tests did reveal that the bones had a high fluorine content and an 'unexpectedly high' concentration of uranium, suggesting that they are very ancient.[37]

The professor to whom Ragazzoni took these bones had his

finger on the pulse of scientific attitudes when he predicted that the academic reaction would inevitably be hostile. He deplored the attitudes of his colleagues, warning that 'by means of a despotic scientific prejudice' such discoveries would be discredited.[38]

We should note that, while these fossil bones are of a similar date to those found in East Africa, there is one very significant difference. These finds at Castenedolo are of individuals anatomically *identical* to modern humans. Most of the finds in East Africa have been of early and primitive creatures, at best perhaps proto-humans.

Yet, to give us pause, there are a very small number of finds in East Africa, of very early date, of people anatomically similar to modern humans.

In 1965, at Kanapoi, at the southern end of Lake Turkana in Kenya, an upper-arm bone, 'strikingly close' to modern human examples, was found and initially dated around 2.5 million years ago.[39] This date was later revised to 4 million or more years ago.[40] At Koobi Fora, east of Lake Turkana, in 1973, some fossil leg bones dated at 2.6 million years ago were found. Richard Leakey declared that they were 'almost indistinguishable' from those of modern man.[41] Also at Koobi Fora, an ankle bone was discovered in 1974, dated from 1.5 to 2.6 million years ago. Anatomist Dr Bernard Wood (now Professor) studied this fossil at length and proved it to be virtually identical to that of a modern human.[42] In 1977 the French team led by J. Chavaillon found an upper-arm bone at Gombore in Ethiopia which they pointed out was the same as that of modern man.[43] This was also dated at over 1.5 million years ago.

Other human remains, equally controversial as those of Professor Ragazzoni, have been found in Europe, Asia and South America. All of them have been the butt of scornful attacks over the years by scientists defending what now seems to be a mistaken evolutionary orthodoxy. Yet orthodoxy itself is getting closer and closer to the heretical.

It is right that we allow the final word to those gatherers of dissident data, Michael Cremo, Richard Thompson and their researcher, Stephen Bernath: 'we conclude that the total evidence, including fossil bones and artefacts, is most consistent with the view that anatomically modern humans have coexisted with other primates for tens of millions of years'.[44]

7

Where Did Our Civilization
Come From?

On the bare Anatolian highlands of central Turkey, thirty-two miles south-east of the Turkish provincial capital Konya, are two ancient mounds hiding the ancient ruins of Çatal Hüyük, the world's first town.

This substantial Stone Age community appeared from nowhere. There are no known sites which reveal where its inhabitants gained their technical skills, their religion with its complex temples or their ability to create an urban trading and farming lifestyle. This highly sophisticated culture suddenly erupted upon the fertile highland plains as though transported mysteriously from elsewhere.

For archaeologists and historians, this city is where civilization begins. It is, in effect, the beginning of the age of settlements and farming, the Neolithic. Its first excavator, Englishman James Mellaart, enthused

> The Neolithic civilization revealed at Çatal Hüyük shines like a supernova among the rather dim galaxy of contemporary peasant cultures . . . Its most lasting effect was not felt in the Near East, but in Europe, for it was to this new continent that the Neolithic cultures of Anatolia introduced the first beginnings of agriculture and stockbreeding and a cult of the Mother Goddess, the basis of our civilization.[1]

Evidence of an unprecedented command of technology was discovered here: hundreds of knives, daggers, arrow-heads and lances, of flint or obsidian, all worked to an incredible and unique level of accomplishment, far in advance of any others known in the Near East at that time. Obsidian, in particular, is an extremely hard volcanic glass and flakes split off can have a cutting edge as thin as one molecule across, far sharper than any modern metal blade.

There also were found highly polished obsidian mirrors, finely pierced beads, jewellery and textile work of the highest standard, including carpets – evidence of a comfortable standard of living. These settlers did not use pottery but had wooden and basketwork which, for its sophistication and excellence, is unparalleled elsewhere at the time.

Their technical accomplishment was so great that we still do not know how they created some of their manufactured objects. We do not know how they polished their hard obsidian mirrors without leaving a single scratch; stone beads have been found, also some of obsidian, which, extraordinarily, have a hole drilled through them which is so fine that a modern needle cannot be pushed into it. It is impossible to think how they could have created them without using very hard metal drills. Yet somehow they managed it.[2] Perhaps one day we shall learn their secret.

A well-developed and elaborate religion thrived, centred, it appears, upon a Mother Goddess who was perceived as three people in one: a young woman, a pregnant woman and an old crone. To serve this cult, even in the very small part of the city excavated to date, over forty shrines or sanctuaries have been excavated although not all were in use at the same time.

In other words, so far as archaeology is concerned, the urban culture at Çatal Hüyük was unique; it had no apparent forerunners, no apparent sites nearby where the talents the inhabitants displayed might have been learned.

The inhabitants must have learned their craft techniques some-where. But this could not have been in any known contemporary communities such as those found at Jericho in the Jordan valley or Jarmo in the Kurdish highlands. For these communities did not display anything remotely resembling the same level of culture and craftsmanship.

It is absurd to believe that this urban sophistication appeared, suddenly, from nowhere, around 8000 BC. It is blindingly obvious that settled culture must have begun developing much earlier and elsewhere.

The question is, where and when?

Surviving the Cataclysmic Ice Age

From around 80,000 years ago an immense ice-cap with huge glaciers reached deep into Europe, Russia, Canada and the United States. An ice-cap, perhaps a mile or more thick in the north, covered all of Ireland, most of England as far south as the London area, and stretched across Europe. In North America an ice-cap almost two miles thick reached as far south as St Louis and Philadelphia; further south still were endless plains of arctic tundra.

This, of course, would not have been an insupportable problem for humans living at the time because the areas of southern Europe, North and Central Africa and Central America would not have been so affected, although it is thought that the general world temperature would have been much lower, the cloud cover and rainfall higher. If humanity had not developed an urban culture by then, it would have been under considerable pressure to do so, for people would have needed shelter from the rain and cold winds.

We have always thought of mankind at this early period as leading a nomadic hunter-gatherer life, seeking shelter when necessary within caves. This much is true, but true only to the extent that remains of humans have been found in caves. We need to be cautious regarding the conclusions we draw from this. It is rather like future archaeologists finding bodies in Second World War bomb-shelters and assuming that this was the norm for twentieth-century culture.

Early man did not just live in caves. Even hundreds of thousands of years ago, shelters were built, some apparently permanent. In France the Terra Amata site near Nice, perhaps 300,000 years old, has revealed what appear to be post holes and stone circles which the discoverer, French scientist Henry de Lumley, argues are the remains of substantial shelters.[3] As is often the case, this site is controversial and not all agree with his conclusion.[4] More certain are the finds at Bilzingsleben, in Germany which are dated to around 400,000 years ago. Archaeologists have excavated three circular structures made of bone and stone with a diameter of nine to thirteen feet. They are considered to be foundations of structures which comprised a permanently occupied site. The most curious find here, which raises many questions about the potentially high level of culture reached by these early people, is an area, paved with bones and stone, twenty-seven feet wide. The director of research, Dietrich Mania, believes that the inhabitants 'intentionally paved this area for cultural activities'.[5]

Potentially portable 'tents' or 'windbreaks' have been found constructed of mammoth bones at the 60,000-year-old site of Molodova on the Dnestr river, Russia.[6] At Dolni Vestonice, in Romania, a group of five dwellings has been found dating up to 28,000 years, the largest being over fifty feet long. Nearby were the remains of a pottery kiln. This was used apparently only for firing small clay figurines since no domestic pottery has been found.[7]

Such solid shelters are fixed; they cannot be moved with a nomadic tribe. Hence a tribe must stay in one place, must domesticate animals and grow crops to supply the needs of food. To supply food for a sedentary population the members of the community must develop specialization of labour and attempt to produce a commodity surplus in order to trade for those goods they cannot grow or make. They need to establish patterns of land usage and ownership, must gather together for mutual aid, for defence and for trade. Such a mutually supportive culture, protected from the elements by well-constructed shelters, and from hunger by effective food production, is the best way for human beings to survive in an erratic, perhaps hostile, environment.

The Sunken Lands

Where would these cultures develop? The answer must be, where cultures have always developed: in the temperate, fertile lowlands, near the rivers for water and communication. Especially, culture would emerge in the delta regions where these rivers entered the sea. It is reasonable to suppose the gradual construction of urban cultures at such sites over the 60,000 years or more of the last Ice Age.

Small boats were undoubtedly a well-used means of transport even long ago. Engravings and paintings of deep-sea fish, such as dolphins and whales, found in the ancient caves, attest to probable maritime activity. That such a technology was potentially available very early is proved by the discovery that boats capable of sailing for days in the open sea were in use in South-east Asia by perhaps 40,000 years ago.[8]

Unfortunately, these broad river valleys where culture most likely developed are never very high above sea-level: the present Indus valley, for example, stretches almost 450 miles before it exceeds 300 feet high; the Mississippi reaches about 550 miles; much of western France is below 300 feet.

At the peak of the last Ice Age, from around 24,000 BC to 14,000 BC, so much water was locked up in the ice-caps that, world-wide, it has been estimated, the sea fell by over 400 feet.[9] By the end of the Ice Age, around 7000 BC, the sea had returned and regained its former level, reaching its approximate present shorelines, indicating *a height rise of 400 feet.*

With the return of the sea we would expect any ancient coastal settlements to be far out on the continental shelf, beneath the waters. It has been proved that most of the present under-sea continental shelf off the coast of the United States was dry land about 9000 BC. Fishermen dragging the sea bottom for scallops and clams have found the teeth of extinct mastodons or mammoths up to 190 miles out to sea, beyond Cape Cod. They have been found at depths of up to 400 feet. The remains of horses, tapirs, musk ox and giant moose also have been found. Similar finds of mastodon teeth have come from a depth of 300 feet in Japan's Inland Sea.[10]

The shells of shallow-water oysters, normally found in tidal estuaries or lagoons, have been discovered at many different sites off the Atlantic coast of the United States, at depths of almost 300 feet. Radiocarbon dating put them at up to 9000 BC.[11] This data gives an indication of the speed at which the water rose; it suggests a very rapid rise in sea-level after this date. For the seas had stabilized by 7000 BC, hence there must have been a rise of 300 or 400 feet over the preceding 2,000 years.

Vegetation has also appeared; ancient twigs, seeds, pollen and peat deposits have all been hauled to the surface by both fishermen and oceanographers; carbon dating has indicated that they too were submerged around 9000 BC. Scientists have also found evidence of sunken shorelines, sands and deposits of peat. All this evidence has led them to conclude that in 13,000 BC the United States continental shelf was a wide coastal plain teeming with wildlife and covered with forests. But after 9000 BC it was the sea floor.

A mapping of the world's land masses at their maximum during the peak of the Ice Age has revealed the true extent of extra land then available. Australia, New Guinea and Tasmania were all one continent; the Philippines, Sumatra, Borneo and Java were together connected to the land mass of continental Asia. Extensive lands extended almost 100 miles south from the tip of South Africa and a dry land passage, interestingly ice-free (while mile-high ice covered Canada and the northern United States), was available between

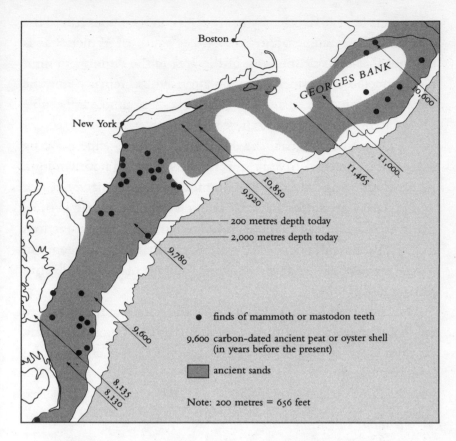

Boston

GEORGES BANK

10,600

New York

11,000

11,465

9,920

10,850

200 metres depth today

2,000 metres depth today

9,780

finds of mammoth or mastodon teeth

9,600 carbon-dated ancient peat or oyster shell
(in years before the present)

ancient sands

9,600

Note: 200 metres = 656 feet

8,135
8,130

Submerged land areas off the coast of the United States: showing
finds of land animal teeth (mastodon and mammoth).

Siberia and Alaska.[12] In Europe the North Sea did not exist, most
of the land being covered with a mile-thick ice-cap. Wide plains
extended from the present English Channel into the Atlantic.

Studies on the Mediterranean area have proved intriguing: huge
temperate watered plains stretched up to 120 miles out from the
present coastline of Tunisia; Malta was connected to Sicily; plains
also generally extended all along the coastline of Spain, France, Italy
and Greece, where many of the islands were joined. But, most
remarkable of all and previously unsuspected, was the existence of

a huge fertile plain, crossed by many rivers, in the upper half of the Adriatic Sea, reaching almost 200 miles south of Venice.[13] It is thought that this was the most fertile area in the region and must have attracted a considerable population whose remains now lie beneath hundreds of feet of sea. It is, of course, almost impossible to search for the remnants of these settlements.

We cannot overestimate the effect of this world-wide flooding caused by the melting ice and the changes it would have wrought to any developing cultures. The memory of its destructive horror would have seared itself into the cultural memory of the peoples living there and been communicated down through the generations in legend and mythology. The world-wide incidence of legends of a great flood could well be a residue of this event in the collective folk memory.

One expert in the field has stated, 'it is not an exaggeration to say that in many parts of the world the largest and most important environmental change of the past 15,000 years has been the rising level of the sea'.[14]

World-wide Flooding

The waters may have come in a terrifying few years of utter disaster, or decades of endless rains and floods. Or they may have crept slowly up over the land during millennia of inexorably rising tides and destructive storm-driven waves. However it occurred, the melting of the last great Ice Age had ended around 7000 BC.[15] The glaciers and ice-caps retreated to the general position they occupy now.

If, year after year, century after century, the tides inexorably rose and, with them, the deterioration of the weather created violent storms and waves large enough to crush the mud-brick or stone houses, what would be the reaction of the population? They would, of course, leave for higher ground, taking what they could and carrying with them their skills in building, agriculture and weaving.

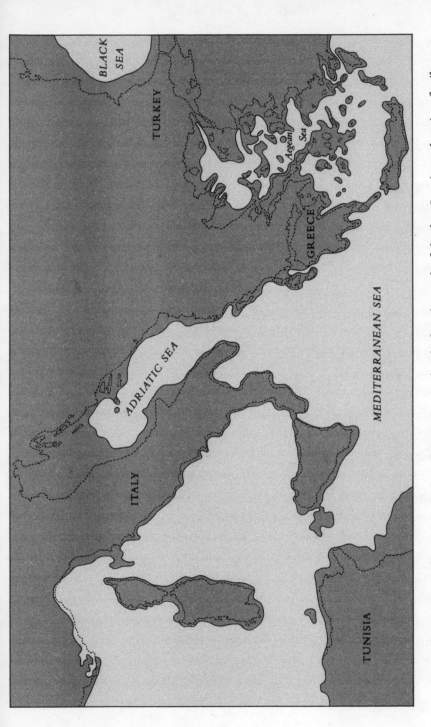

The Adriatic and Aegean Seas before the rise in sea-level after the end of the last Ice Age: showing fertile lands where early civilization may have developed prior to the widespread inundation. (The dotted line gives today's land contours.)

They would also have taken their culture, their religion, their myths, their songs and stories.

They would have no way of knowing how far the gradual flooding of their land might reach, so they would withdraw progressively to higher ground. In the now ancient legends of a world-wide flood which have survived into our time, there is consistent mention of human survival by virtue of boats and high ground.

The ancient Greeks believed that, following a catastrophic, world-destroying flood, survivors rebuilt Greek civilization in Thessaly. Their myth echoes much of the story of Noah. It explained how Zeus, angered with mankind, sent a great flood. Deucalion was warned about this by his father, one of the demigods, and so constructed an 'ark' on which he and his wife rode out the flood. When the waters receded he landed upon the top of Mount Parnassus. Deucalion and his wife then reigned in Thessaly. Their son, Hellen, was regarded as the ancestor of all the Greeks who, in classical times, called themselves *Hellenes*.

Was this tale an embellishment of a real folk memory of the rising sea-levels? And if so, why should Thessaly have been pinpointed as the original homeland of the Greeks?

The Greek philosopher Plato (*c.* 429–347 BC) considered it 'perfectly credible' that this story symbolized a reality. He believed, furthermore, that civilization had existed in Greece prior to this destructive deluge; that towns had flourished on the plains and near the sea; and, further, that the Greeks had known the use of metal. But this catastrophe not only destroyed the towns, it also destroyed the knowledge of mining and working metals. The mines were all flooded and those with the skills necessary to work metal were killed. In consequence, humanity was forced back into a more primitive age which knew only the use of stone tools.

Plato writes of his belief that the only inhabitants who would have escaped were those shepherds in the hills whom he describes as 'scanty embers of the human race preserved somewhere on the mountain-tops', where they later turned to farming.[16] Plato's narrative is surprisingly consistent with recent archaeological and geological conclusions.

But there is one terrifying possibility: could it be that after several thousand years of steady melting, and steady but moderate sea-level rise, the vast polar ice-caps suddenly became unstable and rapidly, completely, collapsed with cataclysmic effect?

Scientific analysis of very deep core samples taken from the Greenland ice-cap in 1989 revealed that around 8700 BC the last cold period of the Ice Age came to an abrupt end. The ice retreated so quickly that major climate changes occurred within twenty years and a major temperature rise of seven degrees centigrade in fifty.[17] This was disaster enough. But the evidence is mounting for the existence of an even worse scenario.

Later studies on new core samples, completed in 1993, revealed an even more dramatic picture of this event: they indicated that the most significant melting and collapse might have occurred in just *one to three years*.[18] This is a record of utter catastrophe.

A gradual 400-foot rise over 2,000 years or so would not go unnoticed. If, for example, since the Romans, the sea-level had risen gradually to this extent, then such a rise would constitute a major factor in our history and culture. Especially if, during that time, it had *always* risen.

But if a catastrophic collapse of the ice sheet occurred over one to three years, allowing a turbulent sea literally to rush across hundreds of miles of plains and forests engulfing in its torrent all the human settlements, this would leave searing cultural scars for thousands of years. Scars which would be expected to find their tragic echo in myths and legends of a devastating flood.

Can it be entirely without relevance, given this date of around 8700 BC for a collapse of the ice-cap and consequent rise in sea-level, that the earliest town, Çatal Hüyük, is in the Anatolian highlands and is dated at around 8000 BC? A town which, as we have mentioned, appeared mysteriously, from nowhere?

Was it founded by survivors of the calamitous rise in sea-levels? If this is so, then the origins of its culture now lie beneath hundreds of feet of sea somewhere in the Mediterranean.

But where?

Interlude I: Why Did Everything Happen 'Suddenly'?

As happens so often, it took an intelligent and resourceful amateur in the field to blow apart the narrow thinking of established experts.

Late in 1962, in the wake of the successes in space enjoyed by Russia and the United States, the American writer Alexander Marshack was commissioned to write a book explaining how humanity had achieved such a level of civilization and scientific excellence.

During the course of his research Marshack interviewed hundreds of experts: top space officials, scientists, military commanders and the presidents of great commercial corporations. But his research did not provide the answers he had expected. He was surprised to find that none of these people had a clear idea of why or even how this cultural advance had occurred.[19]

Concurrent with this frustrating research, Marshack had his wider interests in mankind kindled. He began to mull over the essential similarities of aspiration in different cultures at different eras. He concluded that there 'was no essential difference . . . between the first fully modern man of some 40,000 years ago and ourselves, either in brain size or general skeletal measurement'.[20] Even though the tools used by this early man were, so far as was known, only made from stone, they demonstrated great variation and complexity. Marshack found himself wondering about the origins of civilization itself.

He confronted the 'suddenlys', the fact that all the cultural advances were described in the standard texts as having occurred 'suddenly': agriculture around 10,000 years ago; civilization in Mesopotamia; science with the Greeks. He found it impossible to believe that all these things could have happened like this, without any development. As he wrote, 'They must have come at the end of many thousands of years of prior preparation. How many thousands was the question.'[21]

Interlude II: The True Origins of Civilization

Where could the answers be found? Indeed, what sort of evidence would constitute answers?

Marshack had an idea which, he felt, might allow this question of evidence to be resolved: our modern world is created and bound by a sense of time. Science studies things which occur over time, from the movement of the planets to the swing of a pendulum. And the way in which science conducts this study is also bound by time, for it collects results: summaries or averages leading to theories which predict the likelihood of repetition ahead in time. This sense of time, Marshack argued, begins with agriculture. A hunting lifestyle can be conducted on a day-by-day basis, but a settled agricultural life needs a sense of a year with its cycle of seasons.

Thus, Marshack concluded, in order for early man to change from the primitive hunting and gathering way of life to a settled agricultural existence, he needed to learn a concept of time. Any evidence, then, of a concept of time would also constitute the evidence for the origins of a settled agricultural culture.

He contacted experts with his thesis; in particular, he contacted the French expert on the cave art which dates from the Ice Age period. He asked if any of the art revealed evidence for seasonal or periodic time for the painting. He received the reply that it was suspected to do so, but there was no proof.

But in 1963, when his scientific book was virtually completed, he found a key piece of evidence which was to unsprocket his entire writing schedule. He belatedly looked at an article he had clipped from a scientific journal the year before. It dealt with a small bone tool, a prehistoric engraving tool – a bone handle with a sharp chip of quartz fixed to one end which had been found in a site at Ishango in Zaïre, near Lake Edward. It was dated to 6500 BC. The bone handle had a series of scratched markings down its length. The interpretation given for these markings seemed unconvincing to Marshack. Acting on a hunch, in fifteen minutes of study he had found the explanation.

The scratches, he could demonstrate, were a record of lunar phases: of the sets of new, quarter and full moons during the course of a few months.

Whoever constructed this, then, had a concept of time. Marshack began looking at all the published finds of prehistoric stones and bones which had been scratched, marked or engraved in any way. Hundreds of these, dating back to 35,000 years ago or more, had been found all over Europe but they remained enigmatic. Here, Marshack concluded, with the people who made these objects, were the true origins of our civilization.

Yet why did so many millennia pass before the apparent beginning of culture?

Commenting on this, the writer Colin Wilson throws his hands up in exasperation at the orthodox dating of the rise of urban centres. With man, he says

poised on the brink of civilisation 35,000 years ago, living in a community sufficiently sophisticated to need a knowledge of astronomy, we are asked to believe that it actually took him another 25,000 years before he began to take the first hesitant steps towards building the earliest cities. It sounds, on the whole, rather unlikely.[22]

Interlude III: The Conclusions

Alexander Marshack has argued that all the necessary elements of civilized culture were in place by 35,000 BC. It is obvious that if the elements were in place, then they were in use. Therefore at this time we can expect that somewhere there were settled farmers needing to understand the movements of the moon and sun in order to regulate their agricultural production.

The implications of his thesis are important. Settled farming means trade; trade means communities – villages or towns which in turn mean the specialization of trades, craftsmanship and art, for example. Language, laws and a primitive writing are not far away. In fact, a symbolic system of notation – primitive writing, in effect – seems to have been in use by the prehistoric cave painters.

Where might be the residues? Where might be the farms and towns we would expect? As we have already seen, the best lands for agricultural and trading settlements would be the well-watered river valleys and coastal delta regions.

The maximum amount of land of this type was available, as we have seen, for about 10,000 years during the greatest period of the Ice Age, from around 22,000 BC to 12,000 BC. At this latter date the sea's rise would begin to cause serious disruption. With the rise of water levels, any remaining evidence of occupation – if it was in any form to survive – would be on the seabed.

Settlers of the River Valleys

If Marshack's analysis is correct and a settled culture had developed at least by 35,000 BC, this would allow a very long period of development and refinement preceding the end of the Ice Age. The ice began to melt in 12,000 BC; the ice-cap collapsed catastrophically around 8000 BC, but had stabilized by 7000 BC. This would be a perfectly competent explanation for why we 'suddenly' find urban cultures around 9000 to 8000 BC in the Anatolian highlands – cultures founded by refugees from the flooded lowlands.

After this, with the stabilization of the sea at its new level, mankind perhaps dared venture back down to seek the fertile valleys. This would be one explanation of why the great civilizations of Mesopotamia and the Indus valley come *after* those of the Anatolian highlands, when the reverse would normally be expected.

These suggestions have received support from a recent study by Professor Tjeerd Van Andel of the University of Cambridge and Professor Curtis Runnels of Boston University. It focuses upon the colonization of the Larisa basin region in Greece, north-west of Athens.[23] Here lie the plains of Thessaly, the legendary kingdom of Deucalion, survivor of the Flood.

All over Europe during the latter part of the Ice Age, from 12,000 to 8000 BC, great rivers, swollen by the melting ice and rain, carried large quantities of gravel and silt down from the glaciers and icecaps. These overloaded rivers regularly silted up, flooded and changed their course. Over the years they filled in the valleys with many yards of debris creating wide flood plains.

Greece during the high glacial period was markedly different from the Greece of today. The greatest difference was that prehistoric Greece had many huge coastal plains; today such land is very rare.[24] After the inundation of these Greek lowlands the only inhabitants were small roaming groups of nomadic hunters, killing game with their distinctive bows and arrows tipped with very small sharp pieces of flint.

Around 7000 BC, following the time that the coastline stabilized, there was an influx of a completely new type of people leading a completely different way of life. These immigrants chose, overwhelmingly, to live upon what remained of the fertile and well-watered flood plains which had never been settled by the hunters.

These new people were farmers; they led a settled life, domesticated animals and cultivated crops. They chose the flood plains because the soil was light, easily tilled and well-watered. In addition to their own animals and the crops, there were many local sources of food such as deer, wild boar and water fowl; fish and shellfish also abounded.

But this evidence confronts us with a mystery: we have no idea where these people came from. No artefacts, no pottery, fabrics, nor any other archaeological remains have ever been found which would allow an identification of their origins. All we know is that they came by sea, and they brought their skills with them.

Van Andel and Runnels consider that the most likely source for these immigrants is either from the highlands of Palestine or from southern Anatolia. The latter is considered the most likely since the terrain around Çatal Hüyük, they say, being on a flood plain, is very similar to the area in Greece where these immigrants first settled.

The results of this study opened more questions for its authors: why, they asked, since there was no pressure over land use in Anatolia, did anybody choose to emigrate from what must have been a successful and comfortable situation? And how did they find this particular Greek plain on which to settle? How did they even suspect it existed?

The authors speculate that the Anatolian farmers may have had contact with early traders and seafarers.[25] Something of this sort must be the case since living in a landlocked site such as Çatal Hüyük would not promote the skills associated with building, sailing and navigating boats. It is more likely that they had good, presently unknown, contacts with these mysterious early mariners.

There were, it seems, even at this early era just following the last Ice Age, competent seafarers already exploring the Mediterranean, and perhaps even further afield, perhaps beyond the Pillars of Hercules (the Straits of Gibraltar).[26]

The Earliest Settlers of Greece

The whole episode of the early settlement of Greece suggests less a gratuitous emigration from an already comfortable home than that of a long-awaited return to a lost homeland. One which was far beneath the sea off the coast of Greece. The refugees from the rising seas and destructive rivers had fled when the seas tumbled across their lands after 8000 BC. They took with them to their refuges in the highlands which border the eastern Mediterranean their skills in farming and animal husbandry.

There, their communities survived and it is the remains of these which archaeologists have excavated. It is only due to the destruction of their former homes that these new communities, like Çatal Hüyük, are considered to be the earliest by the archaeologists. When the changes had ceased, when the sea coast had arrived at its more or less modern level, around 7000 BC, the descendants of the original refugees acted upon a long-awaited plan and returned home; rather like the European Jews returning to the Holy Land after 1,800 years of exile.

At about the same time immigrant farmers moved into Crete. It is thought that they also came from the Anatolian highlands.[27] Such maritime colonization both in Crete and in mainland Greece reveals a considerable degree of long-term planning and organization. At the least, they would need to use boats that were competent, to make certain that the seed stock was not ruined by water, as well as large enough to transport livestock.

Archaeologists emphasize that such colonization reveals a completely different mental perspective to that held by the primitive hunter-gatherers who were the earlier inhabitants in the region. It cannot be explained as a natural or accidental development of the hunter-gatherer lifestyle.[28]

Amongst the academics who have studied this phenomenon there

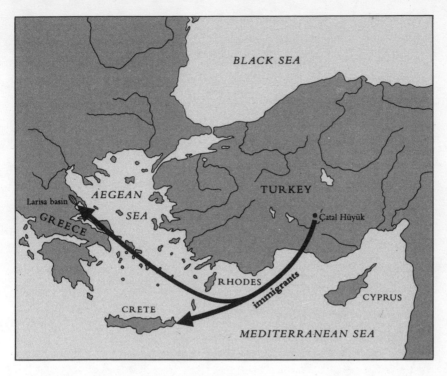

Possible source for the immigration of farmers into Greece and Crete around 7000 BC.

is a growing suspicion that there might be much more going on than they have suspected. Speaking of the Cretan immigration, one study asks whether, on the one hand, it is perhaps unique and so just a local oddity of little importance, or whether it might be 'the tip of a largely invisible iceberg'?[29] Are we seeing just a fragment of what was a widespread and planned immigration and relocation? One which might have been a major factor in the settlement of Greece itself? If this proves true, then the history of early civilization will need rewriting.

The maritime skills by which these travellers reached their destination could not have been recently learned; they must have been part of a sea-going culture for hundreds of years, perhaps millennia.

If a competence in sailing had developed, so too would a competence in navigation and the mapping of routes. We can expect some very early geographical knowledge to have been recorded, somewhere. And, indeed, as we shall see in the next chapter, there are some ancient records which suggest the existence of geographic knowledge which is very extensive indeed.

8

The Story of Atlantis

No one knows when the ancient Egyptian city of Saïs was founded; it has been recorded since at least 3000 BC. It rested unobtrusively beside the Nile, in the delta region, through the millennia until it gained a short period of prominence in the seventh century BC. It became the royal capital for the 26th Dynasty of pharaohs.

The many temples of Saïs were tended by a jealous priesthood who maintained the rituals and guarded the historical writings. For the Egyptians believed that all wisdom and knowledge had been given to them by the gods at the very beginning of their civilization; all subsequent innovation, all rewriting, could only move them further away from that original pure truth.

According to tradition, it was here, in one of the temples of Saïs, that a mysterious story from the distant past was carved in hieroglyphics upon great stone pillars. This was the story of the first empire known to mankind: that of Atlantis. The priest of the Temple explained

Nine thousand years ago in the Atlantic Ocean, the *true* ocean, beyond the Pillars of Heracles was an island larger than Libya and Asia together. Its kings were allied in a great confederation which ruled not only their own island but many other countries; in Africa as far as Egypt and in Europe as far as Tuscany.[1]

He described Atlantis: for most of its coastline, it rose sheer out of the sea, its high cliffs affording good protection both from the stormy Atlantic and any invading army. Beyond its cliffs were forests, lakes, rivers and, rising above them all, wide ranges of mountains with volcanoes and numerous hot springs which were exploited by the populace. In size Atlantis was similar to Spain; about 500 miles long with its northern border level with the Straits of Gibraltar.

It was rich in natural resources: its forests, lakes and marshes harboured a wide range of wildlife, the most prominent – according to the story – being large numbers of elephants. These latter reports could perhaps refer to the extinct mastodon, a variety of elephant very common during the last Ice Age.

The southern half of the island was quite different. There the mountains stopped; they protected a broad and fertile plain almost 250 miles deep and 370 miles wide. This was the agricultural heartland of the nation. Countless farms, villages, towns and temples dotted the landscape, all linked by a network of canals to the capital city. Vessels plied the canals carrying timber from the inland forests and the farm produce for sale in the city or for export through its port.

The capital of Atlantis stood at the southern tip of this great plain. It was built on a circular plan with at its very centre a temple for the god Poseidon and his human wife, Cleito. The immediate surroundings comprised the royal precinct which contained the king's palace. Beyond was the first of the wide concentric canals which surrounded and divided the city. There were three of these canals and each provided harbours for the naval and commercial fleets for which Atlantis was renowned.

The chief god and founder of civilization upon Atlantis was Poseidon. The records claim that he came down from above and chose to marry, from amongst the native population who were then living a simple life on the island, an orphaned girl, Cleito. His eldest son, Atlas, he appointed as first king.

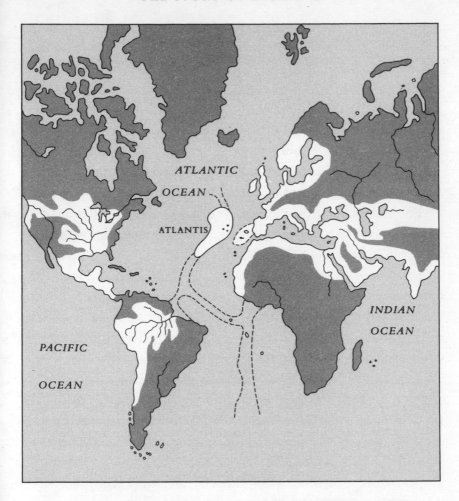

The continent and empire of Atlantis as illustrated by Donnelly in 1882.

Poseidon's cult was celebrated by the sacrifice of bulls. In the centre of the island was his temple and sacred grove within which wild bulls roamed freely. On a regular basis – every fifth or sixth year – the king and his relatives who were the provincial rulers would gather here to renew their covenant with Poseidon and to pass judgement upon affairs of state.

First they were required to hunt and capture a bull: forbidden to use iron weapons they used wooden staves and rope nooses. Once they had taken a bull they would lead it to a metal pillar which stood inside the temple. Upon this pillar were engraved the earliest records and laws of the country. The bull was then sacrificed over the pillar, its blood spilling down over the inscription. The rulers then swore an oath that they would remain true to their law and, to seal this covenant, they all drank from a cup containing a mixture of this blood with some wine. Following this ritual of renewal they would hold court and give their judgements.

For many centuries wisdom and moderation held sway over Atlantis. But, in time, such virtues fell by the wayside and were replaced by avarice and ambition. The wealth and pride of the people lost them the favour of their gods and led them to utter ruin.

They succumbed to the enticements of power; their armies invaded, and sought to hold, a wide empire: the Iberian Peninsula, southern France, North Africa and northern Italy were theirs. Then they tried to take Egypt and Greece. They were finally checked in a great battle in which the Athenians took a leading role.

At some time subsequent to this defeat the gods seemed finally to despair, and utterly destroyed them. Great earthquakes and floods struck the earth. Atlantis, in a sudden and catastrophic manner, was swallowed entirely by the sea.

All that remained was a vast shoal of thick mud which rendered the crossing of the Atlantic Ocean impossible.[2]

The Source of the Story

The story of Atlantis, its period of greatness and its violent destruction was first made public by the ancient Greek philosopher Plato. He was one of the earliest and certainly one of the greatest philosophers of all. He was born around 427 BC, and wrote and taught in Athens until his death some eighty years later. To express his ideas he usually wrote his books in the form of discussions or arguments between friends and associates. While he pressed many historical stories and legends into service in this way, he has never been found to have invented them. He took what he found, as he found it, in order to illustrate his philosophy further.

Late in his life, when his reputation was already at its peak, he wrote two related dialogues, his *Timaeus* and *Critias*. In both of these he depicts Critias – who in reality was an older relative of Plato – telling the story of Atlantis as he had heard it.

Evidently Critias had himself first told the story to Plato who, as was his style, had worked it into the dialogue. But where would Critias have received the story?

Critias explains that it had long been in his family; his great-grandfather had first been told it by a relative, a prominent Athenian, the famous Solon. And along with the story Solon had passed across his detailed handwritten notes. These notes would have been available to Plato, a century and a half later.

Solon was a highly revered figure in Greek history, especially for the Greeks of Plato's day. It would have been unthinkable for Plato to have attributed any falsehood to him. Solon was credited too for being one of the wisest men of his generation, for it was he who had devised the legal system used by Athens.

During a period of considerable civil tension Solon had been asked to form some legal and political settlement which would satisfy all sides. He did so very effectively but, knowing that he would subsequently be the target of men attempting to plead their own causes, he decided to remove himself from Athens so that all would have to find some way of living with the laws as they stood. Accordingly, as soon as the system was in place, he left Athens on an overseas trip, beginning with a voyage to Egypt.

Like most Athenians, Solon had a trade; he was a merchant and ship-owner. Egypt was a likely port of call for him because there was a well-established Greek presence there. The pharaoh Amasis (570–526 BC) had allowed the Greeks to establish the port of

Naucratis as a trading settlement near to his royal capital Saïs, in the Nile delta. It was during his reign that Solon arrived.

Solon resided in Egypt for some years. During this time he visited Saïs, and spoke at length with Sonchis, a priest there; he also visited the Heliopolis where he again became friendly with a priest, Psenophis, who also communicated much of the ancient wisdom held in the temples.[3] Both priests were later regarded as 'the most learned of the Egyptian priests'.

It was in conversation with a priest – perhaps Sonchis – in a temple at Saïs that Solon first heard the story of Atlantis. Perhaps the priest had allowed anger to overcome his usual reserve.

In the temple Solon had begun pontificating upon the antiquity of Greek history when one of the Egyptian priests present, an inordinately elderly man, finally could stand it no longer.

'O Solon,' he cried in exasperation, 'Solon, you Greeks are always children: there is not such a thing as an old Greek.'[4] Solon, taken aback, asked what he meant.

The priest explained, 'You possess not a single belief that is ancient and derived from old tradition, nor yet one science that is hoary with age.'

The priest described the many destructions of mankind in the past: in Greece, for example, there had been a great flood which had swept all the cities of the land into the sea. Because none of the survivors had known how to write, the culture had to start afresh and all memory of the times prior to the disaster was lost. However, the priest continued, in Egypt none of these calamities had caused any such destructions; in consequence, 'all such events are recorded from old and preserved here in our temples'.

Upon hearing this Solon grew excited about the possibility of learning something of the past and eagerly requested the priest to continue. The priest, it appears with an initial reluctance, decided not to withhold the story of Atlantis from Solon. This is an indication that perhaps the priest's anger had got the better of him and had placed him in the position where he was to reveal something about which he would perhaps have preferred to keep quiet. Certainly, the absence of any subsequent information regarding this story could indicate that it was knowledge kept for the inner circle of priests only. Reluctant or not, the priest revealed to Solon the story of what had occurred 9,000 years earlier: he told him the story of Atlantis.

Solon was caught by the drama of the narrative and resolved to work it into a major epic poem like those written by Homer about the Trojan War. After the conclusion of his travels, Solon returned to Athens and began to work on it. But he abandoned it. Perhaps he was staggered at the immensity of the task he had taken on. Whatever the reason, he passed both the story and the notes he had made over to Critias' great-grandfather. It then began its family descent to Plato.

Plato remains the original source for the story. Did he invent it? Against this is the fact that in all his other writing he has never been accused of inventing material. Solon too was a man with a strong reputation for honesty and wisdom. The very specific pedigree for the transmission of the information from Solon to Plato also seems plausible. But could we be dealing with a story to which everyone, including the Egyptian priest, had added details? A story which, beginning mostly true, ended mostly false? It certainly appears to contain elements which could derive from a number of separate sources.

Even Plato knew that what he had was close to the limits of belief, to the extent that he felt the need to state explicitly that it was 'a tale, though passing strange . . . yet wholly true'.[5] In fact, four times in his *Timaeus* he feels compelled to insist that it is true. Such repeated assertions are a measure of his expectation that some of his audience, at least, would refuse to believe it. In this he was correct: his pupil Aristotle rejected it out of hand as a fable.

We can accept that Plato accurately passed on something he, at least, believed to be true. Solon, though, could have garbled some of the information from the priest or fumbled in his rendition of the hieroglyphic texts, some of which, Plato makes clear, Solon translated himself. The Egyptian priest too could have been simply creating a story to outdo the assumptions of antiquity which Solon was claiming for Greek culture. Perhaps in his irritation the priest blended a measure of dramatic fable with true history.

There are three basic problems with the story:

1) That only Plato reports it.[6] Hence it is evident that the story, if true, was not commonly known or recorded elsewhere in ancient Egypt. Later the Greeks under the leadership of Alexander the Great invaded and took control of Egypt; hundreds of Greek scholars were to gain access to Egyptian records. During the subsequent Greek kingdom of Egypt the famous Alexandrian library was built which held all the knowledge available to the ancient world. If any details of this story had made their way into the library, many of those who worked there over the centuries would surely have mentioned it. Neither have any modern archaeologists reported finding any papyrus or inscribed versions of it. But it remains true that much has been lost from ancient Egypt. It also remains true that certain knowledge was always kept secret.

2) That the story asserts that 9,000 years earlier – around 9565 BC – a culture existed which knew the use of metals, ships, dressed stone for building and agriculture. This is typical of the Bronze Age which is known only from around 3200 BC. The story appears to be set over 6,000 years too early.

3) That a huge island holding this culture disappeared beneath the Atlantic in a day and a half as a result of earthquakes. There does not appear to be any other record or corroborating evidence of this catastrophe.

Leaving aside, for the moment, the use of metal, cultures of this level of advancement are not too far away from the early date claimed by Plato. Work over the last thirty years or so has shown that a complex trading culture existed, as we have seen, at Çatal Hüyük in Anatolia; stone city walls and towers were built at Jericho in the Jordan valley very early, perhaps around 7000 BC; metal working, however, began perhaps 2,000 years later.[7] So the assertion of such a culture existing in 9000 BC is not at all impossible – we simply have not yet found any evidence for it. Of course, many cultures have been completely lost; we are still occasionally uncovering remnants of completely unknown empires from the past.

Nevertheless, most investigators have accepted the level of civilization described in the story at face value but have rejected the early date as unrealistic. They have argued that if the story has a core of truth, then this vanished culture should be sought around 1500 to 2000 BC, during the Late Bronze Age, rather than far earlier.

There is little doubt that Atlantis, as described by Plato, reveals a Late Bronze Age civilization. Either we have to consider Plato's date wrong and look in known areas of Bronze Age culture, or we have to decide, against all currently known archaeological evidence, that the Bronze Age began very much earlier – about 6,000 years earlier. Naturally, the scholars have chosen to look at known Bronze Age sites.

Have any great Bronze Age cultural centres simply disappeared? Sunk for ever beneath the waters after volcanic or tectonic catastrophe? In fact, at least two have.

Attention has been drawn away from the Atlantic Ocean – which is regarded as a wild exaggeration – and refocused upon the Mediterranean area. For here, in the revised time period, one cultural centre exploded, and another, racked by earthquakes, sank beneath a lake leaving only wall-shadows under the waters.

The Eruption of Thera

One summer, around 1628 BC, the Greek island of Thera exploded with the force of thirty hydrogen bombs.[8] The middle of the island vanished, vaporized, pulverized and ejected miles into the sky. Instead of the fertile farms and vineyards there was but a very large and very deep crater into which the sea rapidly poured. The few parts of the island which remained at the crater's edge were rapidly and deeply covered by volcanic debris, mostly layer upon layer of superheated ash.

These shattered remnants, uninhabitable for many generations, perhaps for hundreds of years, are the five small Greek islands today collectively known as Santorini – the largest of them being Thera. Like all Greek islands, Thera is now a popular tourist spot, impressing all visitors with its high volcanic cliffs rising steeply out of the deep azure Aegean. Bright white houses clutch at the sharp crater rim like squatting sea-birds ready to leave at the first hint of danger. Wisps of smoke occasionally escape from a small island at the centre of the sea-filled crater reminding visitors that the volcano has not yet forgotten how to erupt.

Thera has its classical Greek ruins: the remains of temples, houses, public buildings and a theatre. But it has been known for many years that deep below the layers of volcanic detritus was solid evidence of a once forgotten civilization. Over the years, erosion has uncovered traces of walls and pottery. And last century small excavations exposed the remains of three houses, one revealing ornate painted decorations. But excavation did not continue: archaeologists were few and funds for digging were limited.

Archaeologists very early on learned that funds were generated by dramatic discoveries and so islands like Crete, with its massive palaces, attracted and absorbed the archaeological interest. For on Crete were dramatic remnants of a huge, sophisticated seafaring and trading civilization which had previously been unknown. Its capital was the impressive palace of Knossos where Sir Arthur Evans began excavating in 1899. This is now named the Minoan culture – after one of its kings, Minos, famous in the later Greek myth of the Minotaur.

A particular feature of Minoan culture was its love of decoration; its pottery was ornately painted and its houses had revealing wall paintings – frescos – which have given us a good idea of Minoan life. Especially, it has allowed us a glimpse at the culture's defining religion, the bull cult.

A peculiarity discovered by the archaeologists was that this widespread and successful culture was suddenly overwhelmed and destroyed. Palace and villa walls were broken, houses were burned, pottery was smashed. Its power too vanished, seemingly overnight. It appeared that suddenly its ships no longer commanded the seas and its traders no longer imported goods from every part of the known world.

Scholars were not slow to see glimmerings of a parallel between Plato's description of Atlantis and this ornate Cretan Bronze Age culture, both of which came to an abrupt end. In fact, within ten years such a link was suggested – albeit anonymously.[9] During the following fifty years further parallels were advanced. Finally, in 1967, one of the most enthusiastic theorists, the Greek archaeologist Professor Spyridon Marinatos, finally began to seek proof under the ground.

Professor Marinatos conducted systematic excavations on Thera for seven years until he died, on the site, in 1974. During those seven years dramatic discoveries were made of parts of a very large ancient town. Two important aspects had been clarified. Firstly, he now had proof that Thera had indeed exploded catastrophically during the height of its Bronze Age culture. And secondly, it was evident that the inhabitants of Thera were closely linked in some direct way with the Minoan culture of Crete. Thera might have been a Minoan outpost, a colony or a close ally. Thus the Bronze

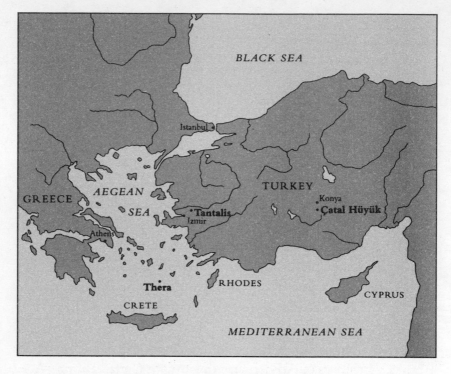

Thera and Tantalis: both possible sites for Atlantis.

Age Atlantis thesis was defined: the explosion of Thera caused the demise of Minoan Crete and its 'disappearance' from the Bronze Age world. Thera – or perhaps Crete – was 'Atlantis'.

Samples from the seabed revealed that debris from Thera was to be found over much of the southern Aegean and allowed an estimate to be made of the depth of ash which probably fell upon Crete: almost eight inches, enough to poison the land. Pumice too was found there together with evidence of widespread destruction: three major royal palaces, four large country villas and six entire towns were destroyed simultaneously. Coastal sites also showed great damage consistent with the destructive effects of tidal waves, tsunamis, which undoubtedly would have followed such an eruption. Walls had fallen outwards and shattered personal objects were found, their pieces widely scattered.

Professor Marinatos, along with many other scholars, believed that these excavations on Thera and Crete had finally solved the mystery of Atlantis. They concluded – and books rapidly appeared in print repeating and reinforcing their ideas – that Plato's story of Atlantis essentially described the Bronze Age Minoan culture of Crete and its sudden demise as a result of the volcanic explosion of Thera. They also concluded that the combined disasters of ash, tidal waves and probably earthquakes so disabled Crete that it rapidly vanished into impotence and obscurity.

But in this conclusion the scholars were to be proved wrong.

The classical Greek world was well aware of Crete and its history. Plato even visited the island with a view to establishing a community there. There was too a rich Greek mythological tradition which revolved around Minoan Crete and King Minos. It is inconceivable that Solon or Plato should have failed to identify Atlantis as Crete if that had been the intention of the original story. That they did not do so is very strong evidence that they were viewed clearly as two separate places. In addition to this, the prime heroic figure in the Atlantis story is Atlas, after whom both the island and the sea were named. Yet there is no Greek myth concerning Crete in which Atlas is accorded a role such as this.[10]

But history and archaeology too finally bring the Thera argument to a conclusion. The much-discussed sudden cessation of Minoan trade simply did not happen. There was no abrupt breaking of links between Crete and its trading partners. The final proof that Professor Marinatos was wrong came when archaeologists discovered layers of volcanic ash from the Thera eruption *beneath* the layers of destruction in Crete, thus proving it to be earlier in time.[11] In addition, the pottery found at Thera has been shown to date from earlier than that found in the destroyed Cretan palaces. It is now thought that the eruption of Thera could be up to 250 years prior to the destruction of the Cretan towns and palaces.[12] This destruction, it is now felt, came through invasion and conquest.

The explosion of Thera did not cause the demise of Minoan Crete. It cannot explain the Atlantis story. This particular thesis is dead. Is all then lost for a classical origin for the story?

The Drowning of Tantalis

According to Plato, prior to the destruction of Atlantis its hitherto victorious army was decisively defeated in battle by the Athenians. Plato then adds a description of life in those early times which is almost intimate in its details.

Plato begins by lamenting the destruction in Greece caused by great erosion. He describes how, in those early days, the land had not yet lost its rich soil and so was covered with forests or arable fields where large flocks grazed. In Plato's day the soil had become much poorer, much less productive. He also gives a detailed description of the acropolis of Athens, its extent and the differing areas inhabited by the military, the craftsmen and the farmers. He describes the buildings and points out that they were all destroyed prior to the buildings which stood in his day. He also notes that a single great spring supplied water but that an earthquake had blocked it up long before his lifetime.[13]

Archaeology has since demonstrated that Plato's description was completely accurate in every way that can be checked. He is not weaving a fantasy but reporting details which were recorded – where, we do not know. This ancient Athens and its inhabitants is known; they belong to the Late Bronze Age dynasty of the kings who ruled from their capital Mycenae until around 1100 BC. It was, in fact, this dynasty which invaded Crete and destroyed its palaces, thus supplanting the Minoan kings in their palace at Knossos. It was also this same dynasty which fought the Trojan War.

It has even been argued by one scholar that it was the Trojan

War which provided the basis of the Atlantis story; that it was simply an Egyptian embellishment of those distant events.[14] This cannot be successfully maintained because Troy remained rather obdurately non-sunken (even though it 'fell'). It can still be visited and seen to be placed very firmly upon dry land. Consequently, Troy has to go the way of Thera: an interesting idea which doesn't work.

Are the Bronze Age links to be explained away, then, as simply a method of providing a dramatic context for the epic poem which Solon had planned? This type of approach is common enough amongst writers and artists: the Renaissance painters often depicted biblical scenes with all the characters in 'modern' dress; the musical *West Side Story* was a recasting of Shakespeare's *Romeo and Juliet* into New York. Was the Bronze Age setting for Atlantis similarly an artistic addition to package an earlier catastrophe?

It might be possible. But before we leave this period we must examine one very close historical parallel to the Atlantis tale which has only recently been recovered from the darkness of history. This concerns the story of Tantalus, the king of Lydia, a kingdom which comprised half of Turkey from around 680 BC until it fell before the onslaught of the Persian armies in 546 BC – just nineteen years before Plato's birth. The last king of Lydia was Croesus, notorious for his love of wealth and luxury.

The scholar and author Peter James, aware of the deficiencies in all other Bronze Age explanations for Atlantis, decided upon another approach. He chose to begin exploring the figure of Atlas, described as the first king of Atlantis.

In Greek myth Atlas had been banished to the west, condemned to forever hold up the sky. And it is his place in the west which gives rise to the Atlantic Ocean location for Plato's story. James wondered whether this placement could be a later addition since Greek ships and merchants only reached the far west during the seventh century BC. Where, he asked, was Atlas banished from?[15] No other modern scholars seems to have asked this question before.

The Greek poet Pindar, writing in the fifth century BC, described Atlas as having been 'banished from his ancestral lands and possessions'.[16] Where were these lands and possessions? James searched all the early traditions and found that they pointed unequivocally to Anatolia – to western Turkey.

Bronze Age Turkey was long ruled by a civilization known as the Hittites. Their mythology featured a figure who, like Atlas, held up the sky. In fact, this Hittite figure may well be the source for the Greek Atlas, for ancient Turkey is the ultimate source for much of Greek mythology.[17]

Furthermore this Hittite Atlas was connected to a bull cult: the figure is often depicted with a bull's head and with hoofs instead of hands and feet. For the later Lydians – whose kingdom covered much of western former Hittite lands – their version of Atlas was the legendary king Tantalus who was reputed to have amassed fabulous wealth.

James discovered that traditions existed concerning Lydia which revealed clear parallels with the story of Atlantis.

The Greek geographer and traveller Pausanias wrote a detailed guide and history for all the places to which he travelled, thus recording many ancient traditions which would otherwise have been lost. One concerned a city upon the Lydian Mount Sipylus which, after a violent earthquake, had vanished into a chasm which then flooded, becoming a lake.[18]

The Roman writer Pliny, working during the first century AD, supplies a further crucial connection: that this vanished city, sunk by an earthquake, had been the old royal capital of Lydia, called Tantalis. The site where it vanished, in Pliny's day, was no longer a lake but a marshland.[19] Pausanias had apparently been unaware of the connection.

The parallels are clear between Atlas and Atlantis and Tantalus and Tantalis. Even the names of the capital cities are uncomfortably close. So has James, as he believed, solved the problem of Atlantis?

In 1994 he travelled to the area, near to the modern Turkish city of
Izmir. He managed to identify the most likely site for the vanished
city, close to the northern slopes of Mount Sipylus where old maps
show the presence of a lake or marsh. In front of the site an ancient,
large, and very worn image of the goddess Cybele could still be
seen carved into the rocky mountain face.[20] She gazed over the site
of Tantalis. All that now remains is to dig.

It is known that Solon, on his travels, not only resided in Egypt
but also visited Lydia. It is possible that he could have heard the
story of Tantalus there from which he created the story of Atlantis.
Indeed, Plato reports that Solon, upon deciding to make use of the
story in his poetry, translated the names into Greek.[21] Did he
translate Tantalus into Atlas?

It is a plausible suggestion and yet it leaves some important
problems unsolved – in particular, the problem of the Atlantic
Ocean location. Let us now look again at Plato's story.

The Atlantic Ocean

There are two major objections to a Bronze Age Mediterranean
setting for the story. Firstly, Plato specifically located Atlantis as
being beyond the Mediterranean and half-way to a great continent.
Secondly, he located it many thousands of years before his time,
before even the 1st Dynasty of Egypt, which was about as far back
as records went in those days. No one expects that every word of
the story is literally accurate, but there are certain points about it
which are anomalous and yet which ring true. The first such point
is an extraordinary geographical one: it indicates that Plato – or the
Egyptian priests at Saïs – knew of the existence of America.

Plato records the geographical location of Atlantis as being beyond
the Pillars of Heracles, that is, beyond the entrance to the Mediterranean sea. Now he and any sailors of the time would have known
well where this was; the Greeks and the Phoenicians were trading

beyond the Mediterranean at the time and had done so for centuries. They traded down the coast of Morocco and also to southern England.

Plato states that, 'it was possible for the travellers of that time to cross from [Atlantis] to the other islands . . .'. Could he mean the West Indies?

He continues, 'and from the islands to the whole of the continent over against them which encompasses that veritable ocean'.[22] Is he speaking of America, the only continent which lies beyond Gibraltar, across the Atlantic, and past a line of islands?

Given that this is geographically the truth, it indicates that someone must have sailed across to America and back, and that knowledge of this reached Plato via the Egyptian priests. It makes us look again at his story and accept that it must contain a kernel of truth. The Egyptians perhaps sailed across the Atlantic at some early stage in their history. Herodotus reports that they sailed around Africa, a much longer trip.[23]

A second indication of the story's validity is also related to seafaring knowledge. Plato records that during the time of Atlantis 'the ocean there was at that time navigable'. And that after the sinking of Atlantis 'that spot has now become impassable . . . being blocked up by the shoal mud which the island created as it settled down'. These words seem to echo sailor's talk; perhaps advice given to those about to sail west for the first time.

It is difficult to explain away these explicit references to the Atlantic Ocean, the West Indies and the continent of America beyond. At least this part of Plato's story must be accurate. And to have this accuracy associated with the lost continent of Atlantis' geographical position must give even the Anatolian theorists pause for thought.

The Ice-free Antarctic

Any thought of early specialized maritime knowledge brings us to a consideration of the unexplained Piri Re'is map of 1513 and of that of Orestius Finnaeus of 1531. These maps, astonishingly, depict the Antarctic continent very accurately as it would be *without its two-mile-thick cover of ice.*[24] They depict it as it has been known *only* since the careful surveys of the 1950s using highly technical equipment. The logical – and apparently only – conclusion is that these maps derive from the work of an unknown early people who were skilled seafarers and cartographers. It appears that somewhere in mankind's unknown past there existed such a culture which traded across the seas beyond the Mediterranean.

What has not been noted, however, is the possible relevance of these maps to the story of Atlantis.

Plato describes Atlantis as being the centre of a great empire founded upon its maritime skills. He states that Atlantis ruled over many other islands in the sea beyond the Mediterranean.[25] The city of Atlantis itself had great inland harbours and shipyards filled with vessels well protected by stone walls. In particular, the largest harbour was 'filled with ships and merchants coming from all quarters, which by reason of their multitude caused clamour and tumult of every description and an unceasing din night and day'.[26]

Two Canadian writers, Rand and Rose Flem-Arth, have suggested that the once ice-free Lesser Antarctica might be the true site of Atlantis. They point out that its geographical position places it at the centre of a 'world' ocean, linking, as it does, the Atlantic, Indian and Pacific oceans, which, after all, are the same ocean split by the continents of America and Africa. They argue that this is the sense in which Plato writes of the 'true' or 'real' ocean which lies outside the narrow 'Pillars of Heracles'. Plato writes that compared to this 'true' ocean the Mediterranean is but 'a haven having a narrow entrance'.[27] This is a very accurate description *when viewed from the perspective of the Atlantic Ocean.*

This is an extraordinary statement for a fourth-century BC Greek to make. In those days the Mediterranean was the heart of the known world and to belittle it in this way again emphasizes the strength and importance of the maritime information to which Plato or Solon had access.

The Flem-Arths propose that the end of the Antarctic Atlantis came when the ice-caps melted catastrophically sending great tidal waves across the 'world' ocean. And with this sudden spread of cold water came a rapid drop in the world's temperature which, in turn, caused a sudden freezing. They point to mammoths being found in Siberia, frozen with fresh grass in their stomachs. All life in Lesser Antarctica met with the same fate. Survivors spread to all the known world bringing their gift of knowledge: of agriculture, architecture and astronomy.

For sheer outrageousness this hypothesis has everything going for it. Everything, that is, except hard facts. But then this should not be allowed to stand in the way of such a delightfully heretical suggestion. Nevertheless, hard facts may be there: the Flem-Arths suggest that archaeologists should begin to dig in Antarctica; below the deep ice may lie, preserved for ever, the frozen remnants of a great city. It is enough to make one reach for one's chequebook. Well, almost.

The Azores

There is one site left to consider, and that is the site at which Plato actually placed his continent of Atlantis. Oddly this seems to have become something of a politically incorrect area for recent theorists, even those working at the fringe.[28] Plato put the island in the Atlantic, its northernmost tip level with the Straits of Gibraltar; it was in the ocean but lay before the islands (the West Indies) and the continent (America).

It has long been known that a great range of undersea mountains runs from Iceland in the North Atlantic all the way to the South Atlantic, a distance of thousands of miles: the Mid-Atlantic Ridge. Occasionally, the very highest peaks of this mountain range break the surface of the water: the Azores, Ascension Island, Tristan da Cunha, all are the tips of these mountains. If Atlantis were a large mid-Atlantic island, it would certainly have included some part of this ridge. The problem is that there is no evidence of any subsidence; the ridge, by all accounts, is rising rather than falling.

There is, of course, another perspective: the land may not have sunk; rather, the sea may have risen.

We have seen in an earlier chapter that the sea-levels rose dramatically and catastrophically around 8000 BC, near the end of the last Ice Age, a date not too far off Plato's date for the destruction of Atlantis. We have seen too how animal teeth brought up by fishermen from the continental shelf off the coast of the United States indicate a rise in sea-level of 400 feet or more.

Oceanographers have produced comprehensive charts of the world's seabed from a century or more of depth soundings. These afford a general guide to the amount of land which would have been exposed during such a period of reduced sea-levels.

The Azores have always been a favourite choice for the residue of Atlantis since a large island in their position would stand level with the Straits of Gibraltar, just as Plato described. And, allowing a certain amount of support is the known fact of the area's seismic activity. Since a major earthquake recorded in 1522 there have been sixteen further strong disturbances, the biggest being one in 1757 which is estimated at 7.4 on the Richter scale.

If we look at the charts for the Azores, a number of facts become evident. The first is that the Azores are most certainly the tops of very tall mountains, over 20,000 feet above the lowest seabed 'plains'.

Secondly, if the sea-level were reduced by 400 feet or more, then, certainly, significantly more land would be exposed. The central islands of Pico and Faial would be joined together and most of the others doubled in size. In addition, up to ten new islands would appear, none very large, but creating a complex archipelago in the area. Probably a good place to live but not providing a very close fit for Plato's description of Atlantis. Curiously, and perhaps significantly, the Piri Re'is map of 1513 which we have already mentioned depicts the Azores, and depicts them in the correct geographical latitude and longitude. But instead of the nine small islands which exist today, it shows seventeen islands, several of them relatively large, up to ten times the size of the present largest island, São Miguel, perhaps about the size of Cyprus.[30] Is this map an accurate rendition of the Azores *pre-inundation*? From *before* 8700–9000 BC? It seems very likely.

To join the Azores into one island would take a drop in sea-level of almost 6,000 feet. This would, however, produce an extremely large island indeed. A more modest drop of 3,000 feet would also give a large amount of land above water but the Azores would be a collection of islands.[31] Of course, it may be, as Plato described, that a massive earthquake lowered the land itself. If this is indeed the case, then the Azores are, without question, the best potential site in the entire Atlantic.

The situation around the remainder of the Atlantic does not reveal any other possible site. While the sea is comparatively shallow in parts of the Mid-Atlantic Ridge, these 'shallows' are still at least 3,000 feet deep.[32] There are, however, curious features called sea-mounts between the ridge and the African continent. A number of these exist today with spot depths as shallow as sixty-five feet. A fall in sea-level would certainly expose them but the islands they would form would be small.[33]

The situation near the Straits of Gibraltar, however, reveals features which render at least part of Plato's geographical comments plausible.

With the sea-level reduced to its Ice Age minimum, extensive lands would reach thirty miles or more out from the Atlantic coast of Portugal, Spain and Morocco. This would give in excess of 8,000 square miles of habitable coastal plains in the Gulf of Cadiz and northern Morocco alone. The Straits of Gibraltar would become a narrow channel about sixty miles long with two small islands at its Atlantic entrance. Some 300 miles due west into the Atlantic, along the site of the present-day Gorringe Ridge, would be a larger island, perhaps the size of present-day Menorca. This is now beneath the sea but parts of it are, even today, as little as sixty-five feet beneath the surface.[34]

The rapid rise in sea-levels at the end of the last Ice Age, would have devastated the wide plains bordering the narrow Gibraltar channel. The entrance to the Mediterranean might very easily have been blocked by hundreds of feet of mud. This then, is one explanation of the impassable mud banks beyond the Straits which Plato mentions.

Survivors of the inundation would have fled, each carrying a story of disaster; through this the story would have entered the oral tradition in those countries of refuge. An oral tradition which was eventually passed on to Solon.

But would this area have had such a technical competence to account for Plato's Bronze Age setting? If we think of it as a description simply of an early but complex society, then it makes sense. The town of Çatal Hüyük had sophistication enough and it dates back to at least 8000 BC. And, as we shall see, the people who built the Sphinx did so thousands of years before the official beginning of the Bronze Age, yet they too lacked little in ability. They may have lacked metal but they had everything else a culture needs – a command of astronomy, mathematics and architecture.

In the end, Atlantis may prove too mysterious and too enigmatic

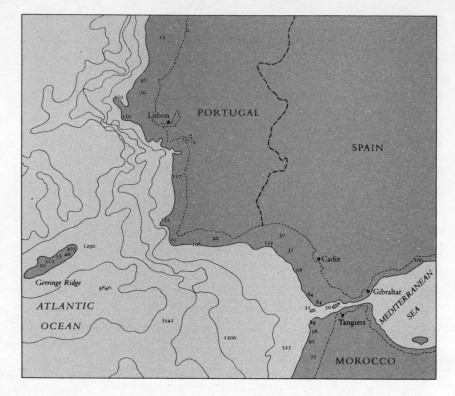

The entrance to the Mediterranean: showing submerged land and present depth soundings. (The soundings are given in metres.)

to be placed in any normal Bronze Age setting. Solon's response may have been correct when he found himself driven to make a great epic poem out of the story. But even with his direct access to the source of the story he found himself unable to deal with it and passed the story on to somebody else to complete.

It appears that we cannot yet know the truth about Atlantis. Nevertheless, the idea that its story along with other elements, perhaps even from across the Atlantic, contains a folk memory of the inundation which occurred at the end of the Ice Age is plausible. This focuses attention upon the sunken lands beyond the Straits of Gibraltar, which we can assume held an active population. Or even,

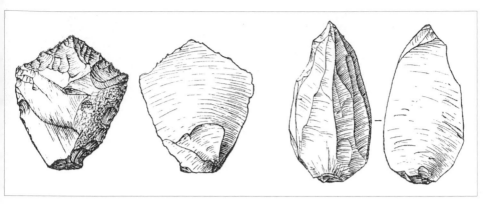

16. Ancient tools found by the famous French prehistorian Abbé Henri Breuil at Clermont, France. Identical to those dating from the last million years of human development, they were, in fact, excavated from Eocene strata; these date from 38 million years ago.

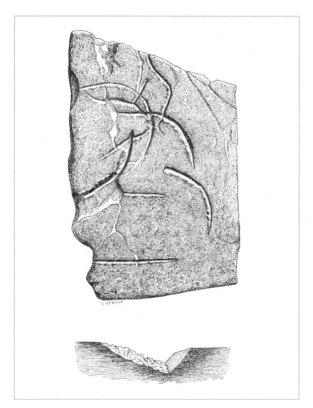

17. (*above*): Drawing of very ancient butchering marks, presumably as a result of human activity, discovered on a fossil whale bone found in Italy last century in rock strata near Siena dating from 2 to 5 million years ago.
Below: A drawing of the magnified section of a butchering mark on a whale bone from the same area and date showing what is obviously the result of slicing action by a sharp object.

18. The pre-dynastic Egyptian carved slate 'Palette of Narmer' from over 3100 BC. Around the centre are depicted two long-necked creatures held in captivity. There is no valid reason to hold that these are mythological.

19. Drawing of a long-necked creature from within the Ice Age cave of Pergouset, France, dated at around 10,000–13,000 BC.

20. Drawing of a group of unknown reptilian creatures incised in a wall of the Ice Age cave of Casares, Spain.

21. Giza: the Pyramid of Khafre and the Sphinx, which shows both modern and ancient repairs to its heavily eroded stone body. The pattern of this erosion and its extent, far greater than on other structures on the Giza plateau, suggest that it is thousands of years older than previously thought.

22. The vertical erosion pattern on the Sphinx enclosure seen here can only have been caused by rainfall; wind-blown sand creates a different, more horizontal pattern.

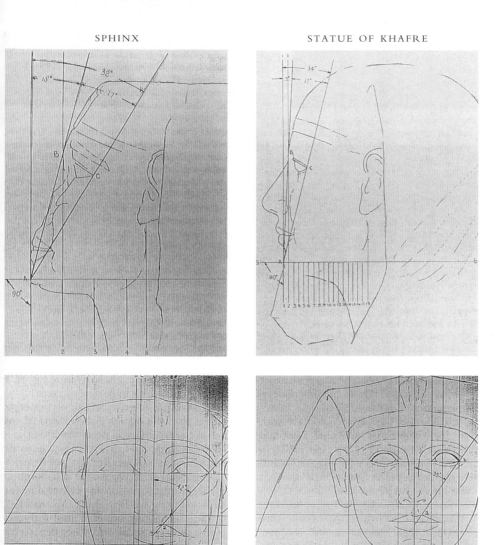

23. Detailed analysis of the head of Egyptian pharaoh Khafre – assumed builder of the Sphinx - and the head of the Sphinx by New York forensic expert Detective Frank Domingo. The difference between the two is so marked that they cannot be representations of the same ruler. The Sphinx is not Khafre.

24. The earliest example of the spiritual *Pyramid Texts*, carved into the interior of the Pyramid of Unas, Saqqara, south of Giza, and dating from around 2350 BC.

25. Wooden coffin of the doctor Seni from El-Bersha, Egypt. The interior contains *The Coffin Texts* painted in black ink, a genre dating from 2000 – 1600 BC.

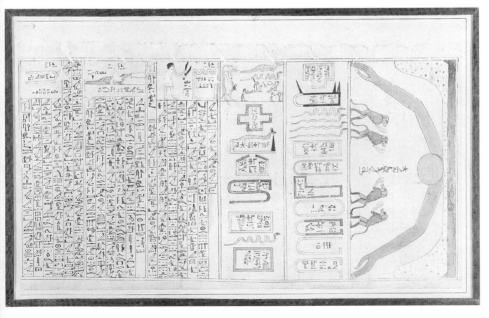

26. The end section of the Egyptian *Book of the Dead* of Userhat dating from around 1400 BC from Thebes. It is completed with a drawing of the sun-god being adored as he rises.

27. Alchemical illustration from Steffan Michelspacher, Augsburg, 1616. The blindfolded alchemist is finally led by the mercurial hare to the seven steps of the alchemical process by which means he climbs into the palace wherein the sun and moon are united.

as has been suggested by the Russian classical scholar V. Kovdriavtsev, upon the edge of the continental shelf off the Scilly Isles.[35]

However, we cannot entirely dismiss a massive cataclysmic earthquake in the Atlantic, for it is certainly possible, however remote this might be. And this would focus attention upon the Azores. For it seems that Plato's report of the Atlantic as the 'real' ocean and his awareness of the limitations of the Mediterranean contain an inescapable element attesting to an Atlantic placement for the heart of the Atlantis story; nowhere else will do.

9

Are the Pyramids and Sphinx
More Ancient than We Think?

For thousands of years the pyramids and Sphinx have reached upwards from their rocky plateau at Giza, their presence seeming to convey an enigmatic message from epochs long since vanished – a message which has exerted an extraordinary compulsion upon many, who arrived simply to gaze but who departed with reluctance carrying a vivid sense that something vital once existed in the world, something now lost to modern life. But precisely what, no one can articulate.

In the early 1990s a storm of controversy hit the world of Egyptology: authors John Anthony West, Robert Bauval, Adrian Gilbert, Graham Hancock and Colin Wilson all went into print on the subject. They fired off an astonishing broadside at the archaeological establishment. The story these authors had to tell was dramatic, always compelling, and often outrageous. Once upon a time, they said, there was a continent called Atlantis . . .

This lost continent, they explain, was the centre of a huge maritime empire where religious mysteries were practised and science had become far advanced. But, contrary to the usual understanding, these authors place Atlantis not beyond the Straits of Gibraltar but much further south, in the continent now known as the Antarctic. Sixteen thousand and more years ago, they explain, this had been generally ice-free, enjoying a climate similar to that of Canada today.

Following upon cataclysmic geological changes, including a displacement of the earth's outer crust, the position of the poles altered. The southern continent shifted to its present position in the polar region and, once this had happened, Atlantean culture was destroyed, quickly hidden beneath two miles of ice and snow as the continent fell into a permanent freeze.

During the latter stages of this catastrophe, during the fourteenth millennium BC, refugees struck out from the south and spread into all the world's continents. Amongst them were high initiates who carried the secrets of Atlantean technology, religion and science. One group of initiates, apparently called in later texts the 'Followers of Horus', settled in Egypt and founded a cult base on the Giza plateau.

These initiates, fearful lest further destructions should ensue, instigated a long-term building plan which would preserve their secret teachings for all time. They devised a method of incorporating these principles into the geometry of their buildings which were designed to be so massive that they would survive any future cataclysm. They expected that, even if their school of initiates should at some future time die out, later civilizations would recover the secrets by decoding clues fixed into the design geometry of these structures. Thus the message of these Atlantean initiates might be protected for aeons, to be transmitted to cultures whose time lay far in the future.

These initiates built the Sphinx and laid out the ground plan of Giza. They may even have built actual structures on the plateau there or perhaps they merely maintained records of the design throughout the succeeding millennia. However this knowledge was preserved, 8,000 years later, in 2500 BC, the pyramids were built in accordance with this ancient plan.

The site of Giza and its secrets was, from the first, protected by the 'Followers of Horus', astronomer–priests whose secret power was such that even 8,000 years later the pharaohs dared not change the complex plan devised for Giza.

Hancock and Bauval write that

> We think the evidence suggests a continuous transmission of
> advanced scientific and engineering knowledge over that huge
> gulf of time, and thus the continuous presence in Egypt, from
> the Palaeolithic into the Dynastic Period, of highly enlightened
> and sophisticated individuals – those shadowy *Akhus* said in
> the texts to have possessed a knowledge of divine origin.[1]

To Hancock and Bauval the Giza complex is truly the sacred heart
of Egypt – if not the world. It is a site so sacred that not one part of
the design could be altered despite the passing of many thousands
of years.

All this provides a wonderful story: a colourful adventure in wild
ideas, anomalous discoveries and unexpected insights punctuated
by repeated challenges to some of the most respected figures in
modern Egyptology. Hancock and Bauval are solidly anti-establish-
ment. Their work in particular diligently notes the denial of contrary
evidence, the prevention of access to sites, the withdrawal of investigation permits, the mislaying of anomalous artefacts and the general
academic disdain for any alternative explanations, however apparently plausible. Theirs is the perfect book to read during a long
flight in order to survive complicated time-zones and lobotomized
airline videos.

But can we believe it?

The Mysteries of Giza

The Pyramids of Giza stand, massive yet mute, upon a rocky plateau
across the Nile from Old Cairo, today at the southern desert edges
of the modern city's suburbs. The Giza plateau, significantly higher
than the surrounding terrain, is about a mile and a half long, half
that wide, and ends with a sharp drop at the edge of the Nile valley.

Egyptologists are confident that the Great Pyramid at Giza was a tomb built by the 4th Dynasty pharaoh Khufu around 2500 BC (there are no certain dates) and that the second large pyramid and the Sphinx were built a little later by the pharaoh Khafre. The latter's son Menkaure, the next ruler, built the third and smaller pyramid.[2]

Each pyramid had, at its east wall, a mortuary temple from which a causeway sloped down to a valley temple situated on the edge of the plateau, near the Nile. It was here that the dead pharaoh, carried by boat down the river, would begin his final journey. At the eastern edge of the plateau squats the Sphinx and its associated temple. In addition, the plateau holds six very small pyramids which are certainly tombs and a regimented host of even smaller *mastabas* – tombs of the nobility. There are also a number of boat pits which contained dismantled wooden boats, one of which, removed from a pit near the eastern side of the Great Pyramid in 1954, when reconstructed, proved to be just over 142 feet long. It showed signs of use suggesting that it might have been the very craft which carried Khufu's remains along the Nile.

The Giza complex is a unity, a coherent organized necropolis site dedicated to glorifying both death and the dead. Elements of this complex are still being discovered. Very recently, during excavations for a sewage system for the nearby Cairo suburbs, the remains of the long-lost valley temple of Khufu were discovered, quickly mapped and just as quickly destroyed by the rapidly progressing construction.

And, to the east, guardian of the entire complex, rests the Great Sphinx; at its forepaws, another temple. At first sight, it is hard to see any difficulty with the interrelationship, the coherence, of these elements. The conventional explanation seems evident; no other is called for. To call any part of the story into question is not only to fly in the face of archaeology but also to deny the evidence of one's own eyes.

The crucial link which, if broken, allows the new and revised version of Egyptian history to be argued is the question of the age

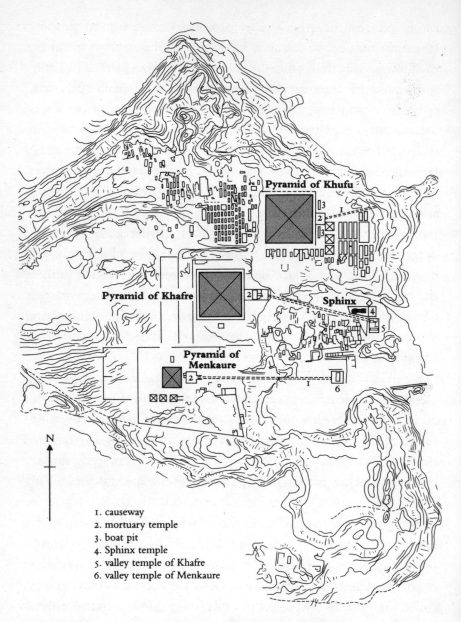

1. causeway
2. mortuary temple
3. boat pit
4. Sphinx temple
5. valley temple of Khafre
6. valley temple of Menkaure

The Giza complex, attributed to the 4th Dynasty (*c.* 2614–2494 BC).

of the Sphinx. For this makes, or breaks, the unity of the Giza complex and therefore the attribution of all its structures to the pharaohs of the 4th Dynasty – Khufu, Khafre and Menkaure. If this unity breaks, if any part of that complex can be proved pre-dynastic – that is, to have originated before the rise of the Egyptian monarchy around 3100 BC – then this throws into disarray the current view of Egypt's past. Such a finding would force Egyptologists to accept the existence of some much earlier, yet technically accomplished, Egyptian culture.

Certainly archaeologists know that the Sphinx is very old. The most obvious evidence is found in its body. Much of the basic stone core, perhaps all of it, was covered in antiquity by a stone facing. It had long been thought that this masonry was added to the roughly cut body of the Sphinx when it was first built, being the means by which final shape was given to the Sphinx's body. But in 1979–80, during a meticulous examination of the Sphinx, a provocative conclusion was reached. In his introduction to an explanation the chief archaeologist, American Dr Mark Lehner of Chicago University, reported, 'We have nowhere observed any kind of working marks on the core body, either in the way of tool marks or of surfaces that would seem to have been left by rough quarrying activity.'[3] Furthermore, he explained, the body of the Sphinx showed the effects of 'severe erosion'. He concluded that, 'the core body of the Sphinx was already in a severe state of erosion when the earliest level of masonry was added'.[4] It is not surprising that Dr Lehner then drew the conclusion that this repair work 'probably' occurred in the 'New Kingdom' period, which dates from around 1500 BC. For this gives him around 1,000 years or so to account for the 'severe' erosion. He would hardly have wished to allow any less.

Unfortunately Dr Lehner's cautious opinion, given in 1980, has been superseded. In 1992 Dr Zahi Hawass, the Director of the Giza complex for the Egyptian Antiquities Organization, reported that analysis of the right rear leg of the Sphinx proved the earliest level of masonry around the body dated instead from the 'Old Kingdom' period, that is, from about 2700 BC to 2160 BC.[5] The pyramids were constructed in the middle part of this period.

Despite the relative obscurity of the publication in which this report appeared and its bland understatement, it was perfectly apparent that some restless genie had finally managed to squeeze its way out of a tightly corked bottle.

For if Khafre had built the Sphinx along with his pyramid around 2500 BC, and if repairs to its heavily eroded body were made before 2160 BC, then this severe erosion covered up by the facing stones must have occurred *in only 340 years* – perhaps less: an extremely unlikely event. In practical terms, given the extent and depth of the erosion, it seems impossible.

Since the obvious conclusion from these rather reluctant admissions is that the Sphinx was already old and eroded when Khafre built his pyramid, perhaps it was Khafre himself who placed the protective facing stonework around its body?

Opposing this argument is the widely held belief that prior to the existence of the strongly wielded central power of the pharaohs – the 1st Dynasty of whom began around 3100 BC – Egyptians did not build in stone and were incapable of the organization needed to construct huge buildings or monuments. Without this authority of command or power of wealth, there was little possibility of either enslaving, or hiring, the manpower needed for such an ambitious building programme.

This criticism, though, ignores the obvious differences between the Sphinx and the pyramids. The pyramids were built stone by heavy stone. The Sphinx was not built, it was excavated out of solid rock, a rather simpler task than constructing a pyramid.

Inevitably showing strong support for the establishment line, Dr Zahi Hawass insisted that archaeologists had 'solid evidence' to prove that the Sphinx was built by Khafre – thus around 2500 BC.[6]

Yet what does this 'solid evidence' consist of? Upon investigation, very little: an eroded inscription, potentially intrusive statues in a temple and a subjective interpretation of the Sphinx's face. Nothing, in fact, which would stand up in court.

Did Khafre Build the Great Sphinx?

Around 1400 BC, the pharaoh Thutmosis IV, obeying the commands of a prophetic dream, cleared all the sand away from the Sphinx. To commemorate this he ordered that a stone bearing an inscription be placed between the Sphinx's paws. This stone still exists, though it has become so badly weathered that much of the text has crumbled away.

It was first uncovered in 1818, at which time line 13 of the text, although damaged, was understood to have mentioned the name of Khafre. Unfortunately, due to the destruction of the surrounding text, its true reading and context could not be established. Soon after, this line too crumbled away entirely. Luckily a British philologist had made a copy and this was published in 1823, revealing that line 13 indeed held the syllable 'khaf'. This was assumed to refer to the pharaoh, Khafre, and translations were made on this assumption.

However, in contrast to the present belief, these early archaeologists were agreed that this reference most likely referred to Khafre not as the builder of the Sphinx but as having *restored* it, just as Thutmosis did later.

For example, in 1904, one of the early masters of the field and a Director of the British Museum, Sir E. A. W. Budge, wrote that the Sphinx 'existed in the time of [Khafre] . . . and was, most probably, very old even at that early period'.[7]

But shortly afterwards, in 1905, any link with Khafre was shown to be extremely tenuous, perhaps non-existent. The Chicago Egyptologist Professor J. H. Breasted noted that there was no trace of a cartouche around the syllable 'khaf', hence this could not refer to a royal name.[8] Without exception, all royal names in dynastic Egypt were written within an oblong frame now called a 'cartouche'. 'Khaf', in fact, simply means 'he rises' — like the sun, for instance.

Despite this, modern Egyptologists still regard this reference to 'Khaf' as demonstrating a strong link between the pharaoh Khafre and the Sphinx. However, doubt seems to have gradually osmosed into certain experts. In 1995 T. G. H. James, Keeper of Egyptian Antiquities for the British Museum between 1974 and 1988, wrote that Khafre '*probably* caused the Great Sphinx to be carved in his likeness'.[9] Such a qualification is revealing.

Two further arguments aimed at linking the Sphinx with Khafre are added by Egyptologists: firstly, because the valley temple — next to the Sphinx — had statues of Khafre in it when excavated (one of which depicted him as a Sphinx), then it must have been this pharaoh who built both it and the Sphinx. This ignores the obvious possibility that the statues might have been added later: a very common occurrence. It is rather like claiming that Abraham Lincoln built Washington because his statue stands there.

Secondly, it is claimed that the face on the Sphinx is similar to the face on these statues of Khafre. This is a highly contentious subjective approach. In an attempt to settle this matter once and for all, the author John Anthony West had the inspired notion to call upon the services of an expert in the field of facial reconstruction, a senior member of the New York Police Forensic Service, Detective Frank Domingo. Domingo visited Egypt in 1992 and his analysis provided strong scientific evidence upon which to conclude that the face of the statue of Khafre is not the same as that of the Sphinx.

All in all, we can see that the evidence hardly justifies the confident attribution of the Sphinx to Khafre given in most common references. The *Encyclopaedia Britannica*, for example, is sublimely confident that the Sphinx dates from Khafre and 'is known to be a portrait statue of the king'.[10]

Indeed, we are forced to accept that there is little hard evidence on which to date the Sphinx to the reign of Khafre. Even Professor

Selim Hassan, who spent many years excavating on the Giza plateau and is a recognized expert on the Sphinx, admitted, 'the general opinion of the ancients was that the Sphinx was older than the Pyramids'.[11] And pointed out that, 'excepting for the mutilated line on the Granite Stela of Thothmosis IV, which proves nothing, there is not a single ancient inscription which connects the Sphinx with Khafra'.[12]

The Date of the Sphinx

Driving rain will gradually, inexorably, erode even stone. Over thousands of years the water splashing relentlessly downwards carves deep fissures into stone leaving a once smooth surface scarred and creased.

When swirling desert sandstorms envelop and batter stone cliffs or carved statues, the erosion rasps great gashes which run horizontally across the face of the stone. It scours out the softer rock leaving clearly separated layers of strata.

In principle, then, it appears relatively straightforward to ascertain the difference between the two types of erosion. If the time-worn ridges run vertically, top to bottom, the culprit is heavy rain; if they run horizontally, end to end, then it is the wind and its abrasive sand. But, of course, erosion is a notorious subject amongst geologists, who are aware of exceptions to every rule and of the constant unpredictability of nature.

In 1978 John Anthony West registered an intriguing fact: the erosion marks on the Sphinx at Giza run from top to bottom – indicating, he surmised, that they were caused by heavy rainfall.

Yet, for all of recorded history, the Sphinx has stood on a dry sandy desert. Indeed, it has usually been virtually covered by sand, ensuring that its lower section would be protected. Nevertheless, its deep erosion is obvious to any observer. Now where does this leave the current archaeological dating of the Sphinx? In trouble, is the immediate answer. For, according to West, it has not rained so heavily in Egypt since before the end of the last great Ice Age, around 10,000 BC.[13]

Or has it?

In April 1991 a group of American scientists received permission to make a geological study of the Sphinx. In particular, they wanted to establish scientifically the facts about the observed erosion patterns. The crucial figure in the team was Professor Robert Schoch from Boston University, a geologist whose field of expertise is the weathering of soft rock.[14]

As we have mentioned, the Sphinx was not built up from stone blocks like the pyramids but was carved from the living rock, a limestone which runs through the plateau in strata of varying degrees of hardness. Originally, perhaps, it seems that a portion of the harder rock protruded above the Giza plateau; this portion was carved as the Sphinx's head. Excavation was then directed downwards, into the softer limestone, producing a wide enclosure but leaving, in the centre, an unexcavated mass of rock which was then further shaped into the body of the Sphinx. The mass of rock quarried from the region of the Sphinx is considered to form part of the interior blocks of one or other of the pyramids. Some of it certainly was used in the building of Sphinx temple.[15] The area is, in effect, a quarry.

Because the bulk of the Sphinx is below the former ground level and sits within a wide excavated enclosure, it very readily fills with sand. Thus, for much of its history its body has been invisible beneath the sand. Only its head protruded above.

Professor Schoch noted that as the Sphinx and the inner walls of the excavated enclosure were carved from the same rock at the same time, geologically speaking they are the same age. They will have both been equally affected by the elements which cause erosion, be they wind-born sand or water in the form of floods or rain.

Furthermore many of the ancient tombs south of the Sphinx but also part of the Giza complex were similarly constructed from the same limestone and, according to conventional understanding, at much the same time. As would be expected, they show distinct effects of erosion caused by wind–blown sand. If the entire complex was constructed at more or less the same era, then the erosion patterns would be expected to remain consistent throughout.[16]

Curiously, Professor Schoch found something quite different. The Sphinx and its enclosure walls showed an erosion pattern quite dissimilar to that of the tombs. This was so distinctive that, according to Schoch, it simply was not possible to see these structures as being of the same age.[17] In stark and startling contrast to the other Giza monuments, 'the body of the Sphinx and the walls of the Sphinx ditch are deeply weathered and eroded . . . It's very deep, it's very old.'[18]

Professor Schoch explained that the erosion he observed on the Sphinx and enclosure walls was

> a classic textbook example of what happens to a limestone structure when you have rain beating down on it for thousands of years . . . It's clearly rain precipitation that produced these erosional features . . . It picked out the weak spots in the rock and opened them up into these fissures – clear evidence to me as a geologist that this erosional feature was caused by rainfall.[19]

Professor Schoch also pointed to the mud-brick royal tombs at Saqqara. Despite their being marked as older than the Sphinx by several hundred years, they reveal no such weathering pattern even though mud-brick is a much more fragile building material than limestone.[20]

It is known that in the past there was an extended period during which much rain fell in North Africa. Long ago, around 40,000 BC, the climate was temperate and sufficient rain fell to maintain vast savanna grasslands teeming with wildlife. Here, on the edges of rivers and lakes, early man created settlements for hunting and fishing.

Then came a very extended arid period which for tens of thousands of years turned the area into desert, just as it is today. But around 8000 BC another rainy period began and much of this desert gradually returned to a vast fertile plain. This epoch lasted – with some intermediate dry periods – until around 4500 BC.[21] A community thrived on the extensive rich pastures, a community which today remains rather mysterious.[22] These people lasted, adapting to steadily reducing water supplies, until perhaps as late as 3000 BC: about the time of the first dynasties of Egyptian pharaohs.

It is this rainy period which most likely caused the deep erosion of the Sphinx.

Professor Schoch is a professional scientist who knows what he is talking about. There is no reason, apart from prejudice, to dismiss his final, dramatic, conclusion: that the Sphinx would seem to date, at the very minimum, from around 7000 to 5000 BC, the major portion of this Neolithic rainy period. Schoch writes

> As a geologist, the current evidence taken as a whole suggests to me that the Great Sphinx of Giza is considerably older than its traditional attribution of *ca* 2500 BC. Indeed, I am currently estimating – based on evidence at hand – that the origin of the colossal sculpture can be traced to at least 7000 to 5000 BC, and perhaps even earlier.[23]

When these conclusions were made public, official opposition erupted. The scientific team was expelled from the site by the Egyptian authorities, fortunately not before they had gathered all the data they needed. And, since 1993, no further geological research has been permitted.

Egyptologists have been vocal in their opposition to Professor Schoch's findings. Geologists have been vocal in their support.

When the findings were publicly presented at the annual meeting of the Geological Society of America in San Diego, in October 1992, the dozens of geologists who saw the evidence were astonished when told that no one had noticed these obvious erosion patterns before. The conclusions of Professor Schoch, that the Sphinx was eroded by rainfall, were readily accepted.[24]

Dr Hawass, an implacable opponent, when asked about all the evidence which would necessitate a revision of the dating of the Sphinx, spluttered, 'There is absolutely no scientific base for any of this.'[25]

But Professor Schoch remains calm in the face of such implacable criticism: 'I've been told over and over again that the peoples of Egypt . . . did not have either the technology or the social organization to cut out the core body of the Sphinx in pre-dynastic times . . .'[26]

This is fair criticism. Certainly, all that is known of pre-dynastic Egypt fails to reveal any such ruler or rulers who could have commanded the requisite manpower and organization. But the studies of this era are still in their infancy. And, in any case, as Professor Schoch rightly points out, this is not his concern. 'I don't see it as being my problem as a geologist . . . it's really up to the Egyptologists . . . to figure out who carved it.'[27] And he adds bluntly, in a direct scientific challenge to the Egyptologists, 'If my *findings* are in conflict with their *theory* about the rise of civilization then maybe it's time for them to re-evaluate that theory.'[28]

Conclusions and Implications

The implications of Professor Schoch's conclusion are wide-ranging. If the Sphinx is removed in time from the rest of the Giza complex, it would indicate that the site had a religious significance long before the rise of the pharaohs. It would also suggest that the temple near the Sphinx also dates from the same epoch. This, in turn, would suggest that the people who lived at that time were not only capable of creating the Sphinx but also sufficiently advanced technically as to be capable of manipulating stone blocks weighing upwards of 200 tons – four times the weight of the blocks used, for example, at Stonehenge.[29] For it is of such huge blocks that the Sphinx temple is built.

If we take these conclusions as a working hypothesis and look again at the excavation records of archaeologists working on pre-dynastic sites, we find that, despite the blunt denials of Egyptologists, it is not quite true that the social organization and technology to create the Sphinx did not exist prior to the 1st Dynasty kingdoms. Furthermore we do not have to invoke Atlanteans as do Hancock and others.

The pre-dynastic period is not well known but certain elements have broken through the surface. We can see hints of what might represent elements of a much greater and much earlier culture. And, significantly, these hints take us to the area of Giza, the site of the Sphinx.

One of the earliest and largest population centres in pre-dynastic Egypt was just across the Nile from Giza, at Maadi.[30] There, very ancient remains have been discovered over an area of forty-five acres. It was excavated between 1930 and 1935 but, as is so often the case, the definitive report has never been published. The remains at Maadi seem to date from around 3600 BC but may well have developed earlier. Only further excavation will tell. It is the only site of its type known but others may have existed, now buried deep beneath the desert sands or under ruins of the later dynastic period.

Maadi was primarily a trading centre, placed as it was on the main route to the Sinai copper mines and at the apex of the Nile delta, a focal point for shipping. Excavations revealed three traits of the town: there is no known earlier site in Egypt so dominated by trade; there is evidence of strong international links with foreigners in residence; and it is one of the earliest known sites of metal working in Egypt.

Trade and metallurgy necessitate a well-organized population. Both involve collection and storage of products, the control of transport, the recording of transactions, of promises and debts. Metallurgy further requires a competence in mining, smelting and manufacturing in order to produce the copper ingots, tools and weapons which have been found. Many of these were undoubtedly produced for export.[31]

We find too at Maadi evidence of some system of civic organization: the town had two areas dedicated to the communal storage of goods. One was a specialized site with sizeable underground cellars filled with goods; the other held a great number of large storage jars buried to their necks in the soil.[32] This is clear evidence of some form of leadership – be it of an individual or a council.

The beginnings of a command over technology are also in evidence. One of the storage cellars had a stone wall, one of the earliest examples of stone being used for building in Egypt. Stone was also used at Maadi for the construction of finely executed jars of basalt, alabaster and limestone, and even of stone as hard as granite and diorite, which take considerably more effort and technical skill to work.

The population residing at Maadi would appear to have possessed the skill and organization sufficient to excavate and carve a monument such as the Sphinx. Did they or their predecessors living in some still unexcavated desert site carve it? Was the population at Maadi the residue of an earlier desert group which, after the rains failed, moved closer to the Nile? Perhaps one day we will be able to answer these questions.

Egyptologists, though, are quick to point out their belief that not a shard of pottery or any other artefacts from the Maadi culture have been found at Giza, thus denying any suggestion of a connection between the two. But in this, they are wrong, as we shall see.

Forgotten by the Egyptologists, evidence once existed. Earlier this century something important *had* been found. And filed into archaeological oblivion.

All museums suffer from an overload of information and objects. A walk into the basement areas of museums or archaeological schools reveals a scene which is always the same: ill-lit corridor walls bearing miles of industrial shelving, all stacked to overload with pots, cardboard boxes, wrapped bundles and all the dusty paraphernalia which excavations throw up, year after year. These may be marked with small numbers or a letter code but, to all practical concerns, they are filed and forgotten.

In the mid 1980s an archaeologist discovered some long-forgotten pots in the basement of the Cairo Archaeological Museum. They revolutionize our view of the Giza plateau, yet, even now, few Egyptologists are aware of their existence or their implications.

In 1907 archaeologists excavated four complete ceramic jars 'at the foot of the Great Pyramid'. Because of this they were attributed to the 4th Dynasty and filed away. However, the archaeologist rummaging through these in the 1980s, Bodil Mortensen, realized with astonishment that these pots were not from the 4th Dynasty at all, but from the settlers living at Maadi – which, we have already noted, flourished 1,000 years or more before the Great Pyramid was built.[33] There was no reason for these pots to have been identified correctly in 1907 because the remains at Maadi were not discovered until 1930.

Mortensen realized further that pots in daily domestic or commercial use are only discarded because they have broken. In any case, any complete bowls left on the surface would have been broken by the later construction work. He concluded then that these must have come from an ancient tomb, a burial at Giza dating from the pre-dynastic Maadi culture. This, then, provides crucial and important proof that, long before the pharaohs, Giza had been marked out and used as a sacred burial site. Evidently, virtually all of these early remains had been swept away by the later building work by the pharaohs of the 4th Dynasty.

What was there, we probably will never now know. But clearly Giza was not a sacred burial area unique to the 4th Dynasty pharaohs: clearly it had long been used as a special site.

There is another intriguing alternative interpretation: perhaps the builders of the Sphinx were brought in from elsewhere? At Maadi there is evidence of close links with Palestine. A number of dwellings in the distinctive underground style of southern Palestine have been found amongst the usual oval Egyptian huts. Perhaps traders or other professionals from Palestine actually lived there.[34]

Probably the largest city in southern Palestine was Jericho. Stone had been used here for construction since around 7000 BC – not long after the end of the last Ice Age and the appearance of Çatal Hüyük – at which time the entire town was protected by an encircling stone wall with a stone tower thirty feet high. At Jericho too, around 5500 BC, shallow underground dwellings were common; dwellings identical to those found at Maadi which might ultimately also prove to be of a similar date.[35] It seems evident that there was a close connection between Maadi and Jericho. Therefore, it would be a simple matter to import the established Palestinian expertise in stone-work to Maadi and thus, of course, to Giza. In fact, it would be rather more surprising if this expertise had not made the journey south.

Other pre-dynastic sites too have Middle Eastern links. A German team have been excavating at Buto, in the delta region, for many years. They have revealed a substantial pre-dynastic centre with strong links to Mesopotamia, a region which also has a very ancient tradition of monumental building dating back, as we have seen, to the end of the last Ice Age. Analysis of their finds is continuing, as is the excavation.

We tend to forget that the earliest form of hieroglyph cannot yet be translated. Neither do we know when, where or how this form of writing developed. Nor, of course, what information it conceals. Perhaps some archaic Rosetta Stone will be found which will provide the key to this script; perhaps some royal or civil library will be discovered in a refuge far beneath the sands. For despite the thousands of dramatic discoveries made in Egypt over the last century of intensive archaeological study, no one has ever suggested that anything but a small part of the history has yet been uncovered.

The Astronomical Connections of the Giza Complex

From the early days of archaeology, Egyptologists have been aware of the astounding precision with which the Great Pyramid was constructed. Its walls are precisely oriented towards the cardinal points of the compass. The accuracy with which this was accomplished is so high that the variation from the exact reading is under 0.06 per cent. This was achieved without the use of compasses, for a building 481 feet high and comprising well over 2 million limestone blocks, each weighing around two and a half tons. Furthermore this pyramid was covered by a precisely fitted casing of even larger, harder blocks of white limestone from a nearby quarry. The other two pyramids are similarly aligned with an equal level of accuracy.

Such accuracy must have been achieved by reference to the stars. To this extent, at least, the major structures of the Giza complex can be seen as having a celestial alignment. But there is a further curiosity. The orderly design shows strange anomalies.

The three pyramids, each oriented to the four cardinal points, are entered by a door in the north. Within, the tunnels and galleries move southwards. Thus we can see that they are planned upon a north–south meridian. Yet the pyramids, so well-planned individually, are aligned with each other in a very curious manner.

They are not aligned together in a line running north–south, as one might expect. Neither are they aligned east–west, as one might think would be a logical alternative. They are instead aligned in a curious dog-leg of a line running south–west. The centre points of the first two pyramids align together exactly; but the third, the smallest, is out of alignment. It falls a little to the east.

This worried author Robert Bauval who, as an experienced construction engineer, knew that buildings are made to plans, not just raised in a haphazard manner. What plan, he wondered, would necessitate on the one hand a very precise alignment to the cardinal compass points and an equally precise north–south meridian but then accept a conspicuously skewed alignment of the structures in relation to each other?

He studied the rocky plateau of Giza from an engineer's point of view. But he could not see any mechanical or geological reason for the misalignment. The smaller, northern pyramid could easily have been placed in the line created by the other two.

Perhaps the builders simply didn't care or perhaps they were sloppy? But this did not fit the evidence of their obsessive precision. Bauval considered that sloppiness and arbitrary siting could not have been part of an attitude otherwise so precise and technically accomplished. Therefore, he concluded, the pyramids were built to a plan and that plan necessitated the misalignment. This posed the question why. What were the origin and meaning of such an apparently eccentric plan?

Bauval began a search of ancient Egyptian ritual and mythology to see whether there could be a clue.

The mythology and the rituals surrounding death and the afterlife had been carved on the interior walls of a number of pyramids, admittedly some time later than those of Giza – being within later 5th and early 6th Dynasty tombs – but undoubtedly recording very early material. These writings are known as *The Pyramid Texts*. They make it clear that after death the king was considered to go to the stars and become the god Osiris. The texts also make it clear that the celestial form of Osiris was a constellation called Sahu.

Two experts on ancient Egyptian astronomy, Otto Neugebauer

and R. A. Parker, discovered that this Sahu was the constellation we now know as Orion. Hence there was an identification of Osiris with Orion.[36] In addition, the terrestrial gate to heaven was called Rostau or Rosetjau. This has been identified with Giza.[37]

This was all very curious. Bauval had noted that the so-called 'airshafts' leading from the Queen's and King's Chambers in the Great Pyramid were aligned with certain stars. One from the King's Chamber aligned with the lower star of Orion's Belt.

He then noted that, relative to the Milky Way, the stars of Orion's Belt formed a line running south–west, identical to that of the three Giza pyramids in relation to the Nile. Furthermore, in the ancient writings, the Milky Way was known as the 'great river'. Could the Nile, Bauval wondered, be seen as the terrestrial equivalent of the Milky Way? And could the three pyramids be seen as the equivalent of the three stars of Orion's Belt?

If Bauval is correct, then the celestial Osiris – Orion – is symbolized by three stars in a south–west pattern to the Milky Way. The terrestrial equivalent, the terrestrial Osiris – the Giza complex – is symbolized by the three major pyramids lying in a south–west pattern relative to the Nile.

Orion's Belt comprises three stars in a line south–west to the Milky Way. The upper star is smaller and offset to the east. The third, smallest Giza pyramid, that of Menkaure, is offset in exactly the same manner. The correspondence seems conclusive. Astonished, Bauval and Gilbert wrote, 'in Giza we had, quite literally, Orion's Belt on the ground'.[38]

Bauval gained some support within the archaeological establishment. A former director of the Egyptian Department of the British Museum for twenty years, and the author of a much-reprinted book on the pyramids, Dr I. E. S. Edwards said that he thought Bauval had 'made a very convincing case'. Dr Edwards had already come around to believing that, 'The stars in Orion's Belt were an important element in the orientation of the Great Pyramid.'[39]

With recent work checking the alignments of the 'airshafts' Bauval was able to determine the stars to which they pointed, and when.

Around 2450 BC, about the date of the building of the Great Pyramid, the southern shaft leading from the King's Chamber pointed at the bottom star in Orion's Belt, the pyramids' equivalent. The southern shaft in the deeper Queen's Chamber pointed at Sirius.

Bauval wondered about the use of the Great Pyramid. A shaft from the Queen's Chamber pointing to Sirius, equated with Isis; a shaft from the King's Chamber pointed at Orion, equated with Osiris. The king and queen, Osiris and Isis, in Egyptian mythology were married, producing a son, Horus. Horus was said to have been the first demigod ruler of Egypt long before the time of the pharaohs. The 'Followers of Horus' were the initiates mentioned in the *Pyramid Texts*. The early pharaohs all had 'Horus' as part of their names. Could the Great Pyramid have been used in some kind of ritual involving a union of the terrestrial and the stellar equivalents? A union of the above and the below?

But there is one structure at Giza which Bauval did not at first consider: the Sphinx, whose gaze is fixed inexorably and for ever towards the eastern horizon, towards the point where the sun rises at the spring equinox.

In a later joint book Hancock and Bauval put forward a date when three astronomical events would occur at the moment of sunrise at the spring equinox: the sun and the constellation Leo would rise, gazed at by the Sphinx; the star Sirius would be just above the horizon; the constellation of Orion would be at its very lowest point in its 25,920 years precessional cycle.

This time, Bauval and Hancock claim, is the 'first time' referred to in the ancient Egyptian texts, when Osiris first gave civilization and kingship to Egypt. They place it at about 10,500 BC.[40]

That is, of course, if the lowest point in a cycle can be taken as a beginning. Most astrologers, ancient and modern, would rather take the highest point – its culmination – as being the end of one cycle and the start of another. This would put Hancock and Bauval's 'first time' in fact midway through the cycle. A new cycle would not begin until around AD 2460.

Nevertheless, it is fair to say that if Hancock and Bauval are correct with their identification and interpretation, then the current theories of Egyptology are in very serious trouble indeed. However, our enthusiasm for such delightful iconoclasm must be tempered. There is one major difficulty which Hancock and Bauval fail to confront with any conviction. They do not give sufficient attention to the crucial difference between understanding a text or a legend literally and understanding it symbolically.

As we shall see in the next chapter, it is beneath the veil of symbolism that the deepest mysteries of ancient Egypt have long been hidden.

10

The Mysteries of Ancient Egypt

The three Pyramids of Giza form what must be the most recogniz-able image of Egypt and, indeed, the ancient world. Yet they are not alone; it comes as something of a surprise to most people to learn that there are around ninety pyramids in Egypt. Most range south from Giza, down the western bank of the Nile for about seventy miles. Beyond these, others stand much further south, at Abydos, for example, at Edfu, Elephantine Island and other sites.

Quite a number are in ruins and none is as large as the Great Pyramid. Even so, many are impressive monuments to ancient building skill. The very first is the 204-feet-high stepped pyramid of the pharaoh Djoser, built at Saqqara around 2650 BC. The last built for a pharaoh is probably that of Amosis, at Abydos, dating from about 1530 BC. The pyramid age, then, was relatively short, lasting a little over 1,100 years.

None of the other sites, however, reveals such a coherent and integrated plan as does that of Giza. None of the other sites is imbued with such an intense aura of mystery and hidden wisdom. Giza continues to fascinate every visitor, from the dust- and trowel-hardened professional to the amateur whose sense of history may be so askew, whose critical faculties may be so dormant, as to ascribe the buildings to extra-terrestrials. But both share an awe at the achievement.

It is a notorious fact that little regarding the pyramids at Giza can be established with certainty. They can be measured and that is about all. We still do not even know how they were built. The Great Pyramid in particular poses innumerable unanswered questions. Simply, there are just too many oddities, too many strange constructional flourishes and eccentricities, all of which took immense effort and organization to achieve; yet for what?

Furthermore, it cannot be proved that Pharaohs Khufu, Khafre and Menkaure were ever buried in their pyramids. They may have been secretly interred elsewhere following the funerary ceremonies in the temples and perhaps in the pyramid. Khufu's mother, for example, was not laid to rest in her large tomb. Instead, she was secretly buried in an underground vault on the Giza plateau with its 99-foot-deep entrance tunnel completely blocked up. Even the entrance was hidden with a final layer of gravel designed to cover all trace of the shaft. Such a use of secret vaults together with dummy pyramids and tombs was not uncommon; it made the task of robbery or deliberate desecration more difficult.

Yet, oddly, the Great Pyramid has three tomb chambers: two are empty and apparently unfinished, the third – the King's Chamber – seems finished but contains an unfinished granite sarcophagus, the top of which is so rough that the saw and chisel marks are still clearly visible. This stands in stark and anomalous contrast to the finely polished walls of the chamber itself. Furthermore, as this sarcophagus is far too large to have been carried up the internal passageways to the chamber, it must have been placed in position during the building of the pyramid, before the King's Chamber itself was finished.

This sarcophagus poses a typical problem, one for which there is a very simple question but no obvious answer: why should it be so rough? Was Khufu trying to save money? Was he defrauded by a silken-tongued builder who knew Khufu would be dead before he noticed it?

The usual explanation is that the initial highly polished coffin was either broken at a very late stage by a flaw in the rock or lost in a shipwreck during its 500-mile journey down the Nile from the quarries at Aswan. Then, in order not to delay the building work, an unfinished coffin was quickly delivered and installed while access to the chamber from above was still possible.

Anyone who believes this nonsense has no business working in Egyptology: while apparently plausible, the explanation has all the appearance of words being thrown desperately into a gaping breach. Given all that we know of the Egyptians and their perfectionism, it is hardly credible that such a casual approach would be adopted.

The rough sarcophagus could have easily been finished off by masons continuing their work inside the King's Chamber during the many years of building which were still to follow. This is very clear. The interior of the King's Chamber, together with the Grand Gallery leading to it, were both made of the same Aswan granite and were both finished with highly polished surfaces. They must have received their final polishing after the stones had been dragged up the causeway and placed in position. The sarcophagus could easily have received the same attention.

One explanation which makes more sense than most is that the rough state of the coffin was deliberate, that, in some manner, it was symbolic, was part of the ritual demands which the builders of the pyramid were seeking to fulfil. But no such ritual demand has been found – or, at least, recognized as such.

On the other hand, despite all the misgivings, the pyramids of Giza may indeed have been tombs. But clearly they were also far more than this. There is little doubt that the pyramids were oriented according to the stars. Without relating to stellar positions such accurate compass alignments would have been impossible. There is also little doubt that the three pyramids were deliberately related to each other in a unified geometric design.[1] The only uncertainty is exactly how far from simple geometry and into the realm of secret religious mystery the implications of this can be taken.

For example: we have seen that if, as authors Bauval and Gilbert suggested, a line is drawn linking the centre points of the two large pyramids, then the third and smaller pyramid is offset; the three create a pattern on the ground corresponding to the three stars of Orion's Belt in the sky.

Conversely, Egyptologist Dr Mark Lehner, while not disputing that a geometrical arrangement is evident, sees it rather as a function of the surveying methods than as an attempt to mark stellar correlations. He points out that a straight line connects the south-eastern corners of each pyramid. Extending this line to the rocky higher ground further to the south-east, at the point of contact, there is a sizeable stone block let into the rock face.[2] During the course of his investigation, Lehner was intrigued to discover that, from the Sphinx temple, at the spring and autumnal equinoxes, sunset occurred along a line drawn through the centre of the temple to the southern base of Khafre's pyramid. He also discovered that at the summer solstice, when viewed from the same site, the sun set 'almost exactly midway between the Khufu and Khafre pyramids'. He points out that it thus creates, on an area of several acres, a huge example of the hieroglyphic sign *akhet* meaning 'horizon'.[3]

Nevertheless, Bauval's interpretation fits the religious texts in a way that Lehner's does not. Does this then mean that Bauval is correct? It is impossible to say. In fact, it is not unlikely that both are correct; neither explanation excludes the other. The surveying pattern may have served to orient the stellar alignment on the ground.

Integration, though, is the keyword for the modern approach to all archaeology, to all attempts to understand the past. The context of artefacts and buildings is the vital clue to their meaning. With his approach, Bauval does seem to be working in the right direction, for evidence is mounting to support the idea of the pyramids forming an integral part of the ritual basis behind the Egyptian understanding of death and the afterlife. A view which is far more complex than simple surveyor's geometry.

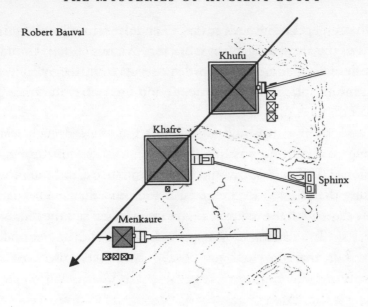

Robert Bauval

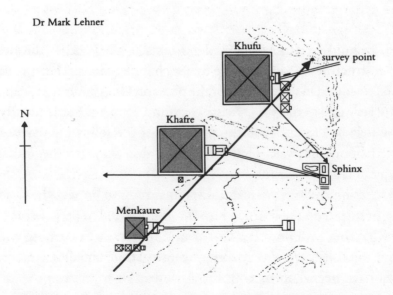

Dr Mark Lehner

The geometry of the Giza complex: two approaches.

In this respect Dr Edwards advanced an intriguing idea about the origins of the ancient Egyptian word for 'pyramid' – *mer*. Could it be, he mused, a compound word made up from the syllable *m*, which means 'place' or 'instrument', and the verb *r*, meaning 'to ascend'?

If this is so, then it would suggest that the inner, deeper, secret meaning of a pyramid was 'place of ascension' or 'instrument of ascension'.[4] The pyramid would be both the place and the means of raising the pharaoh to the gods. A tool, in other words, to be used by those with the requisite secret knowledge, and the requisite magical spells and rituals. What Dr Edwards did not consider, however, is that this tool might also have been used by the living.

Secrets of How to Die

The pyramids at Giza contained no texts at all. Neither did the earlier structures at Saqqara. The first such inscriptions, *The Pyramid Texts*, are found in the pyramid of the pharaoh Unas, built at Saqqara, at the very end of the 5th Dynasty – around 2350 BC. Subsequently these texts are found in all the pyramids of the following dynasty, carved upon the walls of the inner tombs; they are the oldest Egyptian religious writings known.

These inscriptions are magical spells aiming to protect the dead king or queen on the journey into the afterlife and to prepare them for what they will find. For that reason they are a fascinating and enigmatic collection of very complex instructions and descriptions. They have been known now for a century or more, but we still cannot say that we understand them for there are words and concepts which still defy translation and deeper levels of understanding which we are only groping towards.

These texts were certainly not composed by Unas and his priests. They must have existed for a very long time, perhaps even before the pyramid age began. Egyptologists think that parts may have been composed as early as 2700 BC.[5]

The suspicion arises, then, that the pyramids were initially devised not so much as monuments to arrogance but as a means by which the journey into the afterlife could be enhanced, protected, and its successful conclusion ensured. This, of course, is also the object of the spells which were later inscribed inside them; these spells were not simply literary conceits; they had a purpose. In the same way, the pyramids were not simply examples of architectural virtuosity; they too had a purpose: the pyramids and the texts were both vital parts of one unified religious process.

These early *Pyramid Texts* were eventually developed and modified, giving rise to *The Coffin Texts*; and, following further development, to the collection of texts entitled *The Book of the Coming Forth by Day*, generally better known as *The Book of the Dead*, archaic elements of which reach back, it is thought, to very ancient times.

All these texts supplied instructions on how to pass easily into the world of the dead, how to be 'reborn' into the afterlife. There were spells to ensure that all proceeded successfully together with spells for protection against the many dangers which the dead were expected to confront: they conferred knowledge and protection.

The divine author of these texts was the moon-god Thoth. Chapter sixty-eight of *The Book of the Dead* records the recently deceased as 'having the books of the divine words of the writings of the god Thoth'.[6] Thoth was god of writing, of knowledge, of speech and of magic, and the divine guide to the dead. He watched over the judgement of the dead and pronounced and recorded the results. It is not surprising that the burial area of Khemenu (later known as Hermopolis), the centre of the cult of Thoth, has revealed the richest and greatest number of these coffin texts.

In an important development of this spiritual tradition, late in the second millennium BC, the title of *The Book of the Dead* began to contain the word *sakhu*, meaning 'transfiguration', revealing that these texts would 'transform a person into an *akh*' – that is, a 'transfigured spirit that has become one with the light'.[7]

Later still, in the fourth century BC, a series of *Pyramid Texts* and *Coffin Texts* which had been carefully preserved for over 1,000 years in the library of the temple of Osiris at Abydos were produced on papyrus; these were entitled explicitly 'Transfiguration Texts': texts to bring the dead to the divine light.[8] The deep mysticism which undoubtedly always lay behind the Egyptian texts had finally been revealed – but, of course, only to priests in the temple of Osiris. The wider public had no access to this knowledge, which was regarded as highly esoteric and kept secret.

It cannot be a coincidence that the later version of Thoth, the great figure of Hermes Trismegistus, would appear with the same aim of helping a transfiguration into the light – but a transfiguration not of the dead, but of the living.

House of Life

For a temple, such as that of Osiris, to maintain old texts for 1,000 years would not be uncommon; most cult temples maintained a section called the 'House of Life'. This was the ancient Egyptian version of the modern university or seminary: here was a library where papyrus scrolls were maintained and a scriptorium where texts were copied and composed. And here too was a school where the arts of reading, writing and ritual were taught together with astronomy, magic, mathematics, law and medicine.[9] Perhaps these subjects were arranged in different departments as they would be in the modern world: one inscription mentions 'the departments of the Houses of Life dealing with medicine'.[10] The scribes and priests received all the training in the House of Life that they needed to serve the king, the state or the temple.

The overwhelming concern of the House of Life was to maintain the magical tradition. An important task was to ensure that the great sacred books of rituals and spells were protected and copied. It was, too, within the House's precincts that the priests were initiated; priests who, when their training was complete, would conduct the magical rituals in the temples. Opponents were quick to accuse the scribes of the House of Life of sorcery and magic.[11]

Naturally, most of what they studied was held to be secret. Some of the magical spells which archaeologists have translated contain statements requiring that, due to their importance, they should never be revealed to anyone beyond the walls of the House of Life.[12]

This institution was of fundamental importance to ancient Egyptian society, for the sacred texts it maintained were the basis of the sacred rituals which lay at the very heart of Egyptian culture. Without this ritualized nurturing, the culture faced disintegration.

The importance and prestige of the priests of the House of Life was stated succinctly on a Ptolemaic stela now in the Louvre: 'O all ye priests who penetrate into the words of god and are skilled in writings, ye who are enlightened in the House of Life and have discovered the ways of the gods . . . ye who carve the tombs and who interpret the mysteries . . .'[13]

The Invasion of Alexander

In 332 BC the Greek army of Alexander the Great invaded Egypt. It took just a week for him to enter the capital, Memphis, as conqueror. There, it is said, he was crowned. Never again would a native Egyptian rule as pharaoh of Egypt.

On 20 January 331 BC Alexander founded his city of Alexandria where he was eventually to be buried. For almost 300 years it was to be home for the Greek kings and queens of the Ptolemy family dynasty, the last of whom, the famous Cleopatra, died in 30 BC.

Alexander the Great had proved invincible. He was the greatest living conqueror the world had known. Yet, after overseeing the beginning of work at his new city, he abruptly did something very curious: with a handful of men he disappeared into the western desert. He sought a remote oasis which held an ancient temple and oracle of the Egyptian god Amon-Ra, to whom he wished to put certain important questions.

Amon-Ra is perhaps the most resolutely mystical of all the Egyptian gods. Amon was known as the 'hidden' god; Ra was the life-giving sun. The combination denoted the eternal and omnipresent Divine power, the hidden and invisible mystical light which permeates and animates the world.[14]

At some point of his journey, Alexander became lost and almost died before, eight days later, reaching his destination, Siwa Oasis. There, he was ushered into the temple of Amon-Ra closely attended by the priests. In this temple Alexander had the profoundest experience of his life, an experience which ever after influenced his actions but about which he maintained the greatest secrecy. All we know is a bald statement made by the priests that Amon-Ra had adopted Alexander as his son: he had become a 'son of god'.

Alexandria and its Library

After the invasion Greek adventurers poured into Egypt, the majority to profit as members of a ruling class dominating an immensely wealthy country. Others came to learn what they could of the wisdom in the temples, although the priests were notoriously reticent and looked down on the Greeks as being little better than barbarians. But the Greeks loved learning: the kings built the famous library at Alexandria where scholars could live, free of charge, all their needs of accommodation and food being supplied by royal command.

All books were copied into Greek. Histories of every known country were commissioned and the finished works placed in the library. Every ship known to be carrying books which stopped at

Alexandria was required to give them up to the library and accept the copies made as replacements. Private libraries throughout the empire were purchased and brought there. Learning flourished; but of a certain type. For learning also had a political dimension; it encouraged cultural domination. Much as, in the modern world, the power of Hollywood and American television has spread the English language and American values (sports shoes, silicon-enhanced breasts and round slices of processed meat in a bun) the world over.

It seems, at first, that the Egyptian priests thought that the Greeks would arrive, steal everything that moved, and eventually leave. But the Egyptians underestimated their invaders; the Greeks were resilient and masters of the political game. In time the Egyptians realized their mistake; the Greeks were not about to go. And, by virtue of the schools and libraries they had set up, the population of Egypt – especially the children – were being raised and taught Greek language, Greek culture, Greek values.

At some stage, no one knows exactly when, the Egyptian priests realized that their ancient traditions and wisdom was going to be lost. They took steps to preserve it. They changed their approach radically. They began to express their ancient teachings in the Greek language for an audience raised in a Greek culture. They began to teach and they began to initiate. They devised a system which could maintain itself beyond the temples and beyond any religious hierarchy.

In such a manner the sacred Books of Hermes Trismegistus appeared, Hermes Trismegistus (Hermes the Thrice Greatest) being the result of combining the teachings and mysteries of the Greek god Hermes with those of Egypt's god Thoth. This is most likely to have occurred during the second century BC.[15] It is not without relevance that at the cult centre for Thoth, Khemenu, there was a library renowned for its books of magic.

Thoth, who first appears in Egyptian mystery texts as the guide for the dead, in this way reappears as Hermes Trismegistus, the guide for the living.

The Books of Hermes

The Egyptian way of teaching in the temples had always been oral and personal, like a father to a son. While the mode of teaching expressed in the Books of Hermes continued this tradition, it did so in a way which no longer needed the temple ritual structure. It relied instead upon a wide network of initiated teachers, all operating independently: there was no centralized control.

While there were texts dealing with alchemy, magic and astrology, the particular Hermetic books which were focused, above all, upon the mystical path, seem to have first appeared during the first century AD, about the same time as the Christian Gospels and the later Dead Sea Scrolls – in fact, there may just possibly be an Alexandrian connection between the three traditions. These Books of Hermes were later collected into a series known as the *Hermetica*.

These books are dialogues generally concerning a pupil who seeks knowledge or initiation, seeks to experience the Divine mystery directly and immediately. After such an experience, the new initiate then himself – or herself – teaches others. In this way the informal but effective network perpetuates itself.

The Hermetic teachers taught by means of symbolism and allegory – in particular using the terminology of alchemy: the secret of marrying the above to the below in order to gain knowledge of the Divine source.

In these later Books of Hermes the ancient Egyptian wisdom is distilled to its very essence. While there is much magical and alchemical symbolism used, at its heart it focuses upon a divine mystery which even words, symbols and visions can only go so far in communicating. At the end, it is for the initiate to go the final distance. And this final distance is not travelled by faith, or by belief, but by direct knowledge.

One of the most succinct of these books is known historically as 'The Divine Pymander of Hermes Trismegistus'. More accurately it is simply 'The Poimandres', which in Greek means herdsman, or shepherd. Recent work has shown that it derives from an earlier Egyptian title meaning 'The Understanding or Intelligence of Ra', the sun-god.[16] Thoth was one of Ra's sons. This text presents what is certainly the very heart of the secret teaching which emerged from Egypt. It is unashamedly mystical, telling of the Creator and the Creation, together with the experience of both, an experience of transfiguration.

'The Divine Pymander of Hermes Trismegistus': Poimandres

This text is presented in the first person; the writer, a student of the mysteries relates the following:

> Once when I was very still and meditating upon the meaning of existence, a huge being appeared, called my name, and asked me, 'What do you want to hear and see; what do you want to learn and know . . .?'
>
> 'Who are you?' I asked.
>
> 'I am Poimandres,' he said . . . 'I know what you want, and I am with you everywhere.'
>
> I said, 'I wish to learn about the things that are, to understand their nature and to know god.'[17]

Poimandres replied by advising the student to keep everything that he wanted to know at the forefront of his mind. Immediately Poimandres vanished and a vast visionary perspective opened before the student.

'I saw an endless vision in which everything became light – clear and joyful – and in seeing the vision I came to love it.'[18]

Shortly afterwards a darkness appeared, spreading and coiling like a snake. This darkness then became watery, 'agitated and smoking like a fire'; out of it came a huge 'wailing roar'. But then a holy word came out of the light and fire burst from the watery darkness to fly upwards followed by the air until the two of them, fire and air, were suspended high above the mixture of earth and water below. And upon the earth and water the holy word moved.

After this Poimandres asked, 'Have you understood what this vision means?'[19]

The student replied that he should eventually come to understand it. Poimandres explained, 'I am the light you saw . . . your god who existed before the watery nature that appeared out of darkness. The lightgiving word who comes . . . is the son of god.' He then said to the student, 'Understand the light, then, and recognize it.'[20]

Poimandres then related in great detail how the multitude of created things came about and how, even in such complex diversity, the simplicity of the one source of divinity was always accessible. And the student learned all Poimandres had to teach:

> Then he sent me forth . . . instructed on the nature of the universe and on the supreme vision . . . And I began proclaiming to mankind the beauty of reverence and knowledge: 'People, earthborn men, you who have surrendered yourselves to drunkenness and sleep and ignorance of god, make yourselves sober and end your drunken sickness, for you are bewitched in unreasoning sleep.'[21]

People gathered about and the student taught them, exhorting them to leave the 'way of death' and join him in the way of immortality. Some laughed at him, and left; others came and listened. 'I became guide to my race, teaching them the words – how to be saved and in what manner – and I sowed the words of wisdom among them . . .'[22]

Through these Books of Hermes the mystical wisdom from Egypt began to spread far beyond the Nile valley.

It especially spread in its symbolic forms of alchemy, magic or astrology. The inner message, while often obscured by faulty translation or top-heavy prose, was never lost, even during the passing of many centuries.

Nevertheless, it often remained dangerous for the alchemists to speak clearly for they would have readily been persecuted by the authorities, suspicious of any deviation from the official religious viewpoint. The alchemists, then, continued to obscure their true intent in their writings; the twelfth-century adept, Artephius, wrote in his *Secret Book*, 'Poor fool! Will you be simple enough to believe that we teach openly and clearly the greatest and the most important of all secrets?'[23]

11

The Mysterious Art of Alchemy

Terranova di Sibari is a small ragged town sitting unobtrusively at the entrance to a narrow valley which probes deeply into the rugged Calabrian mountains of southern Italy. The river Crati tumbles out of this valley and flows across a rich alluvial plain before entering the sea at the south-west corner of the Gulf of Taranto. Beyond the horizon lie Crete and Egypt.

Near to this small town are a few ruined traces of the ancient Greek colony of Thurii, notable as the city where the historian Herodotus lived out the last years of his life.

Archaeology arrived in the region early in 1879 when Francesco Cavallari began a field survey of the area looking for traces of the long-vanished city. On some lands belonging to a medieval estate he noticed a low plateau, perhaps a mile across, which seemed scattered with graves. Among them were four large mounds up to thirty feet high which he presumed covered ancient burials. He surmised – and he was in fact correct – that he had found the cemetery area of ancient Thurii. He chose to begin his excavations with the large mounds.[1]

As the earth was taken from the top of the most southerly mound, a covering layer of ash was found, the remnants of a ritually burned sacrifice. Beneath this another layer of earth appeared; under it was a second layer of ash from yet another, earlier, sacrifice. In all, eight layers of ash topped by earth were found, demonstrating that repeated ritual sacrifices had been conducted during the burial: the dead man had been given a hero's inhumation. Finally, at the bottom of the mound, Cavallari discovered a tomb: a small but solid rectangular structure built from heavy stone blocks.

On Sunday 23 March 1879 Cavallari, in the presence of a local dignitary and a crowd of spectators, ceremoniously opened the tomb. Inside was revealed a male skeleton facing east with, near to his head, a thin gold plate which proved to have been folded over nine times. When it was opened it was just over thirty-one inches long and almost an inch wide; inside it Cavallari found a second folded plate about two by one inches in size. Both these gold plates held a text in an archaic script dating from the fourth century BC. Mysteriously, the text gave instructions to the dead in a manner more akin to the ancient Egyptians than to the ancient Greeks.

In December that same year another of the mounds was excavated. In it were found three stone tombs, each apparently dating from a different time. Inside each was a skeleton, similarly facing east. And each skeleton had, near its right hand, a small thin gold plate also inscribed with a short text.

Other examples of these inscribed gold plates have since been found or recognized. An English collector living in Rome possessed one which had been found in southern Italy during the eighteenth century. Six more were later found in central Crete. Two were found in graves in Thessaly, Greece. In 1969 another was found in the grave of a woman at Hipponium – now Vibo Valentia – over the mountains from Thurii, on the shores of the Tyrrhenian Sea. Sixteen years later two more were found in Thessaly, this time in the shape of ivy leaves. In total, seventeen have been found, all except one dating from the third or fourth centuries BC.

The texts inscribed on these plates gave directions for the dead, so that they might not get lost on the journey through the next world. They promised too the supreme prize of immortality. In style and content, they bore a distinct resemblance to sections of the Egyptian *Book of the Dead*. Both this and the Greek texts shared the same basic theme: that guardians of the underworld stop and challenge the soul of the dead and that the soul claims identity with one of the gods or with one of the stars.[2] One of the plates found at Thurii praises the dead person as, 'O fortunate and blessed one, you will be a god, no longer mortal.'[3] The similarities could not be simply coincidence. Archaeologists reluctantly realized that these gold plates proved an early and close cultural connection between ancient Egypt and the Greeks, particularly in the colonies of southern Italy.

As a result, the picture of the Greek cultural heritage became a little more complicated.

A Mixture of Mystics

We should not be surprised by this connection. We tend to forget how mobile people – and their ideas – were in ancient times. Scholars, traders, workers with skills, all travelled to and fro, through every frontier, across every sea. The Greeks in particular had a close connection with Egypt; in 570 BC the pharaoh Amasis allowed them to found a special city, Naucratis, as a trading base in the Nile delta. He even allowed them to construct their own temples.

But long before this time, from at least 700 BC, the Greek island of Samos had been forging strong trading links with Egypt. Under Amasis these links became especially strong and their merchants too settled at Naucratis.[4] Not long after the foundation of this city, around 558 BC,[5] a Phoenician trader from Tyre settled on Samos and married a local woman. Their child was to become one of the most influential philosophers of all time: the famous Pythagoras. Like many of his fellow Samians he grew up to travel widely. But, unlike them, he did so for knowledge rather than trade: he became an initiate into the sacred mysteries of every culture he visited.

Pythagoras began his wanderings at an early age when his father sent him to Tyre in Phoenicia for his schooling. He remained there until he was twenty-two when he travelled on to Egypt, where he then lived and studied for many years. During this time he learned to read hieroglyphics, a training which included instruction on their symbolic interpretation[6] – an enigmatic matter about which modern Egyptologists remain strangely silent.

In 525 BC the Persian king Cambyses mounted his invasion of Egypt and Pythagoras was taken, along with many others, into captivity in Babylon. But, once there, he soon began studying with a Zoroastrian magus. After some years he was permitted to leave, first visiting Crete and then Greece. Finally, around 518 BC, he moved to southern Italy, to the Gulf of Taranto, where he founded his famous school, initially at Croton and later further north up the coast, at Metapontum.

The Celestial Music

Much of what Pythagoras taught would have been familiar to the Egyptians: that the soul was immortal and that the dead travelled to the stars.[7] He also taught reincarnation – which Herodotus explicitly states as an Egyptian belief[8] – and the recall of past lives.

Pythagoras' teaching was founded upon a belief in the dynamic harmony of the universe, an ever-changing pattern which could literally be heard as an intermingling of musical notes which Pythagoras claimed to be able to hear. The reason most others were unable to do so, he explained, was because they had become used to it: the constant movement of the planets and stars creates this music and there is no contrasting period of silence which might make it more obvious.

Pythagoras' approach to knowledge was mystical. It was based upon revelation. But to receive this divine gift one had to become purified. And this was the reason for joining his ascetic community. Above all, Pythagoras saw himself as a healer – of both the body and the soul. In particular, he healed by means of musical harmony. In this concern Pythagoras was intensely practical: he saw no distinction between the roles of healer, magician or philosopher. He was quite unlike the later Greek philosophers, who were typified by intellectual theory, unsullied by practical matters.

Pythagoras taught, not by reasoned argument but by the use of symbolism because he considered that to be the best means of expressing a mystical truth. Furthermore, such symbols could be published and yet remain secret; only those with the correct understanding could make sense of them. As we shall see, this is precisely the point with alchemy.

During the lifetime of Pythagoras, and later, profound changes came to Egypt. The Persian domination of 525 to 404 BC opened it to influence from the Zoroastrians and Babylonians. Almost 200 years afterwards the Greeks under Alexander the Great invaded; by then the Greek empire stretched as far east as India and sadhus came west to teach. In this manner, Indian mysticism too – Vedic and Buddhist – entered the Greek world.

By the time of the building of the great library in Alexandria, the capital of Greek Egypt during the third century BC, the city was a melting pot for mystical religious cults. At the same time traditional Egypt continued to maintain its own ancient and esoteric teachings preserved in *The Book of the Dead*, *The Coffin Texts* and *The Pyramid Texts*.

Out of this melting pot, this crucible, came alchemy.

From the Melting Pot

Alchemy, as we know it, first seems to appear in the work of Bolus, a citizen of Mendes, a city in the eastern Nile delta. He died around 250 BC, his life having spanned the reigns of kings Ptolemy I and II and the foundation of the Alexandrian Library. With Bolus we find two great mystical movements in combination. On the one hand, he was immersed in the mystery tradition of Egypt, in particular that of magic – his writings contain many spells, some of which necessitate the use of sound and breath control. On the other, he was committed to Pythagorean thought and healing, even though Pythagoras had been dead for 200 or more years.

Bolus of Mendes was an active Pythagorean. He believed that all matter in its endless diversity was no more than a superficial appearance of an underlying harmonic unity. Accordingly, he considered the forms of matter to be malleable, that one form could be transmuted into another, that lead, for example, could be changed into gold. Yet he was not solely a mystic; he had gained practical skills in chemistry and metallurgy.

In short, Bolus of Mendes was a crucial figure both for the transmission of Pythagorean traditions into Egypt and for the subsequent development of what became known as alchemy.[9] And this was to merge with the later Hermetic writings – the Books of Hermes – which themselves combined Egyptian and Pythagorean mystical themes. They may indeed owe a direct debt to Bolus and his associates. But for the moment this cannot be any more than a suspicion. His true role might be clearer if we had the complete text of a book he wrote, entitled *Physical and Mystical Matters*. Unfortunately only fragments of this have survived the millennia.

Bolus' writings reveal him as intelligent and honest, as always acting from the highest of motives, although it seems that he was regarded as rather conservative by his students. In one of the fragments from his book he complains about the 'young' who refuse to believe in the virtues of the art he was teaching[10] – a cry of frustration which could apply to any era and any teacher ever since.

Through such excerpts, Bolus emerges as a very human figure, an ancient equivalent perhaps of a university professor or church minister: conservative, well-meaning, a safe pair of hands for any tradition. Which simply increases the shock when it is discovered just how much the modern classical establishment dislikes him.

Professor Peter Fraser, for example, author of an otherwise fascinating study of Alexandria under the Greek rulers, complains bitterly about Bolus being a prime force in the 'decline of Alexandrian and indeed of Greek science'.[11] Whatever could it be about Bolus which would cause such animosity? In any case, Greek science had hardly begun; Hipparchus, Hero and Ptolemy were all yet to be born. What is it that has really upset Professor Fraser?

The answer is that here we touch upon a very sensitive point for he academic world which has led to a muddying of the philosophical pool from which Bolus emerges. To put it bluntly, mystical philosophy frightens orthodox academics. It is worth looking, for a moment, at why this should be.

Modern Scholars and the Manipulation of History

Ideas create belief systems: it is these which can cause imperial adventures, mass movements and wars.

Belief systems are rather like a computer program: they serve to handle and interpret data – in this case, observed events in the world – but are themselves neither right nor wrong. That is a function solely of the data, the events themselves.

Thunder and lightning may erupt; the same night a king may die. The meaning of these events is dependent upon which belief system one subscribes to. Many cultures have considered a conjunction of a storm with a king's death as proof of the displeasure of the gods who will then need appeasing by some ritual. Others regard the storm as literally causing the royal death, in which case any ritual appeasement would be too late. Yet another system considers the events arbitrary, unconnected and devoid of any meaning whatsoever. This last is the interpretation fostered by our modern belief system, that underpinned by science.

The modern world can largely be seen as an expression of the belief system created by the ancient Athenian philosopher Aristotle.

For it was he who first advanced the idea that only reason can discover the true nature of our reality. Reason meaning the use of intellectual argument, logic, deduction, scepticism and all other such processes. Aristotle saw no value in revelation.

Christianity, which might be expected to take a contrary view, is also greatly influenced by Aristotle's approach. In the thirteenth century his philosophy was married to Church dogma by Thomas Aquinas; over the succeeding century a pattern of theology was created which has persisted ever since.

But reality encompasses more than that which we can see, touch, smell, taste, measure, weigh and generally record. There is the part of our reality which is after, or beyond, the physical, the so-called metaphysical or supernatural; that part which encompasses things we call divine.

Dogmatic theology tends to localize the divine aspect in particular spheres of its own. Other religious thought has it that the divine cannot be so localized; rather, it *infuses* every part of creation – both the physical and metaphysical. And, further, that this divine part of existence can be directly experienced by anybody – through revelation – given the requisite training or conditions of life.

This is the view put forward by Pythagoras. And by Plato. And by Bolus of Mendes. And by the Hermetic teachings. Of course, it runs in complete opposition to that of Aristotle and his followers.

To support Aristotle's legacy, a concerted – and generally successful – attempt has been made to fragment, isolate and generally impugn all evidence which might suggest that revelation could be maintained within a continuous philosophical tradition. As a result, those such as Pythagoras and Bolus of Mendes are presented as isolated figures paddling futilely against the current of history, the major force of which is assumed to reside upon reason, logic and rationality.

Rather, the example of Bolus of Mendes reveals that an ancient mystical tradition, based upon revelation but with practical aims and deriving in the main from Pythagoras (who himself drew from Egyptian, Babylonian and Zoroastrian elements) not only survived but was maintained through the centuries, eventually to arrive in Egypt where it flourished in a soil already fecund with its own magical and mystical teachings.[12]

Bolus of Mendes was not a sudden spontaneous efflorescence; he was part of a long Pythagorean tradition which has been largely ignored by history. Furthermore this tradition not only continued after Bolus but it thrived and expanded. Often it was expressed as alchemy or as works of Hermes Trismegistus. Despite the absence of written texts, we can be confident of this survival because of the testimony of an alchemist, Zosimus. He flourished over 500 years later in Panopolis, a city beside the Nile in Upper Egypt, now called Akhmim.

According to Zosimus, for these 500 years, the alchemical tradition had been secretly maintained in the Egyptian temples.

Zosimus of Panopolis, an Egyptian Alchemist

Zosimus wrote a great encyclopaedia of alchemy around AD 300; sections of it still survive. But this was only part of his writing: twenty-eight other books were attributed to him. Such productivity suggests more stability than was the case, for the times were far from tranquil, especially for an active alchemist. Zosimus' life coincided with profound changes in the Roman Empire. It moved from the vociferous paganism of Diocletian (emperor 284–305) to the self-righteous Christianity under Constantine (emperor 312–37). Both rulers proved detrimental to the study of alchemy. Diocletian so disliked it that he ordered all texts referring to alchemy to be gathered up and burned. And once Christianity became an accepted and influential religion, it too condemned the art.

Zosimus reveals some very interesting information about the place of alchemy in ancient Egypt. Several times he stresses the important role of the priesthood in maintaining the tradition in secrecy. He explicitly mentions 'those priests who preserve copies of alchemical books in their temples'.[13]

He points out that all workers in alchemy – by which he would have included chemistry – served the pharaoh and were not allowed to work on their own account.[14] Furthermore it was forbidden by royal decree to publish any of the alchemical secrets. Which was why, Zosimus explained, so little information survived regarding the art's history.[15]

Alchemy was certainly still being practised in at least some temples during Zosimus' lifetime. He reported visiting an ancient temple at Memphis in order to make a close examination of an alchemical furnace there.[16] It is known too from other sources that the priests of Memphis were famous in antiquity both for their alchemy and for their skill in magic, which they apparently taught in underground shrines.[17] The Christian theologian Jerome, writing fifty or more years later, reported that even in his day their occult skill remained widely famed.[18]

The alchemical secrets were inscribed in the temples using some form of code, cipher or arcane symbolism. Zosimus writes that they were carved on 'stelae in the darkness and depths of the temples in symbolic characters',[19] adding that even if someone were to be bold enough to obtain entrance to the temples and gain access to these hieroglyphic texts, it would not help them, for, 'If one had neglected to learn the key, one could not decipher the characters . . .'[20]

This reminds us of the comments made about Pythagoras; these are found in a work by Porphyry who was writing about the same time as Zosimus. Porphyry describes three types of writing used by the ancient Egyptians: the common style, hieroglyphics and a symbolic writing.[21] The fact that two unrelated but contemporary writers make identical claims about a 'secret' interpretation of Egyptian writing again raises the question of why the Egyptologists

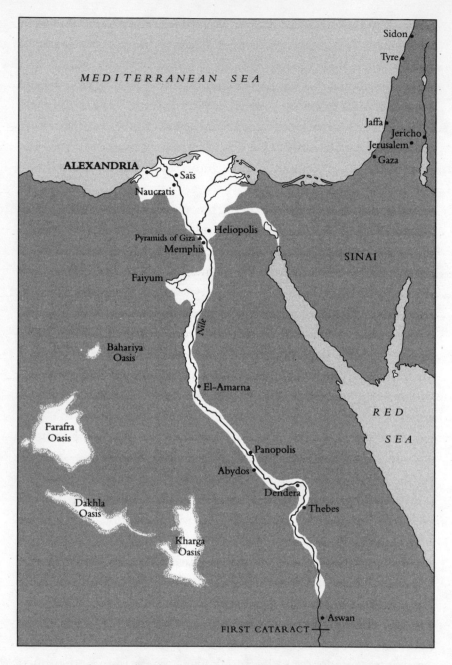

Egypt under Greek rule at the time of the rise of mystical alchemy.

are so silent on this subject. Perhaps such inscriptions have been found but have been misunderstood and mistranslated by archaeologists who are unable to discern the symbolic from the literal.

Zosimus was a dedicated and highly skilled practical alchemist. He reveals too, in his writings, a detailed knowledge of chemistry, in its modern sense, and describes the wide range of technology which was available to the ancient laboratory worker.

Technical Alchemy

Alchemists worked hard at their trade. Many of the technological skills and laboratory techniques known were undoubtedly developed by them. Certainly they developed equipment. They differentiated between some eighty specialist items: furnaces of various types, ceramic dishes and crucibles, glass phials and flasks, files, spatulas, tongs, hammers, sand-baths and water-baths, filters made of cloth and linen, funnels, pestles and mortars, alembics and a host of other instruments and vessels, most of which remain useful today.

Much of their work involved heating. Either gently in horse-dung or water-baths, or fiercely in furnaces fanned ever hotter by sweating assistants plying large leather bellows or blowing through tubes. They heated solids so hot and so long that they were reduced to powder or were vaporized.

And they invented distillation. This led to an active commercial industry for the production of perfumes, such as rose-water, so valued by the medieval Islamic world, made by gently heating rose petals until the aromatic oils distilled out. And, inevitably, during the twelfth century, alchemists discovered that distilling wine gave rise to a medicine which induced conviviality: alcohol.

The alchemists would habitually heat, distil and re-distil the same product over and over again, hundreds of times, for months or for years, in search of their elusive goal, the production of the purest essence of all: the ruby-red Philosopher's Stone. Powder taken from this stone was reputed to have the power of transmuting base metals into gold.

The Arab alchemist Geber described processes involving upwards of 700 distillations before the required changes would occur. Modern chemists have never attempted to replicate these time-consuming procedures so they do not know whether there is any validity in them. As we shall see, there may be.

While there is no absolute agreement over the process by which the Philosopher's Stone was made, most texts list a series of seven stages beginning either with mercury or a mixture of mercury and sulphur. Each stage in the process is generally described as being lengthy, of several months or a year, during which time the furnace must be maintained and kept at a constant heat. The fourteenth-century alchemist and monk John Dastin wrote that when mercury was converted into the red elixir it took the use of a gentle fire for 100 days. If it should go out, the process would need to be begun again.

In some way too, the astrological moment was deemed important. The alchemist Nicholas Flamel is recorded as first having created the 'Stone' around noon on Monday 17 January 1382; then from 'half a pound of mercury' he made the equivalent weight of pure silver. Again, using this 'red stone' at 5.00 p.m. on 20 April the same year, he transmuted a similar quantity of mercury into gold.[22] However we are to take this, by the time Flamel died in 1417, he and his wife had founded fourteen hospitals, three chapels and seven churches in Paris, together with other works at Boulogne.

Alchemical Secrets: The Red Powder

In the seventeenth century, when it developed, experimental science soon began to repudiate its alchemical roots. The early scientist Robert Boyle – discoverer of 'Boyle's Law' – was a firm advocate of the new experimental methods: he wrote contemptuously of the alchemists, 'that their writings, as their furnaces, afford as well smoke as light'.[23] And, obviously miffed by the difficulty and complexity of the alchemical tomes he had struggled to make sense of, he sarcastically noted that if their authors had truly desired secrecy, 'they might less to their own disparagement, and to the trouble of their readers, have concealed it by writing no books, than by writing bad ones'.[24]

Yet over the last two decades it has been conclusively proved that alchemy continued to fascinate Robert Boyle to the point where he conducted his own secret experiments into transmutation. To hide his interest he began writing his reports on these experiments in a highly complicated and varied secret code using the Latin, Greek or Hebrew alphabets. These coded texts were revealed in 1992 to amount to hundreds of pages.[25] It is worth asking who were these texts concealed from? And why? At the very least it is a measure of the seriousness with which Boyle took alchemy.

Boyle, it can now be shown, firmly believed that the transmutation powder existed. And, furthermore, he believed that *adepti* – wise initiates – knew well the secret of its production and use. He made considerable efforts to contact these adepts and gain access to their secrets. We do not know whether he was successful in his quest; but he did make some very curious statements on the subject.

In one unpublished dialogue held in the archives of the Royal Society of London, Boyle speaks of his belief that the 'red powder' from the Philosopher's Stone existed in the hands of the adepts and that it could be used not only to make medicines or to transmute base metals into silver and gold, but also to contact supernatural spirits.[26]

Boyle finally discovered what he termed a 'subtil' mercury for alchemical use but he never revealed how he had made it.[27] He also secretly made, or received, some alchemical powder which he called 'red earth'. At his death, in 1691, he left a portion of this 'red earth' to his friend John Locke, philosopher and Fellow of the Royal Society. Locke passed some on to another friend, Sir Isaac Newton, who from 1703 was President of the Royal Society, and thus at the very heart of the developing scientific establishment.[28]

Newton, a monumental figure in the history of science, shared this strong interest in alchemy. He and Boyle together had secret meetings with alchemists – while at the same time they were publicly deriding them.[29]

Newton's strong interest in alchemy was hidden for many years. At his death, in 1727, many of his papers were burned; many others were marked 'not fit to be printed' and kept by the family. The full extent of his alchemical interests was not discovered until these papers came up for auction in London in 1936. At the auction, 121 lots concerned alchemy. As a result scholars discerned the dominating character of these alchemical interests to his life. It became clear that Newton firmly believed 'that the ancients knew *all* the secrets at one time'.[30]

Professor Betty Dobbs, who studied Newton's papers, concluded, 'It may safely be said . . . that Newton's alchemical thoughts were so securely established on their basic foundations that he never came to deny their general validity . . .'[31]

We are allowed to harbour doubts about the reality of Flamel's or Dastin's success in making the Philosopher's Stone and in transmuting base metal into gold. It was long ago, and perhaps some dramatic licence was taken in the later reports. But, given the scientific rigour exercised by Boyle and Newton towards their experiments, and given the existence of their detailed papers on the subject, we are right to wonder exactly what was occupying their time. Something, certainly. But what are we to make of their long dedication to a lengthy treatment of mercury, hoping to create a wondrous red substance: a stone or an elixir?

In their case, the alchemical process cannot have been exclusively symbolic since Boyle and Newton were well aware of the distinction, and anyway, if symbolic, there would be no reason for Boyle to have used elaborate codes or for Newton to secrete his papers. Could the alchemists have discovered certain techniques yet to be developed by orthodox science but uncovered by Boyle and Newton?

Could repeated distillations or slow heating over long periods of time cause such change within an element or compound that it might literally transmute into a product with quite extraordinary properties?

Has anything of this type ever been demonstrated by modern science?

The blunt answer is, 'Well, er, yes.'

The Threat of Red Mercury

Since the break-up of the former Soviet Union and the loosening of tough central control, criminal organizations there rapidly gained in strength. Once established, they soon began seeking links with overseas crime syndicates. From 1991, high-level meetings were held with Italian crime godfathers from the Mafia, Comorra and 'Ndranghetta. Close links were forged with them, facilitating the laundering of money and the trade in drugs and illicit nuclear materials.[32] The latter had become available with the administrative chaos and shortage of funds in the Soviet nuclear industry and armed forces. There was no such shortage of funds on the part of those regimes desperate to purchase them.

Late in 1993 a disturbing new element appeared. Russian crime syndicates were offering for sale a substance hitherto unknown to the West, called simply 'red mercury'. It was said to be a secret product of the Soviet nuclear industry. On 23 December 1993 five Moldavian nationals were caught trying to enter Romania carrying some pure uranium together with what they said was this red mercury. It was destined for the nuclear black market.[33]

Worried Western scientists sought to establish whether this substance actually existed and, if so, exactly what it was. But in 1994 the US Department of Energy and the International Atomic Energy Agency declared red mercury to be 'bogus'. They argued that it was just another fraud perpetrated by the Russian mafia on would-be purchasers of illicit nuclear goods.[34]

But certain Western nuclear physicists had good reason to think otherwise. And they suspected the accusations of fraud to be motivated by the desire to cover up an unpalatable truth.

In the June 1994 edition of *International Defence Review*, nuclear physicist Dr Frank Barnaby wrote of his conversation with an anonymous Soviet physicist. He had been told that this red mercury was a vital component in a revolutionary type of Russian nuclear bomb. It had proved such an efficient catalyst in the detonation of these devices that they could be built many times smaller and lighter than their Western equivalents.[35]

Dr Barnaby explained that with the use of this red mercury a nuclear bomb weighing only four to six pounds could be constructed. He was concerned since such a weapon could easily be placed in a city centre and detonated. He expressed his fears about the danger of this technology falling into the hands of some terrorist group. His information was that a number of Middle Eastern countries – Israel, Iran, Iraq and Libya – and Pakistan had already illicitly purchased quantities of this substance for weapons production.[36] At least some of these countries are known supporters of terrorist groups and might be expected to pass on either the technology or the finished product.

The reported production of this substance has distinct parallels with the alchemical process. If any alchemists worked in the heart of the Russian military complex with access to modern equipment, it is easy to think of them inventing something like red mercury.

According to the Russian scientist, the recipe for making it is as follows:

1) Antimony sesquioxide and mercuric oxide are heated together at a temperature of 500 degrees centigrade under one atmospheric pressure of oxygen. This heating must continue without pause or fluctuation *for two days*. It produces a substance called mercury antimony oxide. This was not described publicly in the scientific press until as recently as 1968.

2) Next dissolve this mercury antimony oxide in pure mercury, using equal weights of each substance. Seal this mixture in a container and place it inside an atomic reactor. Irradiate it for *about twenty days* at a temperature of 500 degrees centigrade.

3) After this time all excess mercury is tipped off leaving a 'cherry red' substance with a consistency similar to liquid honey. Capsules of this thick fluid are placed inside the nuclear bombs.[37]

It is indeed curious that this manufacturing procedure should involve mercury and such lengthy reaction times. It is curious too that, in addition to mercury, antimony is involved. The twelfth-century alchemist Artephius wrote of a special tincture which contained both antimony and sublimated mercury for which many dramatic uses were promised.[38]

The creation of the initial chemical compound of mercury antimony oxide was admitted only in 1968; red mercury is not yet openly accepted. How many more supposedly impossible substances can be created using chemistry, modern technology and much time? Apart from great patience, perhaps there is more that we can learn from the experiments of the alchemist.[39]

But it was not these chemical techniques which lay at the very heart of alchemy. At its deepest and most secret level the experiment was on none other than the alchemist himself – or herself. Their task was the transmutation of the soul.

We must return to Zosimus, one more time, and listen to what else he has to tell us.

To Make the Heavens Open

The writings of Zosimus make it evident that alchemy, whatever physical secrets it might have concealed, had become a chemical metaphor of the same spiritual quest which is the underlying object of Hermetic thought. A spiritual quest which had to be concealed because all too often it was feared and vigorously persecuted by both civil and religious authorities.

The purification of the first material – the mercury – over a long period of time by means of a steady heat until the 'Philosopher's Stone' is reached was simultaneously a practical ascetic discipline and a symbol of the progress achieved in purifying the inner being of the alchemist. This is how we must understand the statement Zosimus made to a friend, a woman alchemist called Theosebia: 'Perform these things until your soul is perfected.'[40] Alchemy, according to Zosimus, was a divine mystery.

In the previous chapter we looked at 'The Poimandres', the first text in the collection of the Books of Hermes Trismegistus – known as the *Hermetica*. We have seen how it concerns a pupil who is seeking an initiation into a divine mystery. An initiation which reaches its profoundest point as an all-encompassing vision of light. Zosimus, in his text for Theosebia, explicitly referred to 'The Poimandres', as well as to another dialogue in the *Hermetica*, the fourth, called 'The Mixing Bowl'. This focuses upon the links between humanity and divinity. It stresses the ever-present, eternal nature of the source of all being. The 'mixing bowl' was a symbol of baptism or initiation which conferred knowledge and immortality. This same text too mentions reincarnation.

Zosimus advised Theosebia, 'Do not roam about searching for God; but sit calmly at home, and God, who is everywhere and not confined . . . will come to you.'[41]

This process of creating the 'Stone' was often expressed symbolically as if it were a birth following a long gestation. This is put well – if cryptically – by the woman alchemist Cleopatra:

> For just as the bird warms her eggs with her heat and brings them to their appointed term, so yourselves warm your composition and bring it to its appointed term . . . cook it upon a gentle fire . . . Then remove it from the fire; and when the soul and spirit are unified and become one, project upon the body of silver and you will have gold such as the treasuries of kings do not contain.[42]

She continues, 'See the mystery of the philosophers which our fathers swore to you not to reveal or publish. It has a divine Form and a divine Activity.'[43]

The secret remained concealed but was never lost. Indeed, the seventeenth-century English antiquarian freemason and alchemist Elias Ashmole explained, in the introduction to his compendium of British alchemy, which he published in 1652, that the alchemist, 'rejoyceth not so much that he can make Gold and Silver . . . as that he sees the Heavens open . . .'[44]

12

Reincarnation

On 3 December 1990, in northern India at the town of Dharamsala in the Himalayan foothills, the base of the Tibetan
government in exile, a BBC television crew was filming inside a
flamboyantly decorated temple. They were recording a Tibetan
ceremonially dispensing blessings to respectful hosts of queuing
pilgrims who, one after another, were being gradually presented to
him. But this regal Tibetan holy man was a child of only five years,
a small calm figure all but dwarfed by the large and ornate throne
upon which he was sitting.

He sat with great dignity during the three-hour ceremony and
maintained the same composure during the remainder of the day's
elaborate rituals. The reason for all this reverential attention was
that this young boy was regarded as the reincarnation of Ling
Rinpoche, a greatly respected and high-ranking lama who had died
six years earlier.[1]

The Tibetans consider it a normal occurrence for lamas to be
reborn; their new incarnations are sought by various means, either
written clues left by the dying lama or various mystical revelations,
generally delivered by the Tibetan state oracle while in a state of
trance. Accordingly, following the death of Ling Rinpoche, a search
had been made for his new incarnation.

In this particular case, the dead lama having been such a close
friend of the Dalai Lama – the exiled leader of the Tibetans – the

latter undertook to seek the mystical clues within his own meditation and divinations.

His first insight was that the lama had reincarnated, within the year, into one of the Tibetan enclaves in India. So it was within these communities that the search began. By the end of the first year, 690 children had been recorded as possible candidates. Succeeding divinations and mystical insights narrowed the choice of location down to one settlement two hours away from Dharamsala where ten young boys had already been noted.

An official deputation visited these boys but the initial results were not encouraging. None of the children seemed to feel comfortable with the investigators and none gave any indication, any recognition or memory, that might have suggested the reincarnation of Ling Rinpoche.

The visitors noted, however, that one little boy was missing. They were informed that since the initial survey his mother had died and he had been moved to another school, to the Tibetan Children's Village School, in Dharamsala itself.

A senior Tibetan, together with his assistants, then visited the school. As they arrived, one small boy cheerfully approached them and readily took the hand of one of the visitors. They were told that he was the boy they had come to see. It seemed an auspicious beginning.

The next day a more senior deputation interviewed the boy. During their talk they handed him four strings of religious beads; one string had belonged to the dead Ling Rinpoche. Without showing the slightest doubt, the child immediately picked out the beads of the latter and, with his left hand, fingered them in the manner of those trained in their use. It was recalled that Ling Rinpoche had been left-handed in his youth. The deputation became more confident that this child was the one they sought.

The next day the young boy was taken before the Dalai Lama, who later reported:

When I received the boy at my residence and he was brought to the door, he acted just as his predecessor had done. It was plain that he remembered his way around. Moreover, when he came into my study he showed immediate familiarity with one of my attendants . . .[2]

The boy's guardian, who had previously served Ling Rinpoche for many years, remembered

There were many occurrences that confirmed our belief. His behaviour while eating, his smiling. He does lots of things that are typical of the past master . . . He always showed sensitivity in recognizing past associates and students, especially Western students of the past master. He called some close students by their names.[3]

As a result the young boy was accepted and honoured as the reincarnation of the dead lama.

However, intriguing though the events of this story are, it is most unlikely that the procedure followed would go very far towards satisfying a modern scientific inquiry into reincarnation. But such reservations do not enter into the Tibetan approach. Reincarnation has always formed a fundamental part of their belief. Furthermore, they take it for granted that the recently dead lama would be doing what he could to make his new presence felt.

This wide search for incarnations of religious leaders is probably most widely known in the West with respect to the Dalai Lama himself. All Tibetans believe that he is the reincarnation of the previous Dalai Lama, and so on, back to the first who died in 1475. This first, they believe, was a god-like figure who chose to incarnate on earth in order to help where he could. The present Dalai Lama, the fourteenth, was picked out in 1936 as the reincarnation of his predecessor who had died the year before.

The Dalai Lama has since given his own thoughts on reincarnation. 'Death,' he has explained, ' . . . is just a change of clothes.'[4]

The Teachings of Reincarnation

Indian literature is extremely ancient: the oldest, known as the Vedas, dates from at least 4,000 years ago, about the time that the first Babylonian Empire emerged in Mesopotamia. Running through this ancient literature is the concept of reincarnation. One Vedic text, speaking of a man who has died, states, 'Let him reach his own descendants, dressing himself in a life span . . . let him join with a body.'[5] If age of a belief is any measure of its validity, then reincarnation is there with the finest of them. A later Indian text, the *Bhagavad Gita*, explains reincarnation in much more detail: 'As a man leaves an old garment and puts on one that is new, the Spirit leaves his mortal body and then puts on one that is new.'[6]

Generally, in the non-Muslim East, the idea of reincarnation is a perfectly acceptable belief, integrated into even the most modern aspects of the culture. Scientists who are at the very cutting edge of technological progress, who have sent India's own rockets and satellites into space, have done so while at the same time believing in their personal past and future lives. In other words, contrary to Western prejudices, such belief is eminently rational and not incompatible with modern science.

The Hindus and Buddhists believe that every individual is, in reality, an eternal being (each a fragment of the One) which, over many thousands, or many millions, of years returns, again and again, to take on another body. All humanity, they teach, is caught within this cycle of birth and death from which the only escape is enlightenment. The search for enlightenment is the finest aim of any life.

Successive lives are better or worse, pleasant or unpleasant, depending upon the quality of karma (meaning 'action') which might be faced. This karma arises from past actions; it denotes the amount of good or bad which might have accumulated in previous lives: it determines whether, in a new life, a person faces retribution or reward. Naturally, from this concept arises a very strong sense of morality, for each individual's success and eventual freedom from the cycle of rebirth depends upon his or her karma.

It is, perhaps, not surprising that we also find allusions to reincarnation in those texts which came out of Egypt, known as the *Hermetica*. As we have seen, they are primarily concerned with the profound direct experience of Divinity. Nevertheless, the texts contain various asides which make it clear that the full spectrum of Hermetic thought – perhaps given more often in an oral form – did have a recognition of reincarnation. In the text called 'The Mixing Bowl', Hermes is reported as saying, 'Do you see how many bodies we must pass through, my child . . . in order to hasten towards the one and only?'[7] And in the tenth book of the *Hermetica*, 'The Key', Hermes explains what occurs when the soul leaves the body:

> The irreverent soul, however, stays in its own essence, punishing itself, seeking an earthy body to enter – a human body, to be sure. For no other body contains a human soul; it is not allowed for a human soul to fall down into the body of an unreasoning animal.[8]

It is just possible that this is evidence of an influence from the Indian holy men who were certainly teaching in Egypt during the Greek and Roman period, the same period during which the Hermetic books were composed. By our present understanding, none of the earlier Egyptian texts contains the specific idea of reincarnation – achieving the afterlife was the consistent preoccupation. Of course, we may have seriously misunderstood and mistranslated certain crucial passages. There may well be some symbolic understanding of the afterlife that includes a concept of reincarnation which translators have missed.

We are given pause by a very curious exchange found in *The Book of the Dead* which seems to relate both to a cycle of lives and a concept of karma, or something similar.

Unfortunately, this particular part of the ancient papyrus text was damaged and its true sense cannot be determined with accuracy. And that is quite apart from any translation difficulties.

The exchange is between the dead man – in this case the scribe Ani – and the god Thoth. The dead scribe asks, 'How long, then, have I to live?' Thoth answers, 'It is decreed that thou shalt live for millions of millions of years, a life of millions of years.' Ani responds, 'May it be granted unto me that I pass on unto the holy princes, for indeed I am doing away with all the wrong which I did, from the time when this earth came into being . . .'[9]

The Memories of Philip Corrigan

Philip Corrigan was born in 1959. Night after night as a child he had dreamed in vivid detail of having lived in England during the years leading up to the First World War. These dreams were so powerful that never for a moment did he doubt that they were real memories of a previous life.

He always dreamed of the same family in which he was the eldest of three girls. He dreamed of playing in a park, walking with his sisters, going to school; all ordinary events in an ordinary life. Except, of course, that this life was half a century in the past.

And, although he was yet to discover it, this life had come to a terrible end.

Curiously, apparently by sheer chance, when Philip was eleven, his parents moved to a village in the English Midlands, near the city of Bradford. His father had purchased a small shop there. Once settled, along with the continuing influence of his dreams, another certainty grew: Philip realized that he had somehow come back home. He sensed, for the first time, that it was here he had once lived.

But with this certitude grew an ominous feeling, as yet unattached to any specific incident which Philip could remember. Perhaps being closer to the actual site of the past events awoke memories much deeper, long buried because of their horror and pain. Philip gradually realized that in this previous existence he had met with a sudden death. At first he wondered whether it had been the result of some accident. Yet, belying this suggestion, something much darker lingered, something decidedly sinister.

And once, only once, he had dreamed of being violently attacked.

In his early teens Philip began to work on a paper round. On his first day, he was shown a list of the houses and streets to which he had to deliver. Out of the blur of house names and streets jumped 'Ellenthorpe': it seemed very familiar to him.

'Ellenthorpe', he soon discovered, was the name of a large house. It had formerly had a long drive leading up to it; a drive which survived as a rather isolated cul-de-sac called Little Red Lane.

Philip's first view of 'Ellenthorpe' confirmed immediately that it was a house he recalled from his vivid dreams. And something about the lane leading to it unnerved him; he always ran down it as quickly as possible.

He had mentioned this discovery of 'Ellenthorpe' to his parents but, wishing to prise him free of his attachment to the past, they urged him to ignore both the house and the rest of the dreams. They encouraged him to treat it as a fantasy of some kind. With their scepticism and with his growing older and becoming far more involved in his present life, Philip pushed the house and his dreams to the back of his mind. Eventually, in his late teens, the dreams faded.

But the memory did not. Some years later, with queries concerning that life again nagging at the edge of his mind, he took advantage of a period between jobs to make a concerted effort to search into the history of 'Ellenthorpe' and its immediate environs. He sought any historical evidence which might support the events of his dreams and began to speak to all long-term residents of the area in the hope that he might learn sufficient to draw up a picture of everyone who had formerly lived there.

It was during an interview with a local woman that the key to his search came. Her husband appeared and, without any preamble, abruptly said, 'Lad, did you know there was a murder on the driveway to this house?'

Philip suddenly shivered.

'Don't tell me,' he quickly replied. 'It was a young woman, slim, with light brown hair up in a bun, in her twenties. And she wouldn't have had two sisters younger than her, would she?'

The neighbour looked at him strangely.

'How did you know all this?' he demanded, suddenly curious about his young visitor.

Philip was circumspect but gained his confidence. He was told that the murdered girl's name was Lilian Bland, from a local family. Philip was also put in touch with the local historical group and through their contacts was introduced to a researcher who had made a study of the Bland family history.

Philip later recalled

I felt I could trust him, and so told him about my memories, and that I felt I could be Lilian Bland reincarnated. He didn't laugh or dismiss me. He simply said, 'It's a possibility.' I said I always felt she was buried locally, but I didn't know where. He smiled. 'It's 200 yards away. I know where she is, and I know where her boyfriend's grave is too.' Then he said, 'If you come tomorrow to my house, I've got something for you.'

The next day he handed Philip an old newspaper cutting. It was dated 9 January 1914.

The headline was, 'ECCLESHILL TRAGEDY. PRETTY GIRL MURDERED'. It added, 'Her assailant commits suicide. Desperate shooting affray in Little Red Lane.'[10]

According to the report, on 2 January 1914 the owner of 'Ellenthorpe' stated that he was out walking his dog when he heard a woman screaming for help. Quickly afterwards he heard several revolver shots. Running towards the scene he saw a woman lying on the ground, apparently lifeless. A man was standing over her. Then, according to this same witness, the apparent assailant shot himself. The dead woman was Lilian Bland; the man was a former boyfriend, recently returned from America.

The circumstances of the case were suspicious and the subsequent investigation hinged upon the statements made by the only witness to the shooting, the owner of 'Ellenthorpe'. The police naturally concluded that the former boyfriend was the murderer. But, even at the time, certain points of evidence seemed odd. While Lilian's boyfriend had owned a gun, the murder weapon was not this. A half-opened and bloodied razor was found nearby. There was evidence that a struggle had occurred. Yet the two young former lovers seemed very close; witnesses reported that earlier the same evening they had been talking and laughing together. There seemed no apparent reason for the evening to end in murder.

Curious, Philip obtained reports of the case. These convinced him that another person was involved; perhaps he was a rival for Lilian's affections. Perhaps too he had resided at 'Ellenthorpe'. In any case, he had subsequently escaped justice. But, despite his research, Philip failed to discover the true events of that day, either from the reports or from his own residual memories of his life as the murdered Lilian.

> I believe the murder had been blocked out of her mind to protect me in this existence, because if I could remember such horrific things, it would have affected me now. The pain of the murder was there, but the actual memories were blocked out.[11]

Is this story an example of some memory of a previous life, so strong that it forced its way out through dreams and half-conscious feelings despite the scepticism with which our society views such claims? Philip Corrigan, at least, had no such doubts as to its literal reality.

A Search for Scientific Proof

The Western tradition of science (often curiously distinct from the private beliefs of individuals, which might be anything but rational) always seeks proof of any assertion concerning reality: whether of the temperature at which water boils or whether humanity experiences a succession of lives. The scientific method passes no judgement on the importance of the assertion to be proven: all assertions are treated equally. This method requires that any evidence put forward in support of reincarnation must obey certain rules.

First and foremost, this evidence should be accurately recorded by witnesses themselves free from any bias or hidden motive. Second, this information should be verifiable. That is, it should contain facts which can be checked from independent sources.

Unfortunately, as the reader will now be aware, there is a third, unspoken but implicit rule: no new discovery should deviate from what is already 'known' to be true. Of course, this is not science, it is prejudice; but it means that those trying to investigate reincarnation are up against not only science but belief. It makes their task a difficult one.

Without falling into the trap of prejudice we must avoid falling into the morass of the gullible; we must use the principles of science to seek confirmation of the reality of reincarnation. If, for example, someone should claim a memory of a life spent in London 300 years ago, then we should want to be able to draw, from their statements, a list of facts which could then directly be checked in historical archives. We should want addresses, names of family and friends, events of the time with identified actions and principal figures. Importantly, we should want intimate details, some facts difficult to find in anything but the most highly specialized archives but which would be second nature to someone truly living at that time.

Furthermore we should want to be certain that any person

claiming memories of a past life could not have chanced upon the information in any other way. We need to be certain that the information given is free from contamination, either deliberate or unconscious.

In the late 1950s a psychiatrist, Dr Ian Stevenson of the Medical School in Charlottesville, Virginia, sought some answers to the question of past-life recall. He began to study reports of reincarnation using a systematic scientific procedure. Even his critics were impressed by his carefully controlled methods and realized that any criticism of his controversial discoveries would have to follow an equally rigorous method.[12]

The results of Dr Stevenson's initial investigations were published in the United States in 1960, in England a year later. He had looked closely at hundreds of cases where a memory of previous incarnations was claimed. By testing these examples against his scientific criteria, he reduced the number of acceptable cases to just twenty-eight. But these shared a number of strong features in common: all the subjects could remember being specific people living in specific places long before their own birth. Furthermore, the facts which they presented could be subjected to direct verification or rejection by independent research.

One case he reported concerned a young Japanese boy who, from a very early age, had consistently claimed that he had previously been a boy called Tozo, whose father, a farmer, had lived in a village called Hodokubo.

The young boy explained that in his previous life, when he – as Tozo – had still been young, his father had died; shortly thereafter his mother had remarried. But, only a year after this marriage, Tozo too died, of smallpox. He was aged only six. In addition to this information, the young boy gave detailed descriptions of the house Tozo lived in, the appearance of his parents and even the events of his funeral. On the face of it, it seemed as though a real memory of a past life was being recalled.

To test his statements, the young boy was taken to the village of Hodokubo. It was found that his former parents and other people he had identified had certainly lived there in the past. Furthermore he was clearly familiar with the village, which he had never before visited. Without any help, he took his companions to his former home. Once there he drew their attention to a shop which, he said, had not been in existence during his previous life. Similarly, he pointed out a tree unknown to him and which had evidently since grown. Investigation quickly proved that both these assertions were true. In all, his testimony prior to the visit to Hodokubo provided sixteen definite and specific statements which could be checked. When checked, they all proved correct.[13]

In his work Dr Stevenson stressed in particular his high regard for the testimony of young children. He considered that not only are they far less susceptible to conscious or unconscious deception but they are unlikely to have read about, or heard about, the events in the past which they describe.

Stevenson continued his research and in 1966 published the first edition of his influential book, *Twenty Cases Suggestive of Reincarnation*. By this time he had personally studied almost 600 cases which seemed best explained by reincarnation. Eight years later he published a second edition of this book; by that time the case studies had doubled to around 1,200. Among these he had found some which, as he explained, 'do much more than suggest reincarnation; they seem to furnish considerable evidence for it'.[14]

The Case of Imad Elawar

Dr Stevenson heard of a case of past-life recall in a young man, Imad Elawar, living in a small village in the Druze area of Lebanon. The Druze, while considered to be within the Islamic orbit, in fact have a great number of very distinctive beliefs, one of which is reincarnation. There are, perhaps as a result of this acceptance, many cases of past-life recall amongst the Druze community.

Before Imad had reached two years old he had begun talking of a previous life which he had spent in another village, also Druze, called Khriby, where he claimed to have been a member of the Bouhamzy family. He had often pleaded with his parents to take him there. But his father refused and accused him of lying. The young boy soon learned to avoid the subject in his father's presence.

Imad had made a number of statements about his previous life: he mentioned a beautiful woman called Jamileh, whom he was much in love with. He spoke of his life in Khriby, his enjoyment of hunting with his dog, his double-barrelled shotgun and his rifle which, being illegal, he had to hide. He described owning a small yellow car and sharing the use of other vehicles which belonged to his family. He also mentioned witnessing an accident where a lorry ran over a cousin causing such injuries that he soon died. When finally investigated, all these statements were to prove accurate.

In spring 1964 Dr Stevenson made the first of several trips to this mountainous region to interview the young Imad, who was aged five at the time.[15]

Prior to any visit to the village, Imad had made a total of forty-seven definite statements concerning his previous life.[16] Dr Stevenson wished to check the accuracy of each himself and so was determined to take Imad to the village of Khriby as soon as he could. Within a few days it proved possible; together they set off on the twenty-five-mile journey along a rarely travelled road which twisted back and forth through the mountains. Like much of the interior of Lebanon, while both villages had good links with the capital, Beirut, on the coast, there was no regular traffic on the difficult cross-country route between them.

Once in the village Imad made sixteen further statements of recognition: he proved vague on one, wrong on another but correct on the remaining fourteen. And, of these correct statements, twelve concerned very personal incidents or comments on his previous life. It is highly unlikely that this information could have come from any other source than from within the family.

Although Imad had never given the Christian name he used in his previous life, the only figure in the Bouhamzy family who matched – and did so exactly – the information was one son, Ibraham, who had died of tuberculosis in September 1949. He had been a close friend of a cousin who died in a lorry accident in 1943. He also loved a beautiful woman called Jamileh who had moved away from the village after his death.[17]

While in the village Imad recalled further specific details of his previous life as a member of the Bouhamzy family, which were impressive in both their domestic nature and their accuracy. He correctly pointed out, for example, where 'he', as Ibraham Bou-hamzy, had kept his dog and how it was tethered. Neither of these had been an obvious answer. He also correctly identified 'his' bed and described how it had been arranged differently in the past. He revealed too where Ibraham kept his gun. Crucially, he also independently recognized and correctly named Ibraham's sister, Huda. Similarly he recognized and named a brother when shown a photographic portrait.

A convincing exchange occurred with 'his' sister Huda. She asked of Imad, 'You said something just before you died. What was it?' Imad replied, 'Huda, call Fuad.' This was correct because Fuad had left shortly before and Ibraham wanted to see him again, but died immediately.[18]

Without direct, secret, collusion between the young Imad and the elderly Huda Bouhamzy – which seems almost impossible given Dr Stevenson's close attention to the case – there is no conceivable way that Imad could have known these final words of the dying man except for one: that Imad truly was the reincarnation of the dead Ibraham Bouhamzy.

In fact, the case is stronger: out of the forty-seven statements about his past life which Imad had made, only three were proved wrong. Evidence such as this is hard to dismiss.

It might be objected that this incident occurred in a society which believed in reincarnation and so might be expected to encourage any youthful fantasy in this direction. Realizing this, Dr Stevenson reports an intriguing point he has noted: memories of past lives occur not only in cultures in which reincarnation is accepted but also in those where it is not – or, at least, not officially. He has, for example, investigated some thirty-five cases in the United States; there are others in Canada and the United Kingdom. And, as he points out, cases also occur in India amongst Muslim families who have never accepted reincarnation.

It hardly seems necessary to emphasize that this research has rather important implications for the scientific and medical understanding of life. Yet, however obvious this statement is, it will be hotly denied in many quarters. Reincarnation poses a direct challenge to modern assumptions of what it means to be human; assumptions excluding anything which cannot be weighed, measured, dissected or isolated in a Petri dish or microscope slide. In common with many modern assumptions which we have already looked at, these too can be maintained only by ignoring, suppressing or marginalizing the contrary evidence, however sound its source. Dr Stevenson once said to the television producer Jeffrey Iverson that

> Science should pay a lot more attention to the evidence we have pointing towards life after death. Looked at fairly, the evidence is impressive and from a variety of sources. The prevailing orthodoxy is when your brain dies your mind perishes also. That is so deeply believed that scientists fail to understand it is an assumption only and there is no reason why aspects of the mind should not survive death of the brain.[19]

In the West reincarnation has not formed any part of our official cultural belief systems since the demise of the Druids perhaps 2,000 years ago. Any brief experience of this type is dismissed as one of *déjà vu*, fantasy or wish-fulfilment. But, as we have seen in the case of Philip Corrigan, experiences coming through dreams can be so real that the subject can have no doubt whatever that they derive from a previous life. Philip Corrigan's parents dismissed them, yet this did nothing to alter his belief. And, as we have also seen, his subsequent investigation gave support to his position.

Given the basic Christian and scientific beliefs underpinning Western culture, it comes as something of a surprise to discover that belief in reincarnation is more widespread than one would imagine.

In February 1969 a poll carried out in twelve North American and European countries by the Gallup organization found that a surprisingly high percentage of the population declared a firm belief in the reality of reincarnation. In the United States 20 per cent admitted holding this belief; in Germany 25 per cent, in France 23 per cent, in the United Kingdom 18 per cent.

Ten years later, a further poll by the same organization in the United Kingdom showed an increase to 28 per cent in the number of people who accepted the truth of reincarnation. In 1981 a similar poll carried out in the United States disclosed an increase to 23 per cent in those adults professing such a belief. This suggests that a staggering 38 million Americans believe that they have lived before.[20]

Buried Memories of the Past

The basis of psychoanalytic therapy is the bringing of unconscious memories into the conscious mind. Once made conscious, such memories can be dealt with, can be integrated into the personality which is thereby healed and made whole.

Many dysfunctions of the personality – and even of the body – can be traced back to strong, deeply buried hurts, confusions, betrayals, frustrations and similar inharmonious events, which, until brought into the light of consciousness, lie buried like land-mines.

They explode whenever some aspect of life treads upon their particular tract of territory.

Those who work in this field, the therapists, analysts, psychiatrists and counsellors of one persuasion or another, have long been used to the techniques of retrieving these memories from the deep unconscious pits in which they lie, well hidden. Dreams are one universal method used to gain access to these memories. Guided fantasies give another, as do art, word association and, in some cases, hypnosis.

Hypnosis is a very powerful tool and we cannot pretend that we know everything of its effects or possibilities. It has a somewhat murky reputation amongst the psychological establishment – there is the whiff of disrepute about it. And, it cannot be denied, this is hardly helped by the touring hypnotists who place themselves in the entertainment business rather than the therapeutic.

But many therapists continue, cautiously, to use hypnosis as a tool to gain access to deeper and deeper levels of buried memory. And it was while using hypnosis in this way that some therapists noted something very odd happening. Deep memories appeared which had no apparent origin in the patient's life; they seemed to be memories of a past life.

Dr Edith Fiore, an American psychotherapist, described how a patient first brought her face to face with such past-life memories. She wrote, 'He had come to me because of crippling sexual inhibitions. When I asked him, while he was under hypnosis, to go back to the origin of his problems, he said, "Two or three lifetimes ago, I was a Catholic priest."[21] This took her by surprise. Her professionalism took over and she encouraged him to work through what he described as life as a priest in seventeenth-century Italy. The next time they met the patient reported himself free of his problems.

Of course, she was not the first to have discovered an apparent power of hypnosis to recover memories of past lives. The first major case to catch the public's imagination was that of the sensational 'Bridie Murphy' affair in the United States in the 1950s, in which a claim was made of a previous life in nineteenth-century Ireland. In England, a similar storm of support and criticism was caused by hypnotist Arnall Bloxham, whose patients, recalling past lives, received considerable publicity when a BBC documentary was made about them.

Certainly, such cases are fascinating and the subjects provide large amounts of very intricate and intimate detail of their previous lives. Correctly, they came under intense scrutiny and criticism.

Perhaps the most famous of Bloxham's patients was one man who, under hypnosis, recalled serving as a gunner on a British Navy thirty-two-gun frigate commanded by a Captain Pearce during the eighteenth century. The ship's name was apparently ornate and difficult; the sailors, according to the patient, nicknamed her HMS *Aggie*. He never could recall her true name. Perhaps the sailor in those days was unable to read or to pronounce it. Perhaps *Aggie* was short for Agamemnon or something similar.

During his recollections, he used many old-fashioned phrases and nautical or descriptive terms familiar only to sailors of that era. He produced a wealth of detail about life at sea in those days: the stench, the worm-ridden food, the rough clothes and the flogging – which he claimed he escaped because he knew well how to 'lay a gun'.[22]

His first, and only, hypnotic session ended with the drama of a battle. He described, with passion and vivid detail, a fight against a French naval ship just outside the port of Calais. They had been waiting close inshore for many hours, hidden by the morning mist. All the guns were primed and ready. The match-boys were swinging their lengths of smouldering tar-soaked cord to keep them burning, ready to fire the guns. The ship was cruising back and forth as it waited for the French ship to emerge. When it finally did, the English gunners were ready for action.

He described the action: the ships began to close upon each other. The less-experienced gunners were impatient, desperate to fire. He continued his story:

Waiting, waiting! Waiting for the order – steady lads, steady – now hold it, hold it hold it – wait for the order, wait for it – wing those matches, aye sirree – stand clear from behind – NOW you fool. Now up fool now – NOW! – (*screams in exultation as the shot is fired*) – Well done, lads – run 'em up, run 'em up, get 'em up, get 'em up – get 'em up the front – (*shrieks*) – pull that man out, pull 'im out – send him in the cockpit – now get 'im back – get up there – get on the chocks there – run them up again! . . .

The shot in – ramrods – swab it, swab it, you fool, swab it first – the shot in, shot in – come on number four, you should be up by now – shot in, ram it home – prime – swing those matches – aye, aye, sir – ready! . . .

And again lads – you had him then – hurry men – by God you bastard – got him that aim – that's the way to lay a gun – My Christ, they've got old Pearce, they've got Pearce – (*sudden terrible screaming*) – MY BLOODY LEG – (*screaming and moaning uncontrollably*) – MY LEG – MY LEG!'[23]

The patient awoke so shaken that he never again submitted to hypnosis.

This story was so extraordinary and convincing that Prince Philip and the Earl Mountbatten, who both served in the Royal Navy, requested tape-recordings of this apparent past-life recall. They set British Admiralty historians the task of identifying the ship, the captain and the action. Sadly, despite all the wealth of detail, they were never able to. Is this, then, not a true case of reincarnation memory? Is it but a fantasy embellished with fragments from books, films and radio programmes?

The jury is still out.

The Use of Hypnosis

There is no denying that hypnosis is a useful therapeutic tool, but are the statements of past lives elicited under it objectively true? Dr Fiore, for example, makes no attempt to verify the historical accuracy of the stories that her patients relate. She is interested in psychological truth rather than historical truth. She is interested solely in what will help improve the patient. If the patient's psychological disability is cured or eased by virtue of understanding the causes of the problem in terms of reincarnation, then that alone is sufficient for her to take it seriously. This approach is rather like the search for the Dalai Lama; it is fascinating, intriguing, compelling – but hardly scientific.

Dr Stevenson has long been aware of this difficulty. In his own studies on reincarnation, he has stayed well away from the use of hypnosis. He freely admits that the use of it is attractive; it seems to offer the possibility of laboratory conditions for control and verification. But, as he explains, this is an illusion. It has always proved impossible to control the subject's previous exposure to the details expressed in the recall of 'past lives': like novels, plays, films or documentaries.[24]

He explains that these apparent past lives appear to be built up from several sources: they contain pieces of the subject's own personality together with fantasy material drawn from a variety of sources, written or filmed. They are also strongly influenced by what the patient thinks the hypnotist might want. In other words, the patient wants to please the expert by giving the 'correct' testimony.

Stevenson adds that there could also be an element derived paranormally: from clairvoyance, telepathy, a discarnate entity of some type, or from a genuine memory of reincarnation. But all these sources may be present at once, all together contributing to the 'recall'. Such would result in a coherent and fascinating story but not one which is wholly a memory of a past life.

Yet we cannot totally dismiss the recollections, however flawed, evoked under hypnosis. It could be that some genuine past-life memory drags to itself all the related material which the mind gathers over the years. Perhaps in some way, under hypnosis, the subject is unable to discriminate between these sources and so presents all the available information he or she has, woven into a convincing whole.

Some of the statements, some of the recollections, have a quiet dignity, an undramatic sense of validity. These are less easy to dismiss completely. One particular example amongst Dr Fiore's patients concerns a man who spoke of participating in a jousting tournament in England in 1486 – a tournament which, for him, went terribly wrong.

The Joust

'I'm sitting on a horse in my armour . . . I'm – I'm a little bit nervous . . . and I feel like I'm . . . a little bit like I might throw up.'[25]

A patient under hypnosis was describing to Dr Fiore the moments before he was about to enter the lists in a jousting competition in England, during the reign of King Henry VII.

After describing nervously awaiting his turn, he finally spoke of entering the field. Suddenly his body jerked violently. He reported that he had just been knocked off his horse by his opponent. Dr Fiore asked whether he was on the ground.

'No, I had . . . got up . . . I feel more ashamed than I am scared, but . . . I am kind of disoriented . . . I think my stomach is injured.'[26]

His opponent, meanwhile, still on his horse, was circling, waiting for a chance to beat the fallen man with a club. The patient described the difficulties he faced: armed only with an axe, try as he might, he was unable to cause much damage to the mounted opponent. Suddenly the knight charged and trampled over him. And, as the knight did so, he swung with his club – a spiked ball on a chain – landing a fatal blow upon his dismounted opponent's head.

Dr Fiore's patient screwed up his face in agony. She asked where he was. With his voice beginning to fade, he replied, 'I'm lying there in the green . . . I just feel nothing . . . just a kind of a warmth and a . . . red blood, a warm blood is running through my body . . . and I'm just . . . kind of . . . I saw a white light and . . . I just kind of floated away . . .'[27]

He later described his death further:

'I was lying face down and then I floated face down . . . floated up and . . . at first, for about three feet . . . and then I floated upright . . . just floated away . . . A feeling of warmth through my whole body and release in my body . . . I see the whole area. I can see everything.'[28]

Falling into the Sun

One curious case moves further into the broader context suggested by the last. For reincarnation is to be understood as just one aspect of a greater process, a process which begins, not ends, with death.

This case concerns a man who, in his late teens and early twenties, experienced a number of brief but vivid recollections of past lives. None of the experiences lasted for longer than a minute or two but he had no doubt whatsoever of their reality. As he explained, each time he suddenly found himself reliving these past events, his memory *at the time* also returned. Not only did he remember the life but he also knew that he had subsequently forgotten it. It was rather, he explained, like riding a bicycle after many years of driving a car. That moment of sitting on the saddle and pedalling instantly brings back the memory of how to balance and steer; riding becomes second nature – as it had been before. So too with the experience of the past lives; once they are recalled, their reality is self-evident.[29]

But there was a further discovery: upon first remembering each of the previous lives, upon first 'joining' with that life, he realized that he had done so either at the point in that life when he had died or at the point in that life when he had a profound experience.

One life he suddenly joined at the moment when, a Viking warrior, he was standing near the prow of the ship at sunrise as it creaked and thumped through the North Sea. As the sun rose, so too did his sense of the timeless. For an instant – in that life – he, as a Viking warrior, had realized the timelessness and unity of all creation: a mystical experience.

Another life he entered at a similar mystical point, but this time reached as the culmination of an initiation into some ancient mystery rite.

Others he joined at the moment of death: he was a slave in a Roman galley. He experienced again the stench, the nakedness, the sweat, the chains, the oars, the hopelessness and the hatred he felt towards the Romans. Then an enemy battering ram crashed through the side of the ship. A fountain of water gushed in after it. Chained to the boards, he was dragged down with the ship and drowned. It was over in a matter of minutes.

Yet another life he also entered just before death: he experienced being in the cockpit of a crashing Second World War German rocket fighter, a Messerschmitt Me-163. It exploded on landing, as these small fighters, charged with a very unstable fuel, tended to do. He found himself floating away from the wreckage, looking down over snow-covered devastation, and wondering, just as his memory faded, what had happened to beauty, love and truth. These questions dominated his next life, his present one.

He realized that each of these moments, in however many lives, however many years apart, were all the same time. In fact, to call the experience a 'memory' somehow failed to encompass the full breadth of its reality. Somehow, it seemed to him, those lives still existed; they were separated from the present only by time. Each life seemed like one spoke of a wheel, separate at the rim but joined at the centre.

Two or three years after this flurry of reincarnation experiences and when he was maintaining a regular routine of evening meditations, he had an experience which placed all the others into context.

One evening, after his meditation, he slept briefly before suddenly awakening: he seemed to be falling uncontrollably through deepest dark space; he enjoyed the tumbling freedom of it.

Then, before his eyes, a wispy scene began to form itself, rather like smoke gradually coming together and solidifying. As it formed he recognized one of his previous lives. He knew instinctively that he could accept this forming scene, join with it and experience it again. But instead of feeling curious he felt utterly weary. 'No,' he said. 'No. I'm weary, I'm tired of all these lives. I just want to see the Light'.

The scene dissolved. He continued falling at great speed through the darkness of space. Then another scene began coalescing before his eyes in the same manner. Again he recognized it as one of his previous lives. Again he rejected it, stressing his weariness. Immediately it dissolved, leaving him again tumbling through space.

A third time a scene was presented. A third time he stressed his weariness. A third time it dissolved to leave him falling through the endless darkness. Yet this time there was a change. Far in the distance he saw a bright star, a sun far away. And he was falling towards it with ever-increasing speed. Until he fell into the sun.

Suddenly he was sitting, with the bright light coursing through every cell in his body. And with this light came an intense burning, a painful searing experience which exhausted him as he sat there, unable to do anything but allow it to continue.

Abruptly the pain ceased and the sun seemed to rise inside his body. It was, he explained, as though the sun was shining from the centre of his brow and filling him with the purest light. A light which was Divinity itself.

At that instant he knew that all was indeed one: he later laughed at having forgotten such a self-evident truth, one which he had known for ever, but one which he had long searched for. He realized his mistake: no search was necessary; merely a remembering.

Death was seen as a mythical beast; reincarnation as a process as natural as falling rain or the ebb and flow of the tide . . .

It is difficult to measure the above experience by scientific standards. Yet does that make it unworthy of our attention? Does it make it somehow irrelevant to our lives? However far short of objective proof it might fall, it does serve to impress upon us that reincarnation – as it is experienced – is a process which cannot be viewed in isolation. Like this report, others stress that it is an important component of something much greater.

It goes without saying that the experience of past lives is closely tied to the experience of death itself. And with the experience of death we are, paradoxically, in the grip of the greatest mystery of life. A mystery which no amount of fossils, relics or ancient texts can ever truly explain. For any explanation depends upon a perspective which reaches far beyond the limitations of more time and space. And here, in this wider universe, science as we know it is inadequate. To survive, it will have to change.

Notes

NOTE   The full bibliographical details, when not cited here, are to be found in the Bibliography.

Introduction

1. Belitzky, Goren-Inbar and Werker, 'A Middle Pleistocene Wooden Plank with Man-made Polish', p. 351.
2. Letter from Prof. Goren-Inbar, 8 October 1996.
3. Belitzky, Goren-Inbar and Werker, 'A Middle Pleistocene Wooden Plank', p. 352.

1: How Ancient is Humanity?

1. There are a number of differing dates for the Cambrian Explosion: 'nearly 530 million years ago', according to Drs Erwin, Valentine and Jablonski, 'The Origin of Animal Body Plans', p. 126; Prof. Levinton in 'The Big Bang of Animal Evolution', p. 52, puts it at 'roughly 570 million years' before the present.
2. Semaw et al., '2.5-million-year-old Stone Tools from Gona, Ethiopia', pp. 333–6.
3. The Times, 24 December 1851, p. 5, citing as a source the Springfield Republican.
4. Whitney, The Auriferous Gravels of the Sierra Nevada of California.

5. Skertchly, 'On the Occurrence of Stone Mortars in the Ancient (Pliocene?) River Gravels of Butte County, California', pp. 332–7.

6. Becker, 'Antiquities from under Tuolumne Table Mountain in California', pp. 189–200.

7. Holmes, 'Review of the Evidence Relating to Auriferous Gravel Man in California'. See summary in Corliss, *Ancient Man: A Handbook of Puzzling Artifacts*, pp. 670–72.

8. See Cremo and Thompson, *Forbidden Archaeology*, pp. 270–93.

9. Whitney, *The Auriferous Gravels*, p. 264. Whitney personally inspected some of these objects.

10. Ibid., p. 265.

11. Ibid., p. 266.

12. Ibid., pp. 274–5.

13. Ibid., p. 266.

14. Cremo and Thompson, *Forbidden Archaeology*, pp. 376–7.

15. Becker, 'Antiquities from under Tuolumne Table Mountain', p. 194.

16. Holmes, 'The Evidence Relating to Auriferous Gravel Man', p. 453.

17. Becker, 'Antiquities from under Tuolumne Table Mountain', p. 192. See also Holmes, 'The Evidence Relating to Auriferous Gravel Man', pp. 450–53.

18. Cremo and Thompson, *Forbidden Archaeology*, p. 378.

19. Becker, 'Antiquities from under Tuolumne Table Mountain', p. 192.

20. Whitney, *The Auriferous Gravels*, p. 274.

21. Ibid., pp. 275–8. Objects were found in the Californian counties of Amadour, El Dorado, Placer, Nevada, Butte, Siskiyou and Trinity. For dating see Cremo and Thompson, *Forbidden Archaeology*, pp. 386–7.

22. Cremo and Thompson, *Forbidden Archaeology*, p. 392.

23. *Morrisonville Times*, 11 June 1891, p. 1.

24. Cremo and Thompson, *Forbidden Archaeology*, p. 805.

25. Ibid., p. 806.

26. *Morrisonville Times*, 11 June 1891, p. 1.

27. *The Times*, 22 June 1844, p. 8, quoting the *Kelso Chronicle*.

28. Brewster, 'Queries and Statements Concerning a Nail Found Embedded in a Block of Sandstone', II, p. 51.

29. *Nature*, 35, 11 November 1886, p. 36. It weighed 1 pound 11 ounces

and was covered with a thin layer of oxide. It was as hard as steel and had a specific gravity of 7.75. Some of the specialists who examined it considered that it had been artificially produced, others that it was a meteorite.

30. Allan and Delair, *When the Earth Nearly Died*, p. 336.

31. Cremo and Thompson, *Forbidden Archaeology*, p. 454. The original report was published in the *Geologist*, December 1862.

32. Hürzeler, 'The Significance of Oreopithecus in the Genealogy of Man', p. 169; *Science*, 128, 5 September 1958, p. 523.

33. Burroughs, 'Human-like Footprints, 250 Million Years Old', p. 46. See also Cremo and Thompson, *Forbidden Archeology*, pp. 454–8. Found at the O. Finnell Farm, Rockcastle County, near the town of Berea, Kentucky.

34. Burroughs, 'Human-like Footprints', p. 46.

35. Ibid., pp. 46–7.

36. Cremo and Thompson, *Forbidden Archaeology*, p. 456.

37. Burroughs, 'Human-like Footprints', p. 47.

38. Cremo and Thompson, *Forbidden Archaeology*, p. 457.

39. Thulborn, *Dinosaur Tracks*, pp. 229–31. See also Corliss, *Science Frontiers: Some Anomalies and Curiosities of Nature*, pp. 44–45.

40. Cremo and Thompson, *Forbidden Archaeology*, p. 458.

41. See the survey in Corliss, *Ancient Man*, pp. 636–51.

42. Cremo and Thompson, *Forbidden Archaeology*, p. 807.

43. Ibid., p. 808.

44. *Deseret News*, 13 June 1968, p. 14A. See also Corliss, *Unknown Earth: A Handbook of Geological Enigmas*, p. 642; Cremo and Thompson, *Forbidden Archaeology*, pp. 810–13.

45. Cremo and Thompson, *Forbidden Archaeology*, p. 812.

2: Problems with Evolution

1. Denton, *Evolution: A Theory in Crisis*, p. 75.

2. Dawkins, *The Selfish Gene*, p. 1.

3. Gould, *The Panda's Thumb*, p. 149. Although this essay was originally written in 1977, his first challenge was in 1972. (See n. 31, below.)

4. Schindel, 'The Gaps in the Fossil Record', p. 282.

5. Darwin, *The Origin of Species*, p. 293.

6. Ibid., p. 206.

7. Ibid.

8. Ibid., p. 439.

9. Gould, *The Panda's Thumb*, p. 150.

10. An interview by Luther D. Sunderland reported in Mebane, *Darwin's Creation-Myth*, p. 18.

11. Stanley, *The New Evolutionary Timetable*, p. 95.

12. Wesson, *Beyond Natural Selection*, p. 44.

13. Levinton, 'The Big Bang of Animal Evolution', p. 52. See also Erwin, Valentine and Jablonski, 'The Origin of Animal Body Plans', p. 126: 'All of the basic architectures of animals were apparently established by the close of the Cambrian explosion . . .'

14. Levinton, 'The Big Bang of Animal Evolution', p. 52.

15. Wesson, *Beyond Natural Selection*, p. 39.

16. Formerly called *Eohippus*.

17. Denton, *Evolution*, pp. 182–3. See also Eldredge, *Reinventing Darwin: The Great Evolutionary Debate*, pp. 129–31, and Milton, *The Facts of Life*, pp. 122–7.

18. See Milton, *The Facts of Life*, p. 124.

19. Gould, *The Panda's Thumb*, p. 151.

20. Wesson, *Beyond Natural Selection*, p. 50.

21. Phraseology with thanks to Jacobs, *Quest for the African Dinosaurs: Ancient Roots of the Modern World*, p. 242.

22. Wesson, *Beyond Natural Selection*, p. 40.

23. Ibid., p. 41.

24. Ibid.

25. Ibid., p. 14.

26. Leith, *The Descent of Darwin*, p. 78.

27. Stahl, *Vertebrate History: Problems in Evolution*, p. 349.

28. Gould, *The Panda's Thumb*, p. 157.

29. Darwin, *Life and Letters of Charles Darwin*, II, p. 273.

30. Wesson, *Beyond Natural Selection*, p. 18.

31. Gould and Eldredge, 'Punctuated Equilibria: An Alternative to Phy-

letic Gradualism', in *Models in Paleobiology*, pp. 82–115. Gould and Eldredge write (p. 96): 'Many breaks in the fossil record are real; they express the way in which evolution occurs, not the fragments of an imperfect record.'

32. Denton, *Evolution*, p. 310.
33. Ibid. The possibility is one chance in ten to the power of 100; there are estimated to be ten to the power of seventy atoms in the observable universe.
34. Hoyle, *Nature*, 12 November 1981, p. 105.
35. Wesson, *Beyond Natural Selection*, p. 291.
36. Ibid., p. 157.
37. See Gleick, *Chaos: Making a New Science*, pp. 16–18.
38. Wesson, *Beyond Natural Selection*, p. 294.

3: Could 'Extinct' Creatures Still Exist?

1. Welfare and Fairley, *Arthur C. Clarke's Mysterious World*, p. 106.
2. Kaharl, *Water Baby: The Story of Alvin*, p. 91.
3. Soule, *Wide Ocean*, p. 171.
4. See Bille, *Rumors of Existence*, pp. 21–2; Shuker, *In Search of Prehistoric Survivors: Do Giant 'Extinct' Creatures Still Exist?*, p. 123.
5. Shuker, *In Search of Prehistoric Survivors*, pp. 122–3.
6. Ellis, *Monsters of the Sea*, pp. 343–4, quoting D. J. Stead, *Sharks and Rays of Australian Seas*, Sydney, 1963.
7. Shuker, *In Search of Prehistoric Survivors*, p. 123.
8. Ibid., p. 123. See also Linklater, *The Voyage of the Challenger*, p. 244.
9. Shuker, *In Search of Prehistoric Survivors*, p. 119.
10. Ibid., p. 120.
11. Ibid., p. 121.
12. Secretariat, P.O. Box 43070, Tucson, Arizona 85733, United States.
13. Heuvelmans, *In the Wake of the Sea-Serpents*, pp. 473–7.
14. LeBlond and Sibert, *Observations of Large Unidentified Marine Animals in British Columbia and Adjacent Waters*, pp. 5–6.
15. Ibid., p. 63.

16. Ibid., p. 31.

17. Ibid., p. 32.

18. LeBlond and Bousfield, *Cadborosaurus: Survivor from the Deep*, p. 2.

19. Ibid., p. 29.

20. Ibid., p. 40.

21. Ibid., p. 31.

22. Ibid., pp. 94–118.

23. Ibid., pp. 119–20.

24. Ibid., p. 57.

25. Ibid., pp. 51–5.

26. Ibid., p. 57.

27. Shuker, *In Search of Prehistoric Survivors*, p. 81.

28. Ibid., pp. 81–2.

29. Ibid., p. 82.

30. Ibid., pp. 82–3.

31. Ibid., p. 84.

32. Ibid., p. 102. Doubts have since emerged over this video. Suspicions have been raised that it might have been a hoax. See *Fortean Times*, 102, September 1997, p. 29.

33. Shuker, *In Search of Prehistoric Survivors*, pp. 100–102.

34. Ibid., p. 83.

35. Ibid., p. 84.

36. Shuker (ibid., p. 92) reports that fossils of the plesiosaur group, the later elasmosaur, have been found in a rock formation in California which also contains fossils from the Palaeocene period (55–64 million years ago). Unfortunately there has not yet been a proven link between the two types of fossil.

37. See his discussion, ibid., pp. 91–8.

38. Ibid., p. 95.

39. Vartanyan, Garutt and Sher, 'Holocene Dwarf Mammoths from Wrangel Island in the Siberian Arctic', pp. 337–40. See also Lister, 'Mammoths in Miniature', pp. 288–9.

40. Shuker, *In Search of Prehistoric Survivors*, p. 81.

41. Ibid., pp. 108–9.

42. Bille, *Rumors of Existence*, pp. 39–40.

43. *New York Times*, 12 November 1995.
44. For a review of all creatures discovered this century, large and small, see Shuker, *The Lost Ark*.

4: Living Dinosaurs

1. For the story of the expeditions see Mackal, *A Living Dinosaur?: In Search of Mokele-Mbembe*.
2. Kingdon, *Island Africa*, pp. 10–16.
3. Proyart, *Histoire de Loango, Kakongo, et autres royaumes d'Afrique*, pp. 38–9.
4. Ley, *The Lungfish and the Unicorn*, pp. 122–3.
5. Shuker, *In Search of Prehistoric Survivors: Do Giant 'Extinct' Creatures Still Exist?*, p. 19.
6. Heuvelmans, *On the Track of Unknown Animals*, p. 462.
7. Ibid., pp. 434–41.
8. Shuker, *In Search of Prehistoric Survivors*, p. 19.
9. Ibid.
10. Ibid., pp. 19–20.
11. Mackal, *A Living Dinosaur?*, pp. 19–20.
12. Ibid., pp. 21–2.
13. Ibid., p. 23.
14. Ibid.
15. Ibid., pp. 24–5.
16. Ibid., pp. 81–2.
17. Ibid., pp. 77–8.
18. Ibid., p. 82.
19. Ibid., pp. 59, 62, 75–6.
20. Ibid., pp. 179–80.
21. O'Hanlon, *Congo Journey*, p. 323.
22. Mackal, *A Living Dinosaur?*, p. 84.
23. Ibid., p. 139.
24. Ibid., pp. 235–6.
25. Ibid., pp. 257–9.
26. See, for example, Emery, *Archaic Egypt*, p. 45 and plate 3(a).

27. Lorblanchet and Sieveking, 'The Monsters of Pergouset', p. 40. It is illustrated on p. 47. The same room also contains inscribed signs – groups of curved parallel lines as well as a zigzag design with six angles on the left, seven on the right. What these signs record, if anything, is unknown. See pp. 43 and 50.

28. Breuil, *Quatre cents siècles d'art pariétal*, p. 390, fig. 512.

29. Melland, *In Witch-bound Africa*, p. 238.

30. Price, *Extra-special Correspondent*, p. 178.

31. Lt Col. A. C. Simonds, 'Pieces of War', typescript memoir dated 1 July 1985, covering the years 1931–74.

32. The original article was reproduced in *Fortean Times*, 105, December 1997, p. 37.

33. Shuker, *In Search of Prehistoric Survivors*, p. 57.

34. Ibid., pp. 54–5.

35. Ibid., p. 56.

36. Lawson, 'Pterosaur from the Latest Cretaceous of West Texas: Discovery of the Largest Flying Creature', p. 947.

37. Shuker, *In Search of Prehistoric Survivors*, p. 59.

38. Ibid.

5: *The Mysteries of Human Evolution*

1. Johanson and Edey, *Lucy: The Beginnings of Humankind*, p. 22.

2. For many years it was considered that no *Homo erectus* remains had been found in Europe. In March 1994 much of the upper portion of a hominid skull was found in Italy. Dated to about 900,000 years ago, it was called 'Ceprano Man' and has been assigned to the species of *erectus* despite a number of slight morphological distinctions. See Gore, 'The First Europeans', p. 101.

3. See, for example, the chart published in Leakey and Walker, 'Early Hominid Fossils from Africa', p. 62. See also Lewin, *Bones of Contention*, p. 17.

4. See the comments on *Australopithecus* as apes in Leakey and Lewin, *Origins Reconsidered*, for example, pp. 158, 194 and 196.

5. Ibid., p. 120.

6. Lewin, *Bones of Contention*, p. 137.

7. Leakey and Walker, 'Early Hominid Fossils from Africa' p. 62. They named the species *Australopithecus anamensis*.

8. White *et al.*, '*Australopithecus ramidus*, a New Species of Early Hominid from Aramis, Ethiopia', p. 306. In 1995 this species was renamed *Ardipithecus ramidus*.

9. Johanson and Edey, *Lucy*, p. 309.

10. For an extended discussion of this feature and its implications see Morgan, *The Scars of Evolution*, pp. 124–40.

11. Ibid., p. 126.

12. Ibid., pp. 45–6.

13. Ibid., p. 140.

14. Ibid., pp. 88–91.

15. Ibid., p. 111.

16. Ibid., p. 47.

17. Ibid., pp. 175–9.

18. Ibid., pp. 176–8.

19. Ibid., pp. 51–5, quoting work of geologist Paul Mohr.

20. Ibid., p. 51.

21. La Lumiere, 'Evolution of Human Bipedalism: A Hypothesis about Where It Happened', pp. 103–7.

22. Morgan, *The Scars of Evolution*, p. 178.

23. Quoted in More, 'New Skull Turns Up in Northeast Africa', p. 32.

24. See Tuttle, 'Evolution of Hominid Bipedalism and Prehensile Capabilities', p. 92, where he writes that the bone and muscle structure of the creatures such as Lucy 'are quite compatible with the idea that . . . [they] were derived rather recently from arboreal bipeds. Indeed, they too may have engaged in notable tree climbing.'

   See also the chart in Cremo and Thompson, *Forbidden Archaeology*, pp. 730–31, for the list of features which 'Lucy' shared with apes, chimpanzees, gibbons and orang-utans. It appears virtually certain that these were her relatives rather than man, who seems to have existed already in modern form at that date.

25. Leakey, 'Skull 1470', p. 828.

26. Leakey, 'Footprints in the Ashes of Time', pp. 446–57. See also Leakey, 'Tracks and Tools', pp. 95–102.
27. See a summary of statements supporting this in Cremo and Thompson, *Forbidden Archaeology*, pp. 742–7.
28. Tuttle, 'Evolution of Hominid Bipedalism', p. 91.
29. Ibid.
30. Gore, 'The First Steps', p. 80.
31. Cremo and Thompson, *Forbidden Archaeology*, p. 717, quoting Zuckerman, 1973.
32. Quoted in Gore, 'The First Steps', p. 85. Prof. Wood has now moved to George Washington University, Washington.

6: Suppressed Facts Concerning Ancient Mankind

1. Oxnard, *The Order of Man*, p. 317.
2. A show hosted by Walter Cronkite in 1981; see Lewin, *Bones of Contention*, pp. 13–18.
3. White *et al.*, '*Australopithecus ramidus*, a New Species of Early Hominid from Aramis, Ethiopia', p. 306.
4. Gore, 'The First Steps', p. 80.
5. Cremo and Thompson, *Forbidden Archaeology*, pp. 733–4.
6. For example, see Taylor *et al.*, 'Clovis and Folsom Age Estimates: Stratigraphic Context and Radiocarbon Calibration', p. 517.
7. Lee, 'Sheguiandah in Retrospect', p. 28.
8. During the last Ice Age an ice sheet almost two miles thick covered the area. The last warm period when humans could have lived on the site was around 65,000 BC; prior to that another warm period occurred around 125,000 BC.
9. Sanford, 'Sheguiandah Reviewed', p. 7.
10. Ibid., p. 14.
11. Ibid.
12. Ibid.
13. Cremo and Thompson, *Forbidden Archaeology*, p. 353.
14. Ibid., p. 346.
15. Ibid., p. xxx.

16. White *et al.*, '*Australopithecus ramidus*, a New Species of Early Hominid from Aramis, Ethiopia' p. 306.

17. Gore, 'The First Steps', p. 96.

18. Semaw *et al.*, '2.5-million-year-old Stone Tools from Gona, Ethiopia', p. 333.

19. Charlesworth, 'Objects in the Red Crag of Suffolk', pp. 91–4.

20. Capellini, 'Les traces de l'homme pliocène en Toscane', pp. 47–54. For a rendering in English, see Cremo and Thompson, *Forbidden Archaeology*, p. 54.

21. Potts and Shipman, 'Cutmarks Made by Stone Tools on Bones from Olduvai Gorge, Tanzania', p. 577.

22. Capellini, 'Les traces de l'homme pliocène', pp. 47–8.

23. Ibid., p. 52.

24. Cremo and Thompson, *Forbidden Archaeology*, p. 69.

25. Ibid., pp. 70–71.

26. Ibid., pp. 67–8.

27. Gore, 'The First Europeans', pp. 104–5.

28. Ackerman, 'European Prehistory Gets Even Older', pp. 28–30.

29. Cremo and Thompson, *Forbidden Archaeology*, pp. 94, 96 and fig. 3.5.

30. Ibid., pp. 121–50 gives the story of the palaeo-anthropologist, J. Reid Moir, and the reactions for, and against, his discoveries.

31. Breuil, 'Sur la présence d'éolithes à la base de l'éocène parisien', p. 402. An English rendering in: Cremo and Thompson, *Forbidden Archaeology*, p. 158.

32. Breuil, 'Sur la présence d'éolithes'.

33. Cremo and Thompson, *Forbidden Archaeology*, p. 423.

34. Ibid., pp. 427–8.

35. Ibid., p. 428.

36. See the critique of the carbon 14 dating given in Cremo and Thompson, pp. 790–93. They point out that for an intrusive burial it was very odd. The bodies were buried without any coffin or shroud, unlikely for a burial in medieval times. Furthermore the bones of the man and the two children were spread over several square feet with the children's bones mixed up with each other. They conclude:

This constitutes strong evidence that the Castenedolo bones are not the result of recent intrusive burial. We note that the radiocarbon method was not used to date the bones of the man or children, and the significance of the dispersed position of these skeletons in the strata was ignored by most scientists writing about them.

37. Oakley, 'Relative Dating of the Fossil Hominids of Europe', pp. 40–42. See also, Cremo and Thompson, *Forbidden Archaeology*, pp. 432, 757–60, 762–4 and 790–93. They conclude (p. 793):

> In short, there is conflicting evidence about the age of the Castenedolo bones – a carbon 14 date and a nitrogen test . . . in favor of a recent age, an ambiguous uranium content test . . . and a fluorine content test . . . and stratigraphic observations . . . in favor of high antiquity. In almost all cases of anomalously old human bones, scientists choose to accept carbon 14 dates even when they radically contradict the stratigraphic evidence. But is it really fair that all weight should be given to the former and none to the latter? The stratigraphic evidence is unusually strong in favour of a Pliocene age for the Castenedolo bones, whereas . . . the carbon 14 dating is far from perfect.

38. Cremo and Thompson, *Forbidden Archaeology*, p. 429.
39. Patterson and Howells, 'Hominid Humeral Fragment from Early Pleistocene of Northwestern Kenya', p. 65; table 1 gives seven points of agreement with a modern human bone.
40. Oxnard, 'The Place of the Australopithecines in Human Evolution: Grounds for Doubt?', p. 394. See also Cremo and Thompson, *Forbidden Archaeology*, pp. 684–6.
41. Leakey, 'Skull 1470', p. 821. In his paper 'Evidence for an Advanced Plio-Pleistocene Hominid from East Rudolf, Kenya', p. 450, Leakey writes:

> When the femur is compared with a restricted sample of modern African bones, there are marked similarities in those morphological features that are widely considered characteristic of modern *H. sapiens*. The fragments of tibia and fibula also resemble *H. sapiens* . . .

42. Wood, 'Evidence on the Locomotor Pattern of *Homo* from Early Pleistocene of Kenya', p. 136.

43. Cremo and Thompson, *Forbidden Archaeology*, pp. 686–7.

44. Ibid., p. 750. See also Appendix 3 for a summary of the evidence of ancient artefacts.

7: *Where Did Our Civilization Come From?*

1. Mellaart, *Earliest Civilizations of the Near East*, p. 77.

2. Mellaart, *Çatal Hüyük: A Neolithic Town in Anatolia*, p. 211.

3. Cremo and Thompson, *Forbidden Archaeology*, p. 411.

4. Stringer and Gamble, *In Search of the Neanderthals*, p. 157 and n. 44.

5. Gore, 'The First Europeans', p. 110.

6. Stringer and Gamble, *In Search of the Neanderthals*, pp. 156–7.

7. Shreeve, *The Neandertal Enigma*, pp. 277–81.

8. Andel, 'Late Quaternary Sea-level Changes and Archaeology', p. 742.

9. Ibid., p. 736. The effective depth is thought to be up to 426 feet, taking into account the rise of land deprived of the weight of ice. Total loss could be up to 65 feet more. See p. 734.

10. Whitmore *et al.*, 'Elephant Teeth from the Atlantic Continental Shelf', p. 1477.

11. Ibid.

12. This *ice-free* passage would seem to indicate that a displacement of the poles has occurred since. For if this land was free of ice and yet a mile-high ice-cap reached as far south as Philadelphia, the North Pole must have been towards Baffin Island or Greenland; the South Pole would then have shifted towards Australia, thus leaving, perhaps, the area of Antarctica nearest to South America free of ice.

13. Shackleton *et al.*, 'Coastal Paleogeography of the Central and Western Mediterranean during the Last 125,000 Years and its Archaeological Implications', pp. 310–11.

14. Andel, 'Late Quaternary Sea-level Changes and Archaeology', p. 742.

15. Ibid., p. 737.

16. Plato, *Laws*, Book III, p. 167.

17. Dansgaard *et al.*, 'The Abrupt Termination of the Younger Dryas Climate Event', p. 532.

18. Alley *et al.*, 'Abrupt Increase in Greenland Snow Accumulation at the End of the Younger Dryas Event', p. 527. See also Fairbanks, 'Flip-flop End to Last Ice Age', p. 495.

19. Marshack, *The Roots of Civilisation*, p. 10.

20. Ibid., p. 11.

21. Ibid., p. 12.

22. Wilson, *From Atlantis to the Sphinx*, p. 215.

23. Andel and Runnels, 'The Earliest Farmers in Europe', pp. 481–500.

24. Andel and Shackleton, 'Late Paleolithic and Mesolithic Coastlines of Greece and the Aegean', p. 450.

25. Andel and Runnels, 'The Earliest Farmers in Europe', p. 498.

26. Plato, *Timaeus*, p. 41.

27. Broodbank and Strasser, 'Migrant Farmers and the Neolithic Colonization of Crete', p. 237.

28. Ibid., p. 241.

29. Ibid., p. 242.

8: The Story of Atlantis

1. Plato, *Timaeus*, pp. 41–3 (edited and paraphrased).

2. Ibid.; *Critias*, pp. 279–307.

3. Plutarch, 'Life of Solon' pp. 43–76. See also Plutarch, 'Isis and Osiris' in *Moralia*, V, p. 25.

4. Plato, *Timaeus*, p. 33.

5. Ibid., p. 29.

6. Many say that Crantor reported it also. But Proclus reports Crantor and it is clear that this report has been mistranslated. Crantor is simply repeating the assertions of Plato. See James, *The Sunken Kingdom: The Atlantis Mystery Solved*, p. 173.

7. Mellaart, *Çatal Hüyük: A Neolithic Town in Anatolia*, p. 22.

8. The range was 1628 to 1626 BC, derived from a study of tree rings (*Science News*, 125, 28 January 1984, p. 54). The argument in support of this date from tree rings and ice-core analysis has been strongly

criticized in a paper published in 1997. The authors point out that no direct connection has ever been demonstrated between volcanic eruptions and changes in tree rings or ice-core characteristics. See Buckland *et al.*, 'Bronze Age Myths?: Volcanic Activity and Human Response in the Mediterranean and North Atlantic Regions', pp. 581–7.

9. Luce, *The End of Atlantis*, pp. 35–7.

10. See James, *The Sunken Kingdom*, pp. 70–84.

11. Ibid., p. 81.

12. Ice-core samples from Greenland give a date cluster around 1650 BC. See the *Observer*, 1 May 1988, p. 29.

13. Plato, *Critias*, pp. 273–7.

14. Zangger, *The Flood from Heaven*.

15. James, *The Sunken Kingdom*, p. 191.

16. Ibid., p. 191, quoting Pindar, *Pythian*, IV, 289–90.

17. Ibid., p. 195.

18. Ibid., p. 215.

19. Ibid., p. 216.

20. Ibid., pp. 252–3.

21. Plato, *Critias*, p. 279.

22. Plato, *Timaeus*, p. 41.

23. Herodotus, *The Histories*, pp. 283–4.

24. Hapgood, *Maps of the Ancient Sea Kings*, pp. 62–6, 70–78, figs 18, 48, 49 and 52.

25. Plato, *Critias*, p. 283.

26. Ibid., p. 295.

27. Ibid.

28. With the dramatic exception of M. Hope, author of *Atlantis: Myth or Reality*, London, 1991, who jumps with both feet into the void.

29. Kukal, *Atlantis in the Light of Modern Research*, p. 68.

30. Hapgood, *Maps of the Ancient Sea Kings*, p. 68, fig. 47.

31. Admiralty Chart, no. 1950.

32. Admiralty Chart, no. 4407.

33. Admiralty Charts, nos 4104 and 4115.

34. Admiralty Chart, no. 4103; the site of the island is today called the Gorringe Ridge.
35. *Sunday Times*, 28 December 1997, section 1, p. 12.

9: *Are the Pyramids and Sphinx More Ancient than We Think?*

1. Bauval and Hancock, *Keeper of Genesis*, p. 248.
2. In Greek these pharaohs were known as Cheops, Cephren and Mycerinus.
3. Lehner *et al.*, 'The ARCE Sphinx Project: A Preliminary Report', p. 17.
4. Ibid., p. 18.
5. On the authority of Dr Zahi Hawass in 1992 see Schoch, 'Redating the Great Sphinx of Giza', p. 69, n. 14. Dr Hawass wrote, 'It seems that the Sphinx underwent restoration during the Old Kingdom because the analysis of samples found on the right rear leg proved to be of Old Kingdom date.' This calls into question the conventional dating of the Sphinx at *circa* 2500 BC since the Old Kingdom finished around 350 years later. This is not time enough for the depth of erosion seen on the core body of the Sphinx.
6. Hancock, *Fingerprints of the Gods*, p. 348.
7. Budge, *The Gods of the Egyptians*, II, p. 361.
8. Breasted, *Ancient Records of Egypt*, II, p. 324, note e.
9. James, *A Short History of Ancient Egypt*, p. 49. (My italics.)
10. *The New Encyclopaedia Britannica: Micropaedia*, 15th edition, 1995, XI, p. 92.
11. Hassan, *The Sphinx: Its History in the Light of Recent Excavations*, p. 79.
12. Ibid., p. 91.
13. West, *Serpent in the Sky*, pp. 186–7, 229.
14. Prof. Robert Schoch teaches at Boston University's College of Basic Studies. He has degrees in geology and anthropology and a PhD in geology and geophysics from Yale. He has authored many academic papers and books on palaeontology and the principles of geological stratigraphy.

15. Lehner *et al.*, 'The ARCE Sphinx Project', p. 14.

16. Prof. Schoch took as an example the 4th Dynasty tomb of Debehen on the Giza plateau.

17. Schoch, 'Redating the Great Sphinx of Giza', p. 54. This paper is a revised version of his original report entitled *How Old is the Sphinx?* published by Boston University, College of General Studies for presentation at the annual convention of the American Association for the Advancement of Science, Chicago, 7 February 1992.

18. Hancock, *Fingerprints of the Gods*, p. 421, quoting Prof. Schoch at the Annual Meeting of the American Association for the Advancement of Science, 1992.

19. Ibid., quoting Prof. Schoch in NBC-TV film *Mystery of the Sphinx*, 1993.

20. Schoch, 'Redating the Great Sphinx of Giza', p. 54.

21. Wendorf *et al.*, 'Late Pleistocene and Recent Climatic Changes in the Egyptian Sahara', pp. 221–6 and 232–3; also McHugh *et al.*, 'Neolithic Adaptation and the Holocene Functioning of Tertiary Palaeodrainages in Southern Egypt and Northern Sudan', p. 326.

22. Hoffman, *Egypt before the Pharaohs: The Prehistoric Foundations of Egyptian Civilization*, p. 239. Hoffman suggests that, given the discoveries of archaeologists working in the desert, 'It seems as if the food-producing revolution occurred in the [desert regions] many centuries, if not a full millennium before it penetrated the fertile Nile bottomlands.'

23. Schoch, 'Redating the Great Sphinx of Giza', p. 58.

24. West, *Serpent in the Sky*, p. 229.

25. Ibid.

26. Hancock, *Fingerprints of the Gods*, p. 422.

27. Ibid.

28. Ibid.

29. There have been suggestions made that the use of these large blocks is proof of a very early, perhaps pre-dynastic date, for the Sphinx temple. While the early date may be correct it cannot be established through any argument based on this monumental masonry. The use of such large blocks is attested during the 4th Dynasty; the mortuary

temple of Menkaure includes some blocks of this size. See Edwards, *The Pyramids of Egypt*, p. 254.

30. Hoffman, *Egypt before the Pharaohs*, pp. 200–14.

31. Ibid., p. 207.

32. Ibid., pp. 203–4.

33. Mortensen, 'Four Jars from the Maadi Culture Found in Giza', p. 147.

34. Hoffman, *Egypt before the Pharaohs*, p. 201.

35. Mazar, *Archaeology of the Land of the Bible, 10,000–586 B.C.E.*, p. 50.

36. Neugebauer and Parker, *Egyptian Astronomical Texts*, I, pp. 24–5.

37. Quirke, *Ancient Egyptian Religion*, p. 57.

38. Bauval and Gilbert, *The Orion Mystery*, p. 122.

39. Ibid., p. 127.

40. See Hancock, *Fingerprints of the Gods*, p. 456 (where he opts instead for 10,450 BC); Bauval and Hancock, *Keeper of Genesis*, pp. 74–8 and 253–4.

10: *The Mysteries of Ancient Egypt*

1. Dr Mark Lehner, 'Giza: A Contextual Approach to the Pyramids', pp. 140–45, discusses the possibility of solar cycles being a determinant for the layout of the Giza structures. Further, in his 'Some Observations on the Layout of the Khufu and Khafre Pyramids', he theorizes about the layout, levelling, orientation and alignment of the two pyramids.

   Dr Jaromir Malek, 'Orion and the Giza Pyramids', p. 109, writes, 'I have little doubt that there was a definable positional relationship between the Giza pyramids . . .' A long-running discussion continued on this subject through the pages of *Discussions in Egyptology*. For example, in vol. 31 (1995), p. 35, R. J. Cook writes, 'no arguments have yet been advanced which would show that . . . [he or other writers] are wrong in concluding that the Giza group was laid out to an overall site plan. However, any description of this plan must explain why this group was arranged in its particular configuration . . .'

2. Lehner, 'Giza: A Contextual Approach to the Pyramids', pp. 143–5. For a recent summary of all his thoughts on the surveying, alignment

and building of the Giza pyramids, see his *Complete Pyramids*, pp. 106, 129–30 and 212–14.

3. Lehner, 'Giza: A Contextual Approach to the Pyramids', p. 141. Lehner's article reproduces photographs of the sunsets at the solstice and equinoxes. See pp. 140–41.

4. Edwards, *The Pyramids of Egypt*, p. 286.

5. Pinch, *Magic in Ancient Egypt*, p. 51.

6. Budge, *The Book of the Dead*, p. 233.

7. Quirke, *Ancient Egyptian Religion*, p. 159.

8. Ibid.

9. Pinch, *Magic in Ancient Egypt*, pp. 51–3.

10. Gardner, 'The House of Life', p. 158.

11. Ibid., p. 175.

12. Pinch, *Magic in Ancient Egypt*, p. 63.

13. Gardner, 'The House of Life', p. 173.

14. See discussion in Quirke, *Ancient Egyptian Religion*, pp. 17 and 38–9.

15. That this production of Hermetic books was under way by the second century BC is revealed by a manuscript of that date found in a temple library at Memphis. It is a treatise on astronomy with a note at the beginning explaining, 'Within, concerns of Hermes'. Within the same text is a circle containing the zodiacal signs with the note, 'Oracles of Hermes'. See Thompson, *Memphis under the Ptolemies*, pp. 252–3.

16. Kingsley, 'Poimandres: The Etymology of the Name and the Origins of the Hermetica', p. 7.

17. Copenhaver, *Hermetica*, I, 'Discourse of Hermes Trismegistus: Poimandres', p. 1.

18. Ibid.

19. Ibid., p. 2.

20. Ibid.

21. Ibid., p. 6.

22. Ibid.

23. Klossowski de Rola, *Alchemy: The Secret Art*, p. 12. See also *The Secret Book of Artephius*, Edmonds (WA), 1984.

11 : The Mysterious Art of Alchemy

1. For the story of the excavations, see Zuntz, *Persephone*, pp. 288–92.

2. Kingsley, 'From Pythagoras to the *Turba Philosophorum*: Egypt and Pythagorean Tradition', p. 3. See also Kingsley, *Ancient Philosophy, Mystery and Magic*, pp. 256–61 and 308–13; Zuntz, *Persephone*, pp. 370–76, who points out specific parallels with the Egyptian *Book of the Dead*, and Cole, 'New Evidence for the Mysteries of Dionysos', pp. 224–37.

3. Cole, 'New Evidence for the Mysteries of Dionysos', pp. 233–4.

4. Shipley, *A History of Samos, 800–188 BC*, pp. 43, 56 and 73.

5. Rather than the date of 569 normally given: See Gorman, *Pythagoras: A Life*, p. 49.

6. Ibid., p. 58.

7. Ibid., p. 83.

8. Herodotus, *The Histories*, p. 178.

9. Kingsley, *Ancient Philosophy, Mystery and Magic*, pp. 325–6.

10. Lindsay, *The Origins of Alchemy in Graeco-Roman Egypt*, p. 100.

11. Fraser, *Ptolemaic Alexandria*, I, p. 440.

12. Kingsley, *Ancient Philosophy, Mystery and Magic*, pp. 339–41.

13. Fowden, *The Egyptian Hermes*, p. 167.

14. Taylor, *The Alchemists*, p. 25.

15. Lindsay, *The Origins of Alchemy*, p. 335.

16. Taylor, *The Alchemists*, p. 25.

17. Chadwick, *Priscillian of Avila*, p. 21.

18. Fowden, *The Egyptian Hermes*, p. 166, n. 35.

19. Lindsay, *The Origins of Alchemy*, p. 336.

20. Ibid.

21. Porphyry, *Life of Pythagoras*, xii. (Guthrie, *The Pythagorean Sourcebook and Library*, p. 125.)

22. Flamel, *His Exposition of the Hieroglyphical Figures*, p. 13.

23. Boyle, *The Sceptical Chymist*, p. 166.

24. Ibid.

25. Principe, 'Robert Boyle's Alchemical Secrecy: Codes, Ciphers and

Concealments'. See also Hunter, 'Alchemy, Magic and Moralism in the Thought of Robert Boyle'.

26. *Boyle Papers*, Royal Society, VII, f. 138. See the discussion in Baigent, 'Freemasonry, Hermetic Thought and the Royal Society of London', p. 8.
27. Manuel, *A Portrait of Isaac Newton*, p. 177.
28. Ibid., p. 185.
29. Ibid., p. 170.
30. Dobbs, *The Foundations of Newton's Alchemy*, pp. 16–17.
31. Ibid., p. 320.
32. *The Times*, 11 October 1993, p. 10.
33. *The Times*, 24 December 1993, p. 9.
34. *The Times*, 12 December 1994, p. 16.
35. Barnaby, 'Is There a Pure-fusion Bomb for Sale?', p. 79. See also Barnaby, 'The Red Mercury Saga'.
36. Barnaby, 'Is There a Pure-fusion Bomb for Sale?', p. 79. See also Badolato and Andrade, 'Red Mercury: Hoax or the Ultimate Terrorist Weapon?', for further information, especially regarding alleged links with South Africa. This was published in *Counterterrorism Magazine* and is contained in a compilation *Best of Counterterrorism & Security for: 1995 and 1996* at the website: http://www.worldonline.net/securitynet/CTS/pages/mercury.html.
37. Barnaby, 'Is There a Pure-fusion Bomb for Sale?', p. 79.
38. *The Secret Book of Artephius*, p. 6.
39. With the use of prodigious amounts of energy, modern science has discovered that it can indeed turn base metal into gold. Atomic nucleii of elements can be fused together to create other elements. For example, the nucleus of a copper atom (atomic weight 29) can be fused with the nucleus of a tin atom (atomic weight 50) to produce an atom with a nucleus of atomic weight 79: this is gold.
40. Fowden, *The Egyptian Hermes*, p. 123.
41. Ibid., p. 122.
42. Lindsay, *The Origins of Alchemy*, p. 257.

43. Ibid.
44. Ashmole, *Theatrum Chemicum Britannicum*, p. vi.

12: Reincarnation

1. Iverson, *In Search of the Dead*, p. 162.
2. Ibid., p. 165, quoting the Dalai Lama, *My Land, My People*.
3. Ibid.
4. Ibid., p. 166.
5. *Rig Veda*, 10.16.5.
6. *Bhagavad Gita*, trans. J. Mascaró, London, 1962, 2:22.
7. Copenhaver, *Hermetica*, IV: 'A Discourse of Hermes to Tat: The Mixing Bowl of the Monad', p. 17.
8. Ibid., X: 'Discourse of Hermes Trismegistus: The Key', p. 34.
9. Budge, *The Book of the Dead*, p. 598.
10. Carpenter, *Past Lives*, pp. 91, 92 and 93. The story of Philip Corrigan is given on pp. 88–103.
11. Ibid., p. 102.
12. Prof. Kastenbaum writes:

    Stevenson has been exceptional in the systematic way he conducts his studies and the detail in which they are reported. Put simply, those who have not read Stevenson's studies are in no position to have a credible opinion on the evidential basis for reincarnation.

    See Kastenbaum, *Is There Life After Death?*, p. 201.
13. Stevenson, *The Evidence for Survival from Claimed Memories of Former Incarnations*, pp. 15–16.
14. Stevenson, *Twenty Cases Suggestive of Reincarnation*, p. 2.
15. Ibid., pp. 274–320.
16. Ibid., pp. 286–98. On this tabulation are the forty-seven statements made prior to the visit to Khriby plus ten made during the first journey there. Imad made three errors in the forty-seven and three errors in the ten (see p. 285).
17. Ibid., pp. 280–82.
18. Ibid., p. 301.

19. Iverson, *In Search of the Dead*, p. xi.

20. Cranston and Williams, *Reincarnation*, pp. 12–13.

21. Fiore, *You Have Been Here Before*, pp. 4–5.

22. Iverson, *More Lives Than One?*, p. 136.

23. Ibid., p. 145.

24. Stevenson, *Twenty Cases Suggestive of Reincarnation*, pp. 2–3.

25. Fiore, *You Have Been Here Before*, p. 194.

26. Ibid., p. 197.

27. Ibid., p. 198.

28. Ibid., p. 223.

29. Personal communication, 24 May 1997.

Bibliography

Ackerman, S., 'European Prehistory Gets Even Older', *Science*, 246, 6 October 1989, pp. 28–30.

Allan, D. S., and Delair, J. B., *When the Earth Nearly Died*, Bath, 1995.

Alley, R. B., Meese, D. A., Shuman, C. A., Gow, A. J., Taylor, K. C., Grootes, P. M., White, J. W. C., Ram, M., Waddington, E. D., Mayewski, P. A., and Zielinski, G. A., 'Abrupt Increase in Greenland Snow Accumulation at the End of the Younger Dryas Event', *Nature*, 362, 8 April 1993, pp. 527–9.

Andel, T. H. van, 'Late Quaternary Sea-level Changes and Archaeology', *Antiquity*, 63, 1989, pp. 733–45.

Andel, T. H. van, and Runnels, C. N., 'The Earliest Farmers in Europe', *Antiquity*, 69, 1995, pp. 481–500.

Andel, T. H. van, and Shackleton, J. C., 'Late Paleolithic and Mesolithic Coastlines of Greece and the Aegean', *Journal of Field Archaeology*, 9, 1982, pp. 445–54.

Ashmole, E., *Theatrum Chemicum Britannicum*, London, 1652.

Baigent, M., *From the Omens of Babylon: Astrology and Ancient Mesopotamia*, London, 1994.

Baigent, M., 'Freemasonry, Hermetic Thought and the Royal Society of London', *Ars Quatuor Coronatorum*, 109, 1996, pp. 1–13.

Barnaby, F., 'Is There a Pure-fusion Bomb for Sale?', *International Defence Review*, 1 June 1994, p. 79.

Barnaby, F., 'The Red Mercury Saga', *Medicine and War*, 10, 1994, pp. 286–9.

Bauval, R., and Gilbert, A., *The Orion Mystery*, London, 1994.

Bauval, R., and Hancock, G., *Keeper of Genesis*, London, 1996.

Becker, G. F., 'Antiquities from under Tuolumne Table Mountain in California', *Bulletin of the Geological Society of America*, 2, 1891, pp. 189–200.

Behe, M. J., *Darwin's Black Box*, New York, 1996.

Belitzky, S., Goren-Inbar, N., and Werker, E., 'A Middle Pleistocene Wooden Plank with Man-Made Polish', *Journal of Human Evolution*, 20, 1991, pp. 349–53.

Bille, M. A., *Rumors of Existence*, Surrey (BC), 1995.

Boyle, R., *The Sceptical Chymist*, London, 1911.

Breasted, J. H., *Ancient Records of Egypt*, 5 vols, Chicago, 1906–7.

Breuil, H., 'Sur la présence d'éolithes à la base de l'éocène parisien', *L'Anthropologie*, 21, 1910, pp. 385–408.

Breuil, H., *Quatre cents siècles d'art pariétal*, Montignac, 1952.

Brewster, D., 'Queries and Statements Concerning a Nail Found Embedded in a Block of Sandstone Obtained from Kingoodie (Mylnfield) Quarry, North Britain', *Report of the Fourteenth Meeting of the British Association for the Advancement of Science*, London, 1845, Part II: 'Notices and Abstracts of Communications', p. 51.

Broodbank, C., and Strasser, T. F., 'Migrant Farmers and the Neolithic Colonization of Crete', *Antiquity*, 65, 1991, pp. 233–45.

Brown, F., Harris, J., Leakey, R., and Walker, A., 'Early *Homo Erectus* Skeleton from West Lake Turkana, Kenya', *Nature*, 316, 29 August 1985, pp. 788–92.

Buckland, P. C., Dugmore, A. J., and Edwards, K. J., 'Bronze Age Myths?: Volcanic Activity and Human Response in the Mediterranean and North Atlantic Regions', *Antiquity*, 71, 1997, pp. 581–93.

Budge, E. A. W., *The Gods of the Egyptians*, 2 vols, London, 1904.

Budge, E. A. W., *The Book of the Dead*, London, 1960.

Bunney, S., 'First Migrants Will Travel Back in Time', *New Scientist*, 1565, 18 June 1987, p. 36.

Burroughs, W. G., 'Human-like Footprints, 250 Million Years Old', *Berea Alumnus*, November 1938, pp. 46–7.

Campion, N., *The Great Year*, London, 1994.

Capellini, M. J., 'Les traces de l'homme pliocène en Toscane', *Congrès international d'anthropologie et d'archéologie préhistoriques: Compte-rendu de la huitième session à Budapest, 1876*, Budapest, 1877, pp. 46–63.

Carpenter, S., *Past Lives*, London, 1995.

Chadwick, H., *Priscillian of Avila*, Oxford, 1976.

Chadwick, R., 'The So-called "Orion Mystery"', *KMT: A Modern Journal of Ancient Egypt*, VII, 3, 1996, pp. 74–83.

Charlesworth, E., 'Objects in the Red Crag of Suffolk', *Journal of the Anthropological Institute of Great Britain and Ireland*, II, 1872, pp. 91–4.

Cole, S. G., 'New Evidence for the Mysteries of Dionysos', *Greek, Roman and Byzantine Studies*, 21, 1980, pp. 223–38.

Conroy, G. C., 'Closing the Hominid Gap', *Nature*, 360, 26 November 1992, pp. 393–4.

Cook, R. J., 'The Elaboration of the Giza Site-plan', *Discussions in Egyptology*, 31, 1995, pp. 35–45.

Copenhaver, B. P., *Hermetica*, Cambridge, 1992.

Corliss, W. R., *Ancient Man: A Handbook of Puzzling Artifacts*, Glen Arm, 1980.

Corliss, W. R., *Unknown Earth: A Handbook of Geological Enigmas*, Glen Arm, 1980.

Corliss, W. R., *Incredible Life: A Handbook of Biological Mysteries*, Glen Arm, 1981.

Corliss, W. R., *Science Frontiers: Some Anomalies and Curiosities of Nature*, Glen Arm, 1994.

Coveney, P., and Highfield, R., *The Arrow of Time*, London, 1991.

Cranston, S., and Williams, C., *Reincarnation: A New Horizon in Science, Religion and Society*, Pasadena, 1993.

Cremo, M. A., and Thompson, R. L., *Forbidden Archaeology*, San Diego, 1993.

Dansgaard, W., White, J. W. C., and Johnsen, S. J., 'The Abrupt Termination of the Younger Dryas Climate Event', *Nature*, 339, 15 June 1989, pp. 532–3.

Darwin, C., *The Life and Letters of Charles Darwin*, ed. F. Darwin, 3 vols, London, 1887.

Darwin, C., *The Origin of Species by Means of Natural Selection*, London, 1985.

Dawkins, R., *The Selfish Gene*, Oxford, 1989.

Dawson, A. G., *Ice Age Earth*, London, 1992.

Dennell, R. W., Rendell, H., and Hailwood, E., 'Early Tool-making in Asia: Two-million-year-old Artefacts in Pakistan', *Antiquity*, 62, 1988, pp. 98–106.

Dennell, R. W., and Roebroeks, W., 'The Earliest Colonization of Europe: The Short Chronology Revisited', *Antiquity*, 70, 1996, pp. 535–42.

Denton, M., *Evolution: A Theory in Crisis*, Bethesda (MD), 1986.

Dobbs, B. J. T., *The Foundations of Newton's Alchemy*, Cambridge, 1975.

Edwards, I. E. S., *The Pyramids of Egypt*, London, 1993.

Eldredge, N., *Reinventing Darwin: The Great Evolutionary Debate*, London, 1996.

Ellis, R., *Monsters of the Sea*, New York, 1996.

Emery, W. B., *Archaic Egypt*, London, 1991.

Erwin, D., Valentine, J., and Jablonski, D., 'The Origin of Animal Body Plans', *American Scientist*, 85 (2), March–April 1997, pp. 126–37.

Fairbanks, R. G., 'Flip-flop End to Last Ice Age', *Nature*, 362, 8 April 1993, p. 495.

Faulkner, R. O., 'The King and the Star-religion in the Pyramid Texts', *Journal of Near Eastern Studies*, XXV, 1966, pp. 153–61.

Faulkner, R. O., *The Ancient Egyptian Pyramid Texts*, Warminster, n.d. (1969).

Faulkner, R. O., *The Ancient Egyptian Coffin Texts*, 3 vols, Warminster, 1994–6.

Fiore, E., *You Have Been Here Before*, London, 1980.

Flamel, N., *His Exposition of the Hieroglyphical Figures*, ed. L. Dixon, New York, 1994.

Flem-Arth, R., and R., *When the Sky Fell: In Search of Atlantis*, London, 1996.

Forbes, R. J., *Studies in Ancient Technology*, Leiden, 1955.

Forbes, R. J., *The Conquest of Nature*, Harmondsworth, 1971.

Forsyth, P. Y., *Atlantis: The Making of Myth*, Montreal, 1980.

Fowden, G., *The Egyptian Hermes*, Princeton, 1993.

Fraser, P. M., *Ptolemaic Alexandria*, 3 vols, Oxford, 1972.

Galanopoulos, A. G., and Bacon, E., *Atlantis: The Truth behind the Legend*, London, 1970.

Gardner, A. H., 'The House of Life', *The Journal of Egyptian Archaeology*, 24, 1938, pp. 157–79.

Gleick, J., *Chaos: Making a New Science*, London, 1995.

Gore, R., 'The First Steps', *National Geographic*, 191, February 1997, pp. 72–97.

Gore, R., 'Expanding Worlds', *National Geographic*, 191, May 1997, pp. 84–109.

Gore, R., 'The First Europeans', *National Geographic*, 192, July 1997, pp. 96–113.

Gorman, P., *Pythagoras: A Life*, London, 1979.

Gould, S. J., *The Panda's Thumb*, London, 1990.

Grey, M., *Return from Death: An Exploration of the Near-death Experience*, London, 1985.

Guthrie, K. S., *The Pythagorean Sourcebook and Library*, Grand Rapids, MI, 1994.

Hancock, G., *Fingerprints of the Gods*, London, 1995.

Hapgood, C. H., *Maps of the Ancient Sea Kings*, rev. ed., London, 1979.

Hassan, S., *The Sphinx: Its History in the Light of Recent Excavations*, Cairo, 1949.

Heidel, A., *The Gilgamesh Epic and Old Testament Parallels*, Chicago, 1963.

Herodotus, *The Histories*, trans. A. de Sélincourt, Harmondsworth, 1981.

Heuvelmans, B., *On the Track of Unknown Animals*, trans. Richard Garnett, London, 1958.

Heuvelmans, B., *In the Wake of the Sea-serpents*, trans. Richard Garnett, London, 1968.

Hoffman, M. A., *Egypt before the Pharaohs: The Prehistoric Foundations of Egyptian Civilization*, London, 1979.

Holmes, W. H., 'Review of the Evidence Relating to Auriferous Gravel Man in California', *Annual Report of the Board of Regents of the Smithsonian Institution for the Year Ending June 30, 1899*, Washington, 1901, Part I, pp. 419–72.

Holmyard, E. J., *Alchemy*, Harmondsworth, 1957.

Hunter, M., 'Alchemy, Magic and Moralism in the Thought of Robert Boyle', *British Journal for the History of Science*, 23, 1990, pp. 387–410.

Hürzeler, J., 'The Significance of Oreopithecus in the Genealogy of Man', *Triangle*, IV, 5 April 1960, pp. 164–74.

Iverson, J., *More Lives Than One?*, London, 1976.

Iverson, J., *In Search of the Dead*, London, 1994.

Jacobs, L., *Quest for the African Dinosaurs: Ancient Roots of the Modern World*, New York, 1993.

James, P., *The Sunken Kingdom: The Atlantis Mystery Solved*, London, 1996.

James, T. G. H., *A Short History of Ancient Egypt*, London, 1995.

Johanson, D. C., and Edey, M. A., *Lucy: The Beginnings of Humankind*, London, 1990.

Johanson, D. C., and Shreeve, J., *Lucy's Child: The Discovery of a Human Ancestor*, London, 1990.

Jung, C. G., *Civilization in Transition*, trans. R. F. C. Hull, 2nd ed., London, 1974.

Jung, C. G., *Psychology and Alchemy*, trans. R. F. C. Hull, 2nd ed., London, 1974.

Kaharl, V. A., *Water Baby: The Story of Alvin*, Oxford, 1990.

Kastenbaum, R., *Is There Life After Death?*, London, 1995.

Kemp, B. J., *Ancient Egypt: Anatomy of a Civilization*, London, 1995.

Kingdon, J., *Island Africa*, London, 1990.

Kingsley, P., 'Poimandres: The Etymology of the Name and the Origins of the Hermetica', *Journal of the Warburg and Courtauld Institutes*, 56, 1993, pp. 1–24.

Kingsley, P., 'From Pythagoras to the *Turba Philosophorum*: Egypt and Pythagorean Tradition', *Journal of the Warburg and Courtauld Institutes*, 57, 1994, pp. 1–13.

Kingsley, P., *Ancient Philosophy, Mystery and Magic*, Oxford, 1995.

Klossowski de Rola, S., *Alchemy: The Secret Art*, London, 1991.

Kukal, Z., *Atlantis in the Light of Modern Research*, in *Earth-Science Reviews*, 21, 1984.

La Lumiere, L. P., 'Evolution of Human Bipedalism: A Hypothesis about

Where It Happened', *Philosophical Transactions of the Royal Society of London*, B 292, 1981, pp. 103–7.

Lawson, D. A., 'Pterosaur from the Latest Cretaceous of West Texas: Discovery of the Largest Flying Creature', *Science*, 187, 14 March 1975, pp. 947–8.

Leakey, M., 'Footprints in the Ashes of Time', *National Geographic*, 155, April 1979, pp. 446–57.

Leakey, M., 'Tracks and Tools', *Philosophical Transactions of the Royal Society of London*, B 292, 1981, pp. 95–102.

Leakey, M., and Walker, A., 'Early Hominid Fossils from Africa', *Scientific American*, June 1997, pp. 60–65.

Leakey, R., 'Evidence for an Advanced Plio-Pleistocene Hominid from East Rudolf, Kenya', *Nature*, 242, 13 April 1973, pp. 447–50.

Leakey, R., 'Skull 1470', *National Geographic*, 143, June 1973, pp. 818–29.

Leakey, R., and Lewin, R., *Origins Reconsidered*, London, 1993.

Leakey, R., and Lewin, R., *The Sixth Extinction*, London, 1996.

LeBlond, P. H., and Bousfield, E. L., *Cadborosaurus: Survivor from the Deep*, Victoria (BC), 1995.

LeBlond, P. H., and Sibert, J., *Observations of Large Unidentified Marine Animals in British Columbia and Adjacent Waters*, Institute of Oceanography, University of British Columbia, Manuscript Report no. 28, Vancouver, 1973.

Lee, T. E., 'Sheguiandah in Retrospect', *Anthropological Journal of Canada*, 10, 1, 1972, pp. 28–30.

Lehner, M., 'Some Observations on the Layout of the Khufu and Khafre Pyramids', *Journal of the American Research Center in Egypt*, XX, 1983, pp. 7–25.

Lehner, M., 'The Development of the Giza Necropolis: The Khufu Project', *Mitteilungen des Deutschen Archäologischen Instituts: Abteilung Kairo*, 41, 1985, pp. 109–43.

Lehner, M., 'Giza: A Contextual Approach to the Pyramids', *Archiv für Orientforschung*, 32, 1985, pp. 136–58.

Lehner, M., *The Complete Pyramids*, London, 1997.

Lehner, M., Allen, J. P., and Gauri, K. L., 'The ARCE Sphinx Project:

A Preliminary Report', *Newsletter of the American Research Centre in Egypt*, 112, 1980, pp. 3–33.

Leith, B., *The Descent of Darwin*, London, 1982.

Levinton, J. S., 'The Big Bang of Animal Evolution', *Scientific American*, 267, November 1992, pp. 52–9.

Lewin, R., *Bones of Contention*, London, 1991.

Ley, W., *The Lungfish and the Unicorn*, London, 1948.

Lindsay, J., *The Origins of Alchemy in Graeco-Roman Egypt*, London, 1970.

Linklater, E., *The Voyage of the Challenger*, London, 1974.

Lister, A. M., 'Mammoths in Miniature', *Nature*, 362, 25 March 1993, pp. 288–9.

Lorblanchet, M., and Sieveking, A., 'The Monsters of Pergouset', *Cambridge Archaeological Journal*, 7 April 1997, pp. 37–56.

Luce, J. V., *The End of Atlantis*, St Albans, 1975.

McHugh, W. P., Schaber, G. G., Breed, C. S., and McCauley, J. F., 'Neolithic Adaptation and the Holocene Functioning of Tertiary Palaeodrainages in Southern Egypt and Northern Sudan', *Antiquity*, 63, 1989, pp. 320–36.

Mackal, R. P., *Searching for Hidden Animals*, London, 1983.

Mackal, R. P., *A Living Dinosaur? In Search of Mokele-Mbembe*, Leiden, 1987.

Malek, J., 'Orion and the Giza Pyramids', *Discussions in Egyptology*, 30, 1994, pp. 101–14.

Malek, J., 'Graham Hancock, Fingerprints of the Gods: A Quest for the Beginning and the End', *Discussions in Egyptology*, 34, 1996, pp. 135–42.

Manuel, F. E., *A Portrait of Isaac Newton*, Cambridge (MA), 1968.

Marshack, A., *The Roots of Civilisation*, London, 1972.

Mazar, A., *Archaeology of the Land of the Bible, 10,000–586 B.C.E.*, Cambridge, 1993.

Mebane, A., *Darwin's Creation-Myth*, Venice (FL), 1995.

Mellaart, J., *Çatal Hüyük: A Neolithic Town in Anatolia*, London, 1967.

Mellaart, J., *Earliest Civilizations of the Near East*, London, 1978.

Melland, F. H., *In Witch-bound Africa*, London, 1923.

Milton, R., *The Facts of Life*, London, 1993.

More, V., 'New Skull Turns Up in Northeast Africa', *Science*, 271, 5 January 1996, p. 32.

Morgan, E., *The Scars of Evolution*, London, 1990.

Mortensen, B., 'Four Jars from the Maadi Culture Found in Giza', *Mitteilungen des Deutschen Archäologischen Instituts: Abteilung Kairo*, 41, 1985, pp. 145–7.

Neugebauer, O., and Parker, R. A., *Egyptian Astronomical Texts*, 3 vols, Providence (RI), 1960–69.

Norman, J. R., *A History of Fishes*, 3rd ed., London, 1975.

Oakley, K. P., 'Relative Dating of the Fossil Hominids of Europe', *Bulletin of the British Museum (Natural History), Geology Series*, 34 (1), 1980, pp. 1–63.

O'Hanlon, R., *Congo Journey*, London, 1997.

Oxnard, C. E., 'The Place of the Australopithecines in Human Evolution: Grounds for Doubt?', *Nature*, 258, 4 December 1975, pp. 389–95.

Oxnard, C. E., *The Order of Man*, New Haven, 1984.

Oxnard, C. E., *Humans, Apes and Chinese Fossils*, Hong Kong, 1985.

Patterson, B., and Howells, W. W., 'Hominid Humeral Fragment from Early Pleistocene of Northwestern Kenya', *Science*, 156, 7 April 1967, pp. 64–6.

Pinch, G., *Magic in Ancient Egypt*, London, 1994.

Plato, *Laws*, 2 vols, trans. R. G. Bury, London, 1926.

Plato, *The Republic*, trans. P. Shorey, 2 vols, London and Cambridge (MA), 1980.

Plato, *Critias*, trans. R. G. Bury, London and Cambridge (MA), 1981.

Plato, *Timaeus*, trans. R. G. Bury, London and Cambridge (MA), 1981.

Plutarch, 'Life of Solon' in *The Rise and Fall of Athens*, trans. I. Scott-Kilvert, Harmondsworth, 1980.

Plutarch, *Lives*, 11 vols, trans. B. Perrin, London and Cambridge (MA), 1985.

Plutarch, 'Isis and Osiris', *Moralia*, vol. V, trans. F. C. Babbitt, Cambridge (MA), 1993.

Porphyry, *Life of Pythagoras*, in Guthrie, K. S. (comp. and trans.), *The Pythagorean Sourcebook and Library*, Grand Rapids, 1988.

Potts, R. and Shipman, P., 'Cutmarks Made by Stone Tools on Bones from Olduvai Gorge, Tanzania', *Nature*, 291, 18 June 1981, pp. 577–80.

Price, G. W., *Extra-special Correspondent*, London, 1957.

Principe, L. M., 'Robert Boyle's Alchemical Secrecy: Codes, Ciphers and Concealments', *Ambix*, 39, 1992, pp. 63–74.

Proyart, Abbé, *Histoire de Loango, Kakongo, et autres royaumes d'Afrique*, Paris, 1776.

Quatrepages de Breau, A. de, *Histoire générale des races humaines*, 2 vols, Paris, 1887.

Quirke, S., *Ancient Egyptian Religion*, London, 1992.

Renfrew, C., *Archaeology and Language*, London, 1989.

Reymond, E. A. E., *The Mythical Origin of the Egyptian Temple*, Manchester, 1969.

Rightmire, G. P., *The Evolution of Homo Erectus*, Cambridge, 1993.

Rogo, D. S., *Life after Death: The Case for Survival of Bodily Death*, Wellingborough, 1986.

Ruelle, D., *Chance and Chaos*, Harmondsworth, 1993.

Sanford, J. T., 'Sheguiandah Reviewed', *Anthropological Journal of Canada*, 9 (1), 1971, pp. 2–15.

Schindel, D. E., 'The Gaps in the Fossil Record', *Nature*, 297, 27 May 1982, pp. 282–4.

Schoch, R. M., *How Old is the Sphinx?*, Boston, 1992.

Schoch, R. M., 'Redating the Great Sphinx of Giza', *KMT: A Modern Journal of Ancient Egypt*, III (2), 1992, pp. 52–9 and 66–70.

Schopf, T. J. M., ed., *Models in Paleobiology*, San Francisco, 1972.

The Secret Book of Artephius, reprinted by The Alchemical Press, Edmonds (WA), 1984.

Semaw, S., Renne, P., Harris, J. W. K., Feibel, C. S., Bernor, R. L., Fesseha, N., and Mowbray, K., '2.5-million-year-old Stone Tools from Gona, Ethiopia', *Nature*, 385, 23 January 1997, pp. 333–6.

Shackleton, J. C., Andel, T. H. van, and Runnels, C. N., 'Coastal Paleogeography of the Central and Western Mediterranean during the Last 125,000 Years and its Archaeological Implications', *Journal of Field Archaeology*, 11, 1984, pp. 307–14.

Shipley, G., *A History of Samos, 800–188 BC*, Oxford, 1987.

Shipman, P., 'Human Ancestor's Early Steps out of Africa', *New Scientist*, 1806, 1 February 1992, p. 24.

Shreeve, J., *The Neandertal Enigma*, London, 1995.

Shuker, K., *The Lost Ark*, London, 1993.

Shuker, K., *In Search of Prehistoric Survivors: Do Giant 'Extinct' Creatures Still Exist?*, London, 1995.

Skertchly, S. B. J., 'On the Occurrence of Stone Mortars in the Ancient (Pliocene?) River Gravels of Butte County, California', *The Journal of the Anthropological Institute of Great Britain and Ireland*, XVII, 1888, pp. 332–7.

Solecki, R. S., *Shanidar: The Humanity of Neanderthal Man*, London, 1972.

Soule, G., *Wide Ocean*, Folkestone, 1974.

Stahl, B., *Vertebrate History: Problems in Evolution*, New York, 1974.

Stanley, S. M., *The New Evolutionary Timetable*, New York, 1981.

Stemman, R., *Reincarnation: True Stories of Past Lives*, London, 1997.

Stevenson, I., *The Evidence for Survival from Claimed Memories of Former Incarnations*, London, 1978.

Stevenson, I., *Twenty Cases Suggestive of Reincarnation*, Charlottesville, 2nd ed. 1974, reissued 1988.

Stringer, C., and Gamble, C., *In Search of the Neanderthals*, London, 1993.

Sutcliffe, A. J., *On the Track of Ice Age Mammals*, London, 1985.

Tattersall, I., 'Out of Africa Again . . . and Again?', *Scientific American*, April 1997, pp. 46–53.

Taylor, F. S., *The Alchemists*, Frogmore, 1976.

Taylor, G. R., *The Great Evolution Mystery*, London, 1983.

Taylor, R. E., Haynes, C. V., and Stuiver, M., 'Clovis and Folsom Age Estimates: Stratigraphic Context and Radiocarbon Calibration', *Antiquity*, 70, 1996, pp. 515–25.

Thompson, D. J., *Memphis under the Ptolemies*, Princeton, 1988.

Thulborn, T., *Dinosaur Tracks*, London, 1990.

Tuttle, R. H., 'Evolution of Hominid Bipedalism and Prehensile Capabilities', *Philosophical Transactions of the Royal Society of London*, B 292, 1981, pp. 89–94.

Vartanyan, S. L., Garutt, V. E., and Sher, A. V., 'Holocene Dwarf Mammoths from Wrangel Island in the Siberian Arctic', *Nature*, 362, 25 March 1993, pp. 337–40.

Waldren, W. H., and Strydonck, M. van, 'Deed or Murder Most Foul? Ritual, Rite or Religion? Mallorcan Inhumation in Quicklime', in Waldren, W. H., Ensenyat, J. A., and Kennard, R. C., *Ritual, Rites and Religion in Prehistory*, IIIrd Deya International Conference of Prehistory, pp. 146–63, Deya, 1995.

Wanpo, H., Ciochon, R., Yumin, G., Larick, R., Qiren, F., Schwarcz, H., Yonge, C., de Vos, J., and Rink, W., 'Early *Homo* and Associated Artefacts from Asia', *Nature*, 378, 16 November 1995, pp. 275–8.

Welfare, S., and Fairley, J., *Arthur C. Clarke's Mysterious World*, London, 1982.

Wendorf, F., and the members of combined prehistoric expedition, 'Late Pleistocene and Recent Climatic Changes in the Egyptian Sahara', *Geographical Journal*, 143, 1977, pp. 211–34.

Wesson, R., *Beyond Natural Selection*, Cambridge (MA), 1993.

West, J. A., *Serpent in the Sky*, Wheaton (IL), 1993.

White, T. D., Suwa, G., and Asfaw, B., '*Australopithecus ramidus*, a New Species of Early Hominid from Aramis, Ethiopia', *Nature*, 371, 22 September 1994, pp. 306–12.

Whitmore, F. C., Emery, K. O., Cooke, H. B. S., and Swift, D. J. P., 'Elephant Teeth from the Atlantic Continental Shelf', *Science*, 156, 16 June 1967, pp. 1477–881.

Whitney, J. D., *The Auriferous Gravels of the Sierra Nevada of California*, Cambridge (MA), 1880. *Memoirs of the Museum of Comparative Zoology at Harvard College*, VI (1).

Wilson, C., *From Atlantis to the Sphinx*, London, 1996.

Wilson, I., *The After Death Experience*, London, 1987.

Wood, B. A., 'Evidence on the Locomotor Pattern of *Homo* from Early Pleistocene of Kenya', *Nature*, 251, 13 September 1974, pp. 135–6.

Wood, B. A., 'Origin and Evolution of the Genus *Homo*', *Nature*, 355, 27 February 1992, pp. 783–90.

Wood, B. A., 'The Oldest Whodunnit in the World', *Nature*, 385, 23 January 1997, pp. 292–3.

Wu, X., *Human Evolution in China*, New York, 1995.

BIBLIOGRAPHY

Zaleski, C., *Otherworld Journeys: Accounts of Near-death Experience in Medieval and Modern Times*, New York, 1987.

Zangger, E., *The Flood from Heaven*, London, 1992.

Zuntz, G., *Persephone*, Oxford, 1971.

Index

Page references in *italics* refer to illustrations.